D1562425

Dialectical phenomenology

The International Library of Phenomenology and Moral Sciences

Editor: John O'Neill, *York University, Toronto*

The Library will publish original and translated works guided by an analytical interest in the foundations of human culture and the moral sciences. It is intended to foster phenomenological, hermeneutical and ethnomethodological studies in the social sciences, art and literature.

ROSLYN WALLACH BOLOGH

Department of Sociology
St John's University, New York

Dialectical phenomenology
Marx's method

Routledge & Kegan Paul

Boston, London and Henley

First published in 1979
by Routledge & Kegan Paul Ltd
39 Store Street, London WC1E 7DD,
Broadway House, Newtown Road,
Henley-on-Thames, Oxon RG9 1EN and
9 Park Street, Boston, Mass. 02108, USA

Set in Linocomp Times by
Rowland Phototypesetting Ltd
Bury St Edmunds, Suffolk
Printed and bound in the USA by
Vail-Ballou Press Inc, New York

ISBN 0 7100 0335 8

For Dan, Howie and Gary

CONTENTS

PREFACE

In the work that follows, I analyze Marx's theorizing. I do so by concentrating on his method. I formulate this method as dialectical phenomenology. The body of this book spells out this method and illustrates it with a reading of the *Grundrisse: Foundations of the Critique of Political Economy.*

Since its translation into English the value of the *Grundrisse* for understanding Marx's theorizing has become more widely recognized. In 1971 McLellan translated a volume of selected excerpts and in 1973 Nicolaus translated the whole text. The *Grundrisse* is particularly important as it combines the humanistic, philosophical concerns found in Marx's early writings with the technical analysis found in *Capital.*

The following work differs from previous treatments of Marx in several ways. It conceives of Marx's method as a form of anti-positivism. By anti-positivism, I refer to a perspective that consists of questioning taken-for-granted prevailing conceptions of reality, objective knowledge or science. It inquires into how any given knowledge or reality is possible – its grounds or historical presuppositions.

The aim of this work is to show the possibility of theorizing that is conscious of historical grounds or presuppositions as opposed to the unself-conscious mode that has characterized the main tradition of sociology. As Rossides (1978, p. 531) concludes in his analysis of the history and nature of sociological theorizing, 'The only choice open to social scientists is between being historical consciously (or problem-oriented) and being unconsciously historical (ideological).'

Although others have read Marx as a critical and anti-positivistic theorist, they tend to interpret key aspects of his work positivistically. As against these inconsistent readings of Marx (which I discuss in the concluding chapter), this book presents an interpretation of Marx's work as exemplifying a consistently and completely anti-positivistic approach. I argue for this interpretation by analyzing Marx's method of theorizing. The interested reader might begin with the concluding chapter which highlights the similarities and differences between these other phenomenological readings of Marx and my own.

The method of theorizing that I attribute to Marx overcomes the dichotomy between a phenomenological sociology associated exclusively with the micro-level of social life (individuals and their subjective mental states and their face-to-face interaction) and a structural sociology associated with the macro-level (political and economic systems). It combines an analysis of language with an analysis of social life. It does so by suspending a mathematical version of language as composed of static elements, treating language instead as a form of life, a way of (re)producing a social world. Thus it adds the dimension of language but shifts from a notion of language as separate from life to a conception of language as a form of life itself.

Phenomenology has been criticized for reducing the study of social life to a study of the individual. The alternative has been entirely structural, begging the issue that phenomenology raises, the issue of consciousness. The conception of dialectical phenomenology as presented and explained in these pages deals with this issue in a radical way. It treats consciousness not as originating with the individual and mediating the individual's relation to society, nor as an epiphenomenon of external social forces. Rather, it deals with the issue of reductionism by treating consciousness as an ongoing social (historical) accomplishment.

Dialectical phenomenology analyzes theory as a form of production in the same way that Marx analyzes the production of capital. It provides a set of rules for reproducing Marx's method. The rules, explained in chapter 2 and applied to Marx's text in chapters 3–7, offer a way of analyzing knowledge, language and the relations and practices of everyday life. Chapter 1, a metatheoretical introduction, may be better understood if re-read after the other chapters.

ACKNOWLEDGMENTS

I wish to thank George Fischer for his invaluable help, and his much appreciated encouragement and support. He originally suggested that I write this book. Michael E. Brown's stimulating ideas and critical questions were crucial to the development of my own thinking. He, too, gave generously of his time to read and discuss my work.

I would like to acknowledge the deep influence of Peter McHugh who first introduced me to phenomenological thinking.

Colette Amoda carefully read and edited parts of the book. Carlos DaCunha was good enough to read and comment on the completed manuscript. Lindsey Churchill and Peter Manicas read and commented on an earlier draft. Ino Rossi raised some interesting questions on the work.

I am also grateful to John O'Neill for his kindness and help including some excellent suggestions.

The author and publishers would like to thank the following for permission to reproduce copyright material: Northwestern University Press, © Editions Gallimard 1955 and Heinemann Educational Books for M. Merleau-Ponty, *Adventures of the Dialectic*; The Merlin Press Ltd for George Lukács, *History and Class Consciousness* (1971); Penguin Books for Karl Marx, *Grundrisse: Foundations of the Critique of Political Economy*, trans. Martin Nicolaus; Librairie François Maspero for Louis Althusser and Etienne Balibar, *Reading Capital*.

CHAPTER 1

From a reading of Marx to dialectical phenomenology

This work analyzes Marx's method of theorizing. It focuses on the *Grundrisse*, a work considered by many to be the most important of Marx's texts. The complete text has been available in translation only since 1973, although a volume of excerpts edited by David McLellan was published in 1971. The *Grundrisse* combines the humanist concerns of Marx's earlier philosophical work with the technical concerns of political economy that dominate his later work in *Capital*. Because it appears to be the most comprehensive of his works in certain respects, it provides an opportune place to find how Marx links the different aspects of his concerns.

Martin Nicolaus (1968, 1973), the translator of the *Grundrisse*, stresses the importance of understanding Marx's method. Other readers (e.g. Appelbaum, 1978; Piccone, 1975; Postone and Reinicke, 1975) have agreed with his assessment that the eight-hundred-page set of notebooks that comprise the *Grundrisse* offer a unique opportunity and fertile ground for analyzing Marx's method. In fact Nicolaus's reading of the *Grundrisse* enables him to make reference to the 'unknown Marx' (1968).

The usual formulation of Marx's method, dialectical material-ism, stresses the anti-idealistic aspect of his work. This emphasis made sense in light of the philosophical developments in Marx's time. However, given developments in the social sciences, a stress on the anti-positivistic, phenomenological aspect of his work makes more sense today. *Dialectical phenomenology* provides a comprehensive analysis of this aspect of Marx's theorizing.

This work treats Marx's analysis of capitalism as exemplifying a phenomenological mode of theorizing, one that is characterized by inquiry into grounds or presuppositions of our knowledge of social

1

life. Marx's version of phenomenology differs from others in certain specifiable ways. The pages that follow present the distinguishing aspects of my reading of Marx's method, the method of dialectical phenomenology.

Dialectical phenomenology: unity of subject and object

This method of theorizing deals with the separation of subject and object. Instead of assuming that an object's meaning or sense is inherent or given with the object, phenomenology claims that we can know the meaning or sense of an object only in its relation to a knowing subject. The meaning is grounded in or internal to the relation of subject and object. It is not internal to the object, nor is it internal to the subject. This approach is in its nature dialectical.

A subject or purpose presupposes the existence of some object or objects necessary for accomplishing that purpose. The qualities of the object inhere in the object; they do not originate with the mind (Schmidt, 1971, pp. 69–71). However, the object and its qualities are known only in terms of their meaning for purposive activity. The object takes on its meaning from, that is, its salience to a knower derives from, a form of life within which the knower stands.

The term, 'form of life,' comes from Wittgenstein (1967), who uses it in order to stress that language must be understood actively as a form of life and not passively as a totality of names for things that exist independently of subjects. A form of life- or language-game may be understood in terms of unspoken rules or pre-suppositions for knowing an object. These rules constitute a 'game,' a purposive activity, within which acts and words, like moves in a game, come to make sense. Only within the game are the moves or words intelligible as such. Hence forms of life ground objects of knowledge.

I use the term, 'form of life,' to refer to the productive relation of subject to object, the incorporation of an object into the life of a subject. The term, 'form of life,' avoids the narrow economic meaning that the term, 'production,' tends to have. Dialectical phenomenology inquires into the form of life in which an object of knowledge is embedded, its active relation to a subject. From this form of life or relation, the object derives its sense. Dialectical phenomenology treats the object as grounded in a form of life and, therefore, as a social object rather than an object given with nature. In other words, it treats an object as a thing-for-a-subject rather than a thing-in-itself.

Just as the salience of an object presupposes its subject, the subject would not be possible as such without the object and its distinctive qualities. Although a subject might exist, it would not be the same subject if its object were not the same or if its relation to the object changed. Thus objects should be thought of as objective conditions for the accomplishment of some subject. Instead of conceiving of subjects and objects as separate, self-sufficient things, we should think in terms of the activity that links them and makes them possible as subjects and objects, their form of life. For example, the object, tillable land, which seems to be an objective thing in the world, only exists as such for a subject that conceives tilling as a useful activity and distinguishes types of land to this end. Similarly, the subject, tiller of the land, is only possible as such where land may be tilled. This unity of subject and object constitutes the purposive activity of tilling.

If we use the analogy of a game, the subjective aspect would be the players of the game, the objective aspect the material of the game. However, neither the players nor the equipment are possible as subjects and objects of the game without the rules. The rules constitute the purposive activity of the game. They link the player to the means of playing and in so doing make possible the game as a unity of subject and object. The players are possible as players only because of the game that they play. That is, the individual's acts or moves, the very concept of player, is made intelligible by the game, the relation of players and material known as the rules of the game.

Furthermore, to the extent that a game or activity appears to be external to the self-constituting relations of players and material, there will be some sense in which the game denies the social character of its accomplishment. In other words, it will appear as natural rather than historical. This denial of the social or historical brings with it a denial of the self-constituting character of the players. This means that the players appear as natural beings instead of as historical ones who (re)create themselves as such in the course of carrying out the rules of that specific game. Or the players may appear as things, objects that are moved about by an externality. The appearance of a reality as external to the subjects that know and (re)produce that reality belies that reality as a historical and social form of life and denies its subjects as historical social beings.

A form of life in which the rules and objects appear to be separate from and independent of the actors, an unself-conscious form of life, must be distinguished from a self-conscious form of life in which the individuals are not merely passive players, but active re-creators of the game. To the extent that the rules and equipment are consciously re-worked by the players themselves, the players become free subjects of the process, free social individuals. Such individuals would be self-conscious as they would be conscious that their co-operation and their moves were (re)creating the game and that the game was creating the very possibility of their moves. The distinction between active and passive, united and separated, self-conscious and unself-conscious, parallels the distinction between dialectical phenomenology and positivism and between socialism and capitalism. This work addresses itself to these distinctions and the relations between them.

Dialectical phenomenology treats objects as objective conditions for the accomplishment of some activity. Conversely, it treats the activity as a condition for the knowledge of the object. For this type of analysis, no object exists as an abstraction, a meaning that is removed from all purposive activity, all history. Rather, every object is seen as grounded in its form of life. Thus a subject's activity presupposes objective conditions for its accomplishment and those objective conditions presuppose a subject for which they have salience. This active unity of subject and object constitutes a purposive activity, a form of life or subjectivity.

Positivism: separation of subject and object

The distinguishing features of dialectical phenomenology are: 1   its treatment of subjects and objects as united; 2   its treatment of this unity of subject and object as purposive activity or form of life; 3   therefore, its treatment of subjects and objects as grounded in their form of life. In contrast, a concrete or positivistic consciousness presupposes a separation of subject from object – a divided subjectivity. Positivism, in this sense, treats subjects and objects as separate and knowable in that separation, as if the sense of an object could be taken for granted as emanating from the object independently of any relation to a subject. In this way, the object as it is known, that is, the knowledge or meaning of the object, appears to be natural and eternal, rather than social and grounded in a historically specific form of life.

Positivism, as intended in this book, is the treatment of subjects and objects as they appear, separate and independent of each other. This separation makes it possible for positivism to speak of being subjective as a problem of bias, as a distortion of consciousness or observation by the intrusion of a subject. Positivism conceives of the subject not as a social subject in terms of membership in a community, but as a private subject in terms of purposes and attitudes that originate with the individual rather than with a language community, an ongoing form of life. Positivism can also talk of objectivity – letting facts speak for themselves – as if social reality was not a process of dialectical re-creation, a relation of subject to object.

In reacting against a positivistic interpretation of social phenomena, some versions of phenomenology become subjective or idealist. A subjective phenomenology takes two forms. It can be the view that reality is whatever people think of it (instead of whatever social life makes of it) and, therefore, that reality is mind or concepts. It can also be the view that behavior must be understood in terms of individuals' meanings and intentions. Instead of reifying society, this view advocates studying individuals as they go about their activities of constructing reality. Both of these approaches are subjective in that they explain social phenomena as originating with the mind (its categories or concepts) or the individual's mind (his or her intentions or perceptions).

Instead of this subjective version of phenomenology, the analysis that follows derives from a tradition that stresses a reciprocal relation of subject and object which I call dialectical phenomenology. The latter approach rejects the subjectivistic and objectivistic versions of the theory of reflection: the view that objects reflect either subjective meaning or mental concepts and the view that subjective meaning or mental concepts reflect the reality of objects. In agreement with Lukács, dialectical phenomenology sees objectivism and subjectivism as two sides of the same problem:

> In the theory of 'reflection' we find the theoretical embodi-
> ment of the duality of thought and existence, consciousness
> and reality, that is so intractable to the reified conscious-
> ness. And from *that point of view* it is immaterial whether
> things are to be regarded as reflections of concepts or
> whether concepts are reflections of things. In both cases the
> duality is firmly established (Lukács, 1971, p. 200).

The problem is the duality of thought and existence, consciousness and reality. Instead of a duality, dialectical phenomenology
posits a unity. However, this unity is not the result of reducing the
objective to the subjective or the reverse. The object does not lose
its distinction from the subject. Rather, both are united in a
process, an active relation of subject to object. This relation may
be understood as production in the sense of a subject's appropriation of an object, the incorporation of an object into the life or
intentional activities of a subject:

> Thus thought and existence are not identical in the sense
> that they 'correspond' to each other, or 'reflect' each other,
> that they 'run parallel' to each other or 'coincide' with each
> other (all expressions that conceal a rigid duality). Their
> identity is that they are aspects of one and the same real
> historical and dialectical process (Lukács, 1971, p. 204).

Socialism, capitalism and fetishism

This distinction between dialectical phenomenology and positivism
corresponds to a distinction between self-conscious socialism and
capitalism. The correspondence can be seen in Marx's treatment
of subject and object. As noted above, a form of life refers to an
active, purposive relation of subject and object. This is also what
we mean by mode of production – the subject (re)produces itself
in the appropriation and production of its object. The form of life
that constitutes capitalism, for Marx, separates subject (labor)
from object (objective conditions of its production). This separation occurs with the mediation of capital between labor and its

object. In a self-conscious form of life (socialism) there would be no mediation and no separation. Subject and object would be united. Labor would directly realize itself as social in the relation to its objective conditions, the social activity of production. It would not have to convert itself into wage labor or exchange value before it could appropriate its object.

Because of the separation of subject from object in capitalism, the subject, labor, appears as an independent thing separate from its object, which takes the form of the commodity, gold or money. The object appears not as socially produced human wealth, but as a separate natural thing that has value in itself, a thing without grounds. Marx refers to this appearance and treatment of objects as the fetishism of commodities. In fetishism, the meaning or value of the object seems to reside exclusively with the object, rather than with the subject's active relation to the object.

A comparison with Freud's work (1959) may help us better to understand the similarity between a positivistic treatment of objects and Marx's notion of fetishism. Reciprocally, Marx's notion of fetishism may help us better to understand Freud's work. According to Freud, the meaning or salience of an object resides in the subject's relationship to the object. A fetish develops when the subject becomes divided. This means that the subject becomes of two minds, possessed of opposing tendencies toward the object. Given the internal conflict, the subject denies (represses) one side of itself. Or the object may appear as a divided object such that in one aspect, the object attracts while in its other aspect, it repels. Because of the opposing aspects, one side of the object becomes repressed.

The repressed subject may (re)present itself as a bodily symptom or its repressed object may (re)present itself as a fetish. Which form it takes, bodily symptom or fetish, may depend on which aspect of the relationship is denied more strongly, which side involves greater conflict. A bodily symptom may be due to repressing more strongly the subjective side, the desiring itself. A fetish may be the result of more strongly repressing the object of the desire. A conflictual relationship or form of life may (re)-produce itself one-sidedly as a compulsion in which the active desiring appears to control the subject, or as an obsession in which the passive object seems to take possession of the subject.

In either case, a divided subject-object (re)presents itself one-

7

sidedly as pure subject (physical impulse or bodily symptom) or pure object (a fetish or obsession), rather than as a relation. According to Freud, actively re-membering or self-consciously reliving in relation to the therapist the conflict that represses and separates the relation of subject and object enables the patient to become self-conscious, to reconstitute itself as a self-conscious relation of subject and object.

Similarly, for Marx, actively re-membering the separation of subject and object provides the solution to the problem of the split between subjectivity and objectivity, idealism and materialism, mind and body. Marx's theorizing founds itself in this disunity and in the active struggle that the disunity produces. This ongoing tension or conflict does not end except by overcoming the disunity, thereby making possible a self-conscious mode of self-production, socialism, as opposed to the repressed mode of production, the divided subjectivity that we have with capitalism.

A self-conscious subject is one that (re)produces itself and knows itself in its relation to its object and knows and produces (the meaning of) its object in relation to itself. Capitalism, an unself-conscious form of life, represses unity by separating subject from object. The separation entails a divided object, the exchange value and use value of the commodity form, which in turn presupposes a divided subject, proletariat and bourgeoisie. A divided objectivity (re)presents itself as a fetish, an object whose value seems to be independent of a subject. A divided subjectivity (re)presents itself as internal conflict, class struggle.

It is important to recognize that the struggle of which I speak does not impose itself, from some large external entity conceived as society, capitalism, social structure or form of life, on passive individuals as if struggle and opposition were independent of persons and their strivings, as if individuals were passive objects moved about by external forces of society. To say, as I do, that the strivings and struggles are made possible by a form of life and that individuals are not the authors of their acts, therefore, needs some clarifying.

A form of life that appears as external to its members, and denies itself as a self-constituting process, also denies its members as self-constituting, and therefore free, social individuals. This denial contradicts its positing of individuals as free and equal. This self-contradictory character of the form of life puts individuals in an untenable position. They presume themselves to be free yet they seem not to be free; they presume themselves to be historical, social subjects yet they appear to be ahistorical, natural things; they presume themselves to be the end to which their activity aims and yet they appear as means to some other end.

Individuals, then, find themselves internally divided. In striving to realize one side of themselves as free, social subjects, they find that they are opposing the other side of themselves, the side in which they appear as and are treated as commodities or things, means for some end that is external to themselves. In other words, the very striving to assert the self as a free, social individual which is made possible by this form of life opposes another side of this same form of life – the aspect in which the self appears as an unfree thing, a commodity or exchange value. Marx conceives of this opposition, this divided form of life, as class struggle. Although the motive force of class struggle is the individual's striving to realize itself as a free, social individual, it must be stressed that a specific form of life grounds or makes possible class struggle and such striving. In other words, the very striving of the individual to realize itself as a free, social subject would not be possible in another form of life, another mode of social reproduction. On the other hand, this form of life that makes possible the free, social individual at the same time denies or suppresses this possibility.

The struggle engendered by a divided subjectivity makes possible the conception of history as a movement toward self-consciousness, toward self-conscious (self) (re)production. In other words, class struggle becomes understood analytically or metaphorically as a movement toward a self-conscious form of life, a mode of (re)production whereby the relation of subject and object realizes itself actively and consciously as a self-constituting unity.

Hegelian readers of Marx may refer to this struggle or movement as the history of reason that culminates in self-consciousness. But for Marx, self-consciousness is always self-conscious (re)production. Thus reason is not some abstract thing in the world, consciousness, but a rational form of life by which the human subject realizes itself as such, a mode of (re)production. In this sense, (re)production refers not merely to the making of things, but also to the activity whereby the human works on, i.e. transforms, what is given as object and in the process develops new needs and abilities, i.e. transforms itself as subject. Human history, then, is the self-constitution of the human subject through production.

For Marx, the capitalist division of labor and alienated labor refers to a divided subjectivity, a separation of subject from object. This is why I conceive of Marx's theorizing as dialectical phenomenology, corresponding to self-conscious socialism. Dialectical phenomenology is the treatment of the separate thing-like appearance of subject and object as a problem, as symptom of a repressed relation and a repressed consciousness – the separation of subject from itself, from the conditions for its possibility and realization. This is how Marx analyzes capitalism. In addition to accomplishing his critique of capitalism in terms of subject and object, Marx's method of dialectical phenomenology distinguishes itself from and constitutes a critique of bourgeois political economy's method of theorizing.

Theorizing as mode of production

A method of theorizing may be reformulated as a mode of production. Just as Marx's work on capital inquires into capital's mode of production and does not simply treat capital as a thing-in-itself, I read Marx's text in terms of its mode of production. This mode of production or method of theorizing, I formulate as dialectical phenomenology. Just as I treat Marx's work as a product of its mode of production, dialectical phenomenology, I read Marx as (re)presenting the categories of classical and bourgeois political economy as products of their mode of production, capitalism.

This work shows how a positivist mode of theorizing corresponds to a capitalist mode of production and how dialectical phenomenology as a mode of theorizing corresponds to a socialist mode of production. Reading Marx phenomenologically and as dialectical phenomenology means reading his analysis of capital in terms of a separation of subject and object as his main achievement. Capitalism, according to this analysis, then, becomes interchangeable with positivism. Both capitalism and positivism treat the separation of subject and object as natural. Furthermore, the opposition of subject and object that comes with their separation

10

parallels the opposition between socialism and capitalism and between dialectical phenomenology and positivism. Each of these pairs may be thought of as a metaphor for each of the others.

Marx's analysis of political economy and my analysis of Marx's theorizing display the same commitment. His method and mine require treating objects of knowledge as products and, hence, as presupposing a mode of production. Grounding objects in their mode of production constitutes the distinctive feature of this theorizing. However, the reader should be cautioned that the term, 'mode of production,' must be understood broadly and existentially as referring to human life experiences conceived as a reciprocal relation of subject and object. It refers not only to the production of economic goods as in some interpretations of Marx, but more fully to the social production of any object of knowledge and its corresponding subject.

It should also be stressed that the production of knowledge as intended here does not refer to processes of mind conceived abstractly and universally. Rather, it means a social mode of production, knowledge that is reflexively tied to the social conditions of its production. As distinguished from an exclusively economic interpretation and from an exclusively idealistic interpretation, mode of production becomes understood as form of life. By grounding capital in a form of life, I read Marx as showing the existential issues implied in the production of capital, e.g. the (re)production of human activity, and hence the self, as a commodity or thing that is alien to the producers or actors themselves. Similarly, by grounding Marx's text in a form of life, I try to show the existential concerns implied in his theorizing, e.g. the struggle for self-conscious self-production.

Dialectical phenomenology begins within a positivist, empiricist approach to social phenomena. However, it orients to the overcoming of positivism. It does this by showing how social phenomena which appear as things without grounds are possible, how they are embedded in a form of life. Dialectical phenomenology presupposes the empiricist mode as its other, that which it negates but which it requires as a condition of its own possibility. Hence it is not a self-sufficient program in itself, but a critical program. This means that, by the very act of showing grounds, an inquiry into the possibility of a concrete, positivist consciousness negates that consciousness and constitutes a critique. Similarly socialized labor, as the grounds of capital, by its very presence, negates capitalism's denial of grounds and constitutes an internal opposition to or critique of capitalism.

Reflexivity and grounding

Because dialectical phenomenology treats all objects as grounded in a form of life, a phenomenological analysis of a text inquires into the grounds of the text. It formulates a form of life for which the text becomes a necessary result and a necessary condition. The formulation provides for the possibility of the text; it brings the text to life by showing the text's embeddedness in a form of life. By inquiring into grounds, a phenomenological analysis of a text makes for a self-conscious or reflexive reading.

The reader becomes a reader with the process of making sense of the text. Similarly, a text only becomes a text with a reading. The meaning of a text comes neither from the text, nor from the reader. Rather, the reader encounters the text within a form of life that grounds the text. A reading is, therefore, never innocent or original. It always presupposes a form of life. A reading, then, is a re-reading, a re-reading of a form of life that grounds the text and makes it meaningful. A reflexive reading displays its own grounds as it self-consciously inquires into the grounds of its text.

The notion of a text's grounds refers to that which is necessary for or presupposed in reading (or writing) the text as an intelligible and conceivable social accomplishment. By inquiring into how Marx is able to make sense to me as a reader, I am also inquiring into how I as reader am able to make sense of Marx. Thus, I conceive of the reading as a self-conscious or reflexive reading.

Because a reader and its text are constituted in the work of reading, an inquiry into grounds of a reading is an attempt to do self-conscious work, unalienated labor. Needless to add, by self-conscious I do not refer to a personal self but to a conception of self as reader.

In contrast to Gouldner's conception (1970, pp. 489–512), this version of a reflexive reading is not one in which a reader makes personal values or perspective explicit. (I am using the terms 'text' and 'reader' broadly to refer not just to a written work but to any social object and the subject that makes sense of the object.)

Rather, a reflexive reading inquires into the grounds of the reading, of the sense of the text, not of the reader or of the author as a personal individual. John O'Neill presents a similar critique of Gouldner's notion of reflexivity: 'Because he has neglected to consider the philosophical foundations of reflexive sociology he is obliged to make his choice of a sociology a political choice' (1972, pp. 219–20). Unlike Gouldner's conception, in other words, the grounds of a work are not personal or political choices. Rather, they refer to that which is internal to or presupposed by a work as a meaningful object. Grounds are inherent in the accomplishment of that work, in the meaning that the work has for a reader. They provide for the possibility of the work; they are that without which the text could not exist as such. Grounds are form of life. They constitute a process of production – the production of the work as a meaningful object. Grounds are a way of seeing an object as having a history, a subjectivity in relation to which the object has meaning.

In order to anticipate misunderstandings of the notion of grounds, I list some common interpretations of the term as they might be applied to an analysis of Marx's work. None of these, it must be stressed, constitutes phenomenological grounds as I will be using the term:

Personal motives – such as considering Marx's analysis to reflect his private sympathies or ambitions.

External causes – such as attributing his analysis to his personal position in a social structure.

Personal experiences – such as deriving his views from childhood socialization.

Underlying assumptions – such as imputing to him a version of human nature that informs his work.

Taken-for-granted notions – such as seeing his work as based on a commonly held view that workers were being exploited or unfairly treated.

Objective conditions – such as seeing his work as the observing and reporting of external conditions or occurrences in the world.

In formulating a phenomenological analysis as a concern for grounds, I do not mean any of the above. Phenomenological analysis must conceive of objects as universals and not as particulars, as social products, not as individual creations. Therefore, grounds of a social product, Marx's theorizing, cannot be located in the individual or his or her personal situation. Rather, grounds are given with a form of life that is presupposed by the work.

This version of phenomenological grounds can be compared with John O'Neill's version of reflexivity. Instead of reflexivity as awareness of the 'infrastructures' of knowledge in culture, class and biography (O'Neill, 1972, p. 225), the standard notion of a sociology of knowledge, O'Neill develops the concept of 'reflexivity as institution,' which may be likened to a self-conscious form of life. He does not conceive of reflexivity as awareness of personal conditions of a knowing subject. He likewise rejects a notion of reflexivity as 'resting upon a transcendental subjectivity.' For O'Neill, 'the ultimate feature of the phenomenological institution of reflexivity is that it grounds critique in membership and tradition' (1972, p. 234). Grounds are given with membership, not with the personal situation of an individual. They are internal to a work. They constitute its form of life, the membership and tradition it presupposes.

Because grounds are given with membership, not with the personal situation of an individual, in referring to the grounds of an objectivity one treats the objectivity as a historically specific universal. Thus one might talk of the grounds of science, a historically specific universal, independently of the personal conditions of particular scientists. Of course the personal conditions of particular scientists, *qua* scientist, include the conditions that are presupposed by science itself. Similarly, the personal conditions of any individual life include the conditions presupposed by the historical activities in which that life participates, i.e. the historical grounds of those categories in terms of which that life knows itself.

In treating an object as a universal, one distinguishes between a historically specific universal and an abstract universal. To illustrate, one could use Marx's work as an example of theorizing in general and then analyze the conditions for theorizing. That would be treating it as an abstract universal. Or, one could analyze the conditions for Marx's theorizing that distinguish it from other types of theorizing. This would be treating it not as an absolute, but as a possibility, a historically specific object or product. Others make the same distinction between an abstract universal and a concrete universal (e.g. Gould, 1973–4).

In this work, I treat Marx's work as a historically specific form of theorizing, a historically specific universal. As a universal and not a particular, it is conceived as a type of theorizing that is independent of the particularity of its author or social setting. In other words, it is conceived not as a personal achievement, nor as a result of its setting in time and place, but as a social achievement. This means that it is rule guided. The rules refer to its reproducibility. In other words, the theorizing is reproducible in principle and not just by accident. This analysis makes explicit the conditions or rules that can reproduce that theorizing.

The historically specific conditions (rules or grammar) necessary for reproducing the theorizing are its presuppositions or grounds. These conditions are not personal to the author but are impersonal. They are presupposed in the reading. A reflexive reading locates a text within a set of conditions. These conditions make possible the text as it is known to the reader. The totality of a phenomenon and its conditions, an object and the relations and practices it presupposes, constitute a form of life. Science can be formulated as a form of life as can capitalism.

Dialectical phenomenology is similar to a sociology of knowledge in relating the object of knowledge to social conditions which make that object possible (intelligible) as such. However, dialectical phenomenology treats those social conditions as internal to the knowing of the object, as internal to the object as it is known. Thus one must analyze the knowing – the form of life within which the object makes sense. This differs from a sociology of knowledge approach that locates the origins outside of the knowing as coming from some external cause or set of conditions, as if, for example, capitalism were external to some theory, concept or idea and somehow caused it.

In his work on capital, Marx can be read as analyzing a category or object by tracing how it operates within a form of life. This reading suggests that an object of knowledge operates within something. If the form of life is formulated as a mode of production, then the object is a *force* of production. Accordingly, if the form of life is formulated as a mode of theorizing, then the object is a *category* of the theorizing. A force of production and a category of theorizing are analogous terms. The terms 'category' and 'force of production' call attention to the embeddedness of an object (physical or mental) within some form of life. The implication of embeddedness is opposed to the conception of objects as things in themselves.

Thus objects are analyzed as universals, not particulars. Furthermore, these universals are not treated as given with the mind or nature or language. Rather, they are treated as grounded in a historically specific form of life.

Dialectic and critique

In the text that follows, I refer to the tension between a positivist, empiricist program and a phenomenological one that negates the former as a dialectic of the concrete and the analytic. The term, 'concrete,' takes on a technical meaning. It refers to the appearance of social phenomena as ungrounded things. Concrete theorizing treats social phenomena as they appear before analysis. In concrete theorizing, concepts are abstractions, names for things whose meanings are simply given; they are ungrounded in specific, historical forms of life. The term, 'analytic,' refers to the knowledge of social phenomena as grounded in their forms of life. That phenomenology is dialectical, refers to a dialectic of the concrete and its grounds. A display of that dialectical relation dissolves the concrete, 'objective' thingness in which our world now appears to us.

I adopt the term, 'analytic theorizing,' from the works of Peter McHugh, Alan Blum and their collaborators (1974, pp. 2–17). As used by these theorists, analysis shows how a phenomenon comes to make sense. Its logical opposite is concrete theorizing in which the sense of a phenomenon is taken as given. The distinctive feature of analytic theorizing is its inquiry into grounds: 'analysis is the concern not with anything said or written but with the grounds of whatever is said – the foundations that make what is said possible, sensible, conceivable' (McHugh *et al.*, 1974, p. 2).

Its opposite, concrete theorizing, treats its object as complete in itself. McHugh and Blum treat no speech or text as complete or ahistorical; they treat a speech or text as embedded; they treat it as a result of participating in a form of life. Thus analysis treats its object as a history, a product with origins in a process of production. It, therefore, sees concrete speech as a denial of itself as an achievement, a denial of its own history:

Concrete speech, which treats itself as secure, contradicts itself because the very occurrence of intelligible speech makes reference to its achievement (and speech which treats itself as secure claims that it is first, natural, and has no history) . . . .Analysis brings to light the contradiction . . . by treating the speech as an appearance of that which grounds it (McHugh *et al.*, 1974, p. 17).

A reflexive reading or analytic approach formulates a relation of object to ground. This must be contrasted with a reading that sees only objects without grounds, a passive reading. A passive reading treats the text as a report about or explanation of things in the world. An animated reading treats the text as presupposing some form of life that is not stated, but which provides the animus for the text, a problem or contradiction that the text resolves. Analysis shows how a report or its objects come to make sense. It, therefore, can be understood as violating the text; it violates the 'surfaces and conventions' of the text in order to see the author as 'saying something other than what he speaks' (Blum, 1973, p. 24). For Blum, analysis 'treats all material, data, and text as exemplary, as having the status of examples for inducing the analyst to re-collect and re-orient to some fundamental problem which the surface structure of the example conceals' (*ibid.*).

Instead of treating a phenomenon as immediately sensible, analysis treats a phenomenon as a universal that presupposes and derives its sense from a historically specific form of life. A reflexive reader formulates a form of life which animates the text for the reader.

A concrete reading renders the text as dead but memorable, correctly or incorrectly. The analytic renders Marx a living theorist. That is, it makes it possible to be Marx; it makes it possible for the text to be a work in process. This is not to say that Marx has a use today or that Marxist formulae are correct empirically, etc. These are still readings of a past work only applied today and not a living work in progress. An animated reading brings Marx to life, makes him contemporary – not appropriate today, but *living*.

By grounding a phenomenon in a form of life, phenomenology reveals a tension. It displays the tension between an object as it appears – without grounds – and as analysis knows it – with grounds. Dialectical phenomenology does not reveal grounds as an end in itself. It does so in order to show its own possibility as critique of an unself-conscious form of life in which objects appear not to have grounds. Dialectical phenomenology is a critique, not a positive thing in itself. Its own possibility as a mode of theorizing is grounded in the dialectic of the concrete and its negation.

An animated reading

An animated reading begins with what must be unstated, what Althusser (Althusser and Balibar, 1970, pp. 21, 28) calls an omission or silence. These grounds provide for the possibility of what is stated, the problematic of the reading. Multiple interpretations of a text reflect the multiplicity of problematics or forms of life in light of which a text can be read (Blum, 1973, p. 24; O'Neill, 1972, p. 239).

However, Althusser, as we shall see in the concluding chapter, confuses an analytic problematic with a concrete problem. An analytic problematic refers to questioning how a given object of knowledge, a formulation, is possible in the sense of sensible or meaningful. Particular events or occurrences do not constitute grounds in the sense in which I intend the term. Rather, grounds refer to a form of life, a relation of subject and object, in terms of which some object becomes possible, comes to be known as such.

Against a self-conscious mode of production as ground, for instance, production that is not self-conscious comes to be seen as such and comes to stand out as problematic. By describing production as unself-conscious, Marx invokes the possibility of self-conscious production as its negation. Similarly, my description of Marx's mode of theorizing presupposes a mode of theorizing that is other than Marx's – its opposite or negation against which Marx's work can be seen as such, i.e. as a mode of theorizing. In providing for the possibility of Marx's theorizing, I implicitly make problematic this other mode of theorizing. In other words, my point of departure, that to which my reading is committed – self-conscious theorizing as illustrated in Marx's work – presupposes and makes problematic this other mode of theorizing. Some grasp this other mode as concrete speech or unreflexive theorizing, others as empiricism, and still others as positivism. Marx characterizes it as bourgeois theorizing. The tension or dialectic of the two modes of theorizing makes my reading of Marx possible. The (phenomenological) analysis is grounded in this dialectic.

Given Marx's grounds, commitment to a self-conscious form of life, he is able to show the unself-conscious character of bourgeois political economy. Conversely, that commitment itself is only intelligible as a commitment given a form of life that is not self-conscious. Hence, Marx's work is reflexively tied to an unself-conscious form of life as a condition of its production. This accounts for why Marx titles his works critiques and why Marxian theorizing, formulated here as dialectical phenomenology, can only be a critique. By showing grounds of an object, dialectical phenomenology shows the ideological (ungrounded) character of that object. Dialectical phenomenology is, therefore, the critique of ideology where ideology refers to all forms of knowledge that are divorced from their conditions of production (their grounds).

Marx's analysis of political economy is a critique of a form of life in which a social object comes to be treated independently of its grounds. Treating an object in such a way fetishizes it; treating its concept that way reifies it. Whereas other phenomenologists (e.g. Berger and Pullberg, 1966, p. 61; Berger and Luckmann, 1966, pp. 89–92) treat reification as a universal problem – a problem of forgetting – given with social life (O'Neill, 1972, pp. 219–20, 225–6, and *passim*, is an exception here), Marx's analysis of capital shows how its fetishism and reification, its forgetting, is produced by and *necessary* to its historically specific form of life.

An animated reading formulates the rationality of a text, the form of life that provides its sense for the reader. The text then becomes an occasion for rethinking the rationality of that form of life. In reformulating political economy, Marx invites us to reconsider the rationality of political economy. Similarly, in reformulating Marx's theorizing, I invite the reader to reconsider the rationality of Marx's work. I do not mean by rationality the logical relations between propositions. Rather, the rationality to which I refer is that which the work recommends as a form of life. What reason recommends that form of life? Hence, a reflexive reading is an invitation to a critical dialogue, a dialogue on the rationality of a form of life.

Concepts versus abstractions

Dialectical phenomenology begins with a difference between two modes of theorizing, between a concrete that forgets and an analytic that remembers grounds. A concept that is analytic, as opposed to an abstraction, conveys the relationship of knower and object. It is simultaneously the intentionality of subject and the salience of object. In other words, a concept presupposes a form of life, an internal relation of subject to object. This purposive relation may be said to produce the concept as it is understood.

Ollman (1971, pp. 27–31), too, explains how, for Marx, concepts contain their relations to other things as internal to their meaning. However, he does not conceive of the totality of internal relations as a production, a dialectical relation of subject and object. Totality, for Ollman, is a totality of everything related to everything else internally. For Marx, on the other hand, the internal relations that make up a totality are the relations by which a subject (re)produces itself and its knowledge of the object – a relation of subject to object. It is with such a conception of totality or form of life that I interpret Marx's term, 'mode of production.'

Concepts treated concretely are merely used without remembering that they are produced by and in turn reproduce a form of life. What is lost in this is knowing as a subject's history. If we do not identify Marxist theorizing with the use of his concepts, but with a method of theorizing that makes those concepts possible in the first place, we can understand the sense of Lukács' notion of orthodoxy as referring to Marx's method of theorizing:

> Orthodox Marxism . . . does not mean the blind acceptance of the results of Marx's inquiry, nor a 'belief' in this or that thesis, nor the interpretation of a 'holy' text. Orthodoxy in regard to Marxism refers exclusively to method (Lukács, 1971, p. 77).

Beginning with a given concept, Marx formulates the internal relation of subject and object that it presupposes. However, in doing so Marx shows that the initial concept was inadequate. It concealed rather than revealed the relation. Hence he develops a new formulation that more adequately expresses the relationship. For instance, beginning with the category, money, Marx shows its inadequacy. He analyzes the value form, money, as a relation among exchangers based on the amount of labor (average socially necessary labor time) used in producing the object of value. Marx's analysis shows how the category of money fails to convey this relationship; it conceals it. Beginning with an ungrounded concept of value as a thing in the world, money, Marx ends with the labor theory of value and its grounding in the exchange relation. From this point, he then develops the analysis of capital as a development from the money form of value.

A self-conscious form of life would produce concepts that convey a relation of subject and object. A critique of bourgeois economy's unself-conscious mode of theorizing consists in showing the one-sided character of the categories of political economy: they appear to be objects only independent of any subjectivity. Following Marx, we may call such categories, abstractions.

Marx uses the term, 'abstraction,' to refer to objects that appear to be independent of any subjectivity or purpose or to refer to a subject or purpose that appears independent of any objective conditions of existence. The economic terms, labor and value, are examples of abstractions. They appear to be things in themselves. Opposed to abstractions are concepts or objects that make reference to their grounds, a subject-object relation. Abstractions are self-contradictory because they exclude that which is necessary to and presupposed by their existence (Rovatti, 1973b, pp. 66–7; 1972, pp. 87–106).

A contradiction occurs when a term refers to two mutually exclusive things, A and not-A. This is the case with the category, exchange value. It is both a use value and not a use value. A commodity has a calculable exchange value regardless of the demand or need for it, i.e. regardless of any use value. Hence, in determining exchange value, all consideration of use value is excluded. On the other hand, in order to *realize* its exchange value, the commodity must have use value. The contradictory character of exchange value is not a result of or a stage in the development of consciousness. It is not a mistake in thinking that the mind can correct. Rather, the exchange relationship presupposed by exchange value is a contradictory relationship. The exchange relationship mediated by exchange value assumes that the mediation (money) is both identical with the objects of exchange and not identical with them.

21

We have seen how exchange value is an abstraction and a self-contradictory thing because it excludes use value in its determination and yet its very existence presupposes use value. In other words, value is treated as an object, money, exclusive of any subjectivity. At the same time, it is impossible for a commodity to have exchange value without a subject for which the commodity has use value.

Marx's method begins with a given knowledge, an abstraction, and then analyzes the internal relationship of subject and object presupposed by the abstraction. The analysis reveals the one-sided or abstract character of a term which expresses only an object or a subject. It reveals the inadequacy of the abstraction to its object (subject-object relation). This method of theorizing is only possible given the separation of subject and object – the abstract character of exchange value, the contradictory character of the commodity form which on the one hand denies that which on the other hand it presupposes.

Thus, Marx's dialectic – showing the relation that is hidden in the abstraction – is a method that is only specific to a particular form of life. In that form of life, the relation of subject and object, production, is mediated by an externalized abstraction. Because the mediation is external to subject and object, it takes the place of either subject or object without being identical with that which it replaces. Hence, it appears as subject independent of a relation to object or object independent of a subject. The mediation is an abstraction from the relation of subject and object, an abstraction that denies its origins.

Grounding modes of theorizing

Although Marx does not explicitly address the issue, Marxist theorizing implicitly recognizes its own conditions of existence. Its self-critique and self-analysis – the limits of its existence – are implicated in its practice. Phenomenology shows that what appears as an object exclusively is an abstraction from a relation of subject and object, a forgetting of the unity of subject and object. The dialectic shows the contradictory character of an object that is an abstraction. It shows that the abstraction *qua* abstraction denies or rejects that which is essential to it. However, unlike other dialectical or phenomenological theorizing, Marx's method as formulated here accounts for the separation and the forgetting.

Marx's analysis of the commodity shows that the forgetting, which is the basis of the dialectic and of phenomenology, hence of dialectical phenomenology, is a necessary feature of the production and exchange of commodities. Marx shows that the latter could not be accomplished without the forgetting. The forgetting, in turn, is made possible by the commodity form itself – the separation of exchange value from use value and its embodiment as a universal commodity, money.

Dialectical phenomenology, as a critique of the one-sided character of abstraction, is also a critique of the alienated character of production, the production of commodities or exchange values. As such, dialectical phenomenology ceases to exist when the commodity form and its concomitant, alienated labor, abolishes itself, when subject and object are self-consciously united in production. Thus dialectical phenomenology is located in and limited to a form of life dominated by the commodity form.

Analytically, the commodity form refers to any object whose value or sense is divorced from its subject, i.e. abstract labor. Therefore, dialectical phenomenology becomes possible with any relationship in which a subject fails to recognize itself in its object or fails to recognize that its object is implicated in itself; hence, inadequacy of the concept. The abstraction with which a subject grasps its object is a symptom of a divided object, of a divided relationship. An abstraction is a symptom, an inadequate concept. The notion of a symptomatic reading comes from Althusser and Balibar (1970).

A symptomatic reading begins with the abstraction as a symptom, recovers the relationship that it presupposes, and completes itself by providing a new concept that expresses the totality which the abstraction expressed one-sidedly. What is distinctive about the symptomatic readings that Marx and Freud do as opposed to that of Hegel, for instance, is that the former ground the inadequacy of a concept, an abstraction or symptom, in a specific form of life – exchange and commodity production or a one-sided relationship of dependency and power. Hegel and other phenomenologists differ from Marx in that they see the failure of recognition, the inadequacy of the abstraction, as inherent in the development of mind or in the nature of being or social life.

By inquiring into grounds of an object other phenomenologists recognize the alienation of the object from its subject. However, they do not do dialectical phenomenology if they fail to show how the alienation and hence their own inquiry as critique are made possible, the conditions of their own existence. Such analysts do not provide grounds for the separation of object from subject which, in turn, makes their inquiry possible. This makes their phenomenology undialectical and ahistorical. It becomes a method that is external to its content. Although it reveals the dialectic of other things, the separation of subject and object and the contradictions that this entails, it does not recognize the origin of the separation and, therefore, its own grounds – its specificity to a form of life that produces the separation as a social accomplishment.

Hegel's phenomenology reveals the dialectic of objects and, therefore, the historicity of forms. As such, it is implicitly critical of a bourgeois conception of itself and its categories as eternal. It, therefore, 'forms the springboard for the Marxian critique of bourgeois society' (Postone and Reinicke, 1975, p. 138). Similarly, O'Neill (1972, p. xi) reads Hegel as providing a 'critique of alienation as estrangement from action as expression.' However, Hegel's critique differs from Marx's in not being able to ground itself in a historically specific form of life. In responding to Nicolaus's 'Introduction' to the *Grundrisse* with respect to Hegel's contribution to Marx's theorizing, Postone and Reinicke state:

> On the other hand, it remains within the bounds of bourgeois modes of thought, as analyzed by Marx, insofar as it does not self-consciously, from the standpoint of a historically-becoming revolutionary subject, consider its own relation to its historical context . . . the historically specific motion of the forms, driven forward by their particular immanent contradictions, is posited transhistorically. That is, the *Weltgeist* is posited as Subject and the dialectic as the universal law of motion: History as the product of the labor of the Concept (1975, p. 138).

For Marx and Freud, in contrast to Hegel, the alienated object and its corresponding method of analysis or reconstruction are both historically specific. Marx and Freud provide a formulation of how self-alienation is possible. They each describe a process for which repression or self-alienation is necessary. Marx does not provide such an analysis until the *Grundrisse* and the analysis of exchange value. Before that his analysis was dialectical – he was aware of the contradictions of alienated labor and capital – but ungrounded.

He had not yet grounded the object – alienated labor or capital – or his analysis as subject in the specific process of its production. In the early works, he does a critique of the human condition of alienated labor; in the later works, he analyzes the specific moments of production, the historically specific conditions of alienated labor.

Thus his early analysis could not account for the possibility of its object (alienated labor or capital) as a historically specific product, nor of its own possibility as reflexively tied to its object. Historically specific product means not that it develops at a certain period of time, but that it presupposes historical conditions of production – that it does not just occur or emerge or develop naturally through the intentions of a subject or the features of an object, but that the intentions of a subject and the characteristics of its object reciprocally act on each other. Historically specific production refers to the mutually constituting practices of a specific subject and its specific object.

Marx's method of theorizing is reflexively tied to the conditions of its production – the forgetting that makes analysis as re-membering possible. To analyze, is to see the separation and then bring back together the separated aspects. Forgetting results from the one-sided concept of exchange value as embodied in money and capital. Thus the very recognition of exchange value precludes the recognition of use value which is its other side. Because exchange value is an abstraction that must exclude use value, the existence of capital as the ongoing production of exchange value requires that use value be unacknowledged or expelled from consciousness. Hence, repression. As a remembering of that which must be forgotten, dialectical phenomenology is grounded in the conditions that produce forgetting. Its grounds are the form of life which it negates.

Similarly, Freud's method of theorizing (the psychoanalytic method) is reflexively tied to the conditions of its production – repression or the forgetting that results from a one-sided relation of dependency and power such that a dangerous desire, one that threatens the ongoing relationship, must be unacknowledged or expelled from consciousness.

A critique of one-sided consciousness does not simply account for knowledge in terms of the positions of different knowers. Rather, it accounts for the positions themselves as part of a process or purposive activity. Therefore, it is not an alternative consciousness given with a different position and perspective. It is not an alternative consciousness in the sense of one among others. As a critique it is not simply a criticism from a certain perspective. Rather, it is a negation of that consciousness which is its object.

It is a negation that develops by attempting to complete bourgeois or positivistic consciousness. By uncovering the missing side of the relation that bourgeois consciousness represents one-sidedly, the dialectic shows that mode of consciousness to be a denial, a repression of that which it needs to exist. Hence, it shows positivistic consciousness not to be merely inadequate as if it could be fixed or made more adequate, but to be essentially inadequate, necessarily incomplete.

The completion of positivistic consciousness by the dialectic negates positivism as such. The completion of positivistic consciousness destroys it. In order to exist, it must be one-sided; it must deny or repress that which it presupposes. Such denial is a necessary condition for, as well as product of, bourgeois theorizing. The Marxian critique of consciousness is, therefore, grounded in and limited to bourgeois consciousness:

> One of the most powerful aspects of the critique of political economy is that it understands itself as historically determinate and can account for its existence as critique in the process of analyzing and criticizing bourgeois forms. Any attempt to transform it into a positive science falls into inconsistencies – for it is then posited as the historically unique exception standing above the interaction of form and content, social forms and forms of consciousness, which it postulates as its own basis (Postone and Reinicke, 1975, p. 136).

In other words, dialectical phenomenology postulates a reflexive relation of consciousness and object comparable to the relation of form and content. For dialectical phenomenology, consciousness is always implicated in its object. Therefore, to posit dialectical phenomenology as a form of consciousness that is universal, a method of theorizing that is independent of the historicity of its object, is to exempt it from its own premises about consciousness. Hence, it could not understand itself. Postone and Reinicke, therefore, criticize Engels, on the one hand, and Lukács, on the other, for attributing a transhistorical character to the dialectic:

> As a positive science it would no longer be capable of understanding itself. This is the case with every form of transhistorical dialectic, whether inclusive of nature (Engels) or not (Lukács). In either case dialectic must be grounded ontologically – the one in Being in general, the other in social Being. However, that reality and/or social relations in general are essentially contradictory, can only be assumed, not explained. Dialectic as transhistorical totalizing category can only be dogmatically posited – at the cost of its own self-reflexive understanding (*ibid.*, p. 136).

Marx's method not only shows how things are constituted in labor or social relations, but it also shows how producing capital requires forgetting or repressing this knowledge.

In revealing that which bourgeois theorizing represses from consciousness, Marx's theorizing may be thought of as a re-presentation of proletarian theorizing. The proletariat personifies that which capital must forget – the unity of use value and exchange value. Whereas the bourgeoisie must forget, the proletariat must remind. In its opposition to capital, the proletariat makes for the possibility of self-conscious activity, the possibility of a subject self-consciously united with its object, the possibility of a reading that unites a text with its ground. The proletariat and proletarian theorizing become metaphors for self-teaching, for animated reading, for re-membering grounds and form of life.

Theorizing as rule guided

Form of life refers to the totality of presuppositions necessary for recognizing an object – for understanding its sense. These presuppositions may be likened to rules for making sense. Hence, the recognition of an object may be thought of as a rule-guided accomplishment. The overriding rule with which I read Marx is: Treat Marx's work as a display of reflexive theorizing.

I ground Marx's text in a form of life. I also read Marx as grounding political economy. Grounding a phenomenon may be thought of as treating it as a display of a form of life which it presupposes. To read Marx reflexively, is to treat every aspect of his work as a display of its own possibility. This means treating the work not as a self-sufficient thing, but as a product of its mode of production, its grounds. In other words, treating something as a possibility means recognizing that its sense is made possible, that is presupposes grounds, that it is not a natural thing. To read Marx as doing reflexive theorizing is to read him as treating every aspect of his object as displaying its form of life.

For a reflexive theorist, the task is to formulate the form of life that the object displays. The form of life in which I ground Marx's work is reflexive theorizing. I treat Marx as an exemplar of a mode of theorizing. Furthermore, I read Marx as grounding the categories and theorizing of political economy. He treats the theorizing of political economy as an exemplar of the capitalist mode of production.

Marx accomplishes the analysis by examining the presuppositions of this mode of production. The categories such as money, capital, circulation, value may be likened to the moves of a game. The game or activity has the aim of producing and expanding wealth or exchange value, i.e. the production and reproduction of capital. Marx's analysis shows how the categories are not independent, self-sufficient things or names of things. Rather, they presuppose a 'game' which makes them possible. The rules of the game correspond to the constraints of the mode of production. In other words, Marx grounds the categories in a form of life by describing rules or presuppositions of the game which makes those categories intelligible.

I do a similar analysis of Marx's mode of theorizing by formulating it as a form of life, a set of reading rules, practices that accomplish Marx's mode of theorizing. These rules make possible Marx's categories. Such rules must not be seen as means for accomplishing something else – as when one utilizes certain practices as means to create sympathy or rally the oppressed, for example. Rather, the practices themselves constitute a form of life, a purposive activity. The practices are not a means for accomplishing some external end; they are a *display of an accomplishment*. That is, the practices themselves constitute the accomplishment, the activity and its meanings. Analysis formulates a form of life that grounds the work. I ground Marx's work in a form of life which is not stated, but which the work presupposes and displays: self-conscious production.

A reflexive reading is a self-conscious production. Because the reader and the text are constituted as such with the reading, reading may be understood as production, as human history. I conceive of reading as a (re)production and a text as a product of a reading. Therefore, I do not treat Marx's theory, which is itself a reading, as a given thing to be explicated, validated, corrected or dismissed. I am not concerned with ferreting out and discussing Marx's view on or theory of particular social phenomena as meaningful in itself. Rather, I treat the *theory* as a *product*, as the substantive result of a mode of production, a process of theorizing. My aim is to explicate that process. I do this by addressing the question of how Marx's theory is possible, how it is produced. This means that, instead of treating Marx's text as an external reality (or the subject matter about which he theorizes as external to his theorizing), I treat it as a reality whose meaning is (re)produced by a reading or a mode of theorizing.

I treat *theorizing* as *production* and, therefore, as a history – a self-constituting relation of subject and object. My reading, as subject to Marx's text as object, constitutes a (re)production of Marx's text. The inquiry into grounds provides a method of reading that reproduces Marx's theorizing as dialectical phenomenology. A positivistic reading that treats Marx's categories as references of an 'objective' world (re)produces a concrete version of Marx. Just as Marx's reading of political economy founds itself in the negation of readings by classical and bourgeois economists, my reading of Marx founds itself in the negation of positivistic readings of Marx.

This work is not intended as an assessment of the empirical validity of Marx's theories as literal statements about the world. Neither is it intended as an examination of the logic of his arguments. Rather, it engages the phenomeno-logic of the work, the relations between its formulations and its grounds. This relation is its method.

I reformulate Marx's critique of political economy as a method of theorizing in terms of four rules. This version of rules is identical with Marx's term, 'moments.' There are three reasons for formulating these as rules.

The first reason for treating them as rules, rather than as themes or topics in Marx's work, is to show how they constitute a totality that is a process, a methodic or rule-guided activity – a mode of production, rather than an end product such as a collection of related themes or a theory. In constituting a totality, each of the rules presupposes the others. They are treated separately for purposes of exposition only. In other words, the rules are not discrete steps in a process, but aspects of an accomplishment. The accomplishment is reflexive reading or self-conscious theorizing.

Second, the rules allow the theorizing to be seen as a social accomplishment, a history. As such it is in principle reproducible rather than a personal achievement of an individual genius or an accident. The rules illuminate aspects of Marx's work such that a violation of any one would result in a failure to do Marx's type of theorizing. A violation of any one would also preclude any of the others.

Such a violation would result in the type of work that Marx opposes, theorizing that he labels bourgeois. Hence, a third purpose for the rules is to show the difference between Marx's *analytic* theorizing and the type of theorizing which Marx's work makes problematic, what Marx calls bourgeois and I call *concrete*.

The rules highlight the problematic aspects of this other theorizing. In other words, the rules allow Marx's work to be seen in terms of a method that distinguishes it from other theorizing. The rules or conditions for producing Marx's mode of theorizing constitute the grounds of Marx's work. Earlier, I called these grounds a commitment to self-conscious activity. The rules specify ways in which self-conscious activity is accomplished.

The rules and the order in which I discuss them are:

1   Recognize and treat concepts as grounded in an historically specific form of life. This is the *principle of analysis*.
2   Recognize and treat individuals as grounded in an historically specific form of life. Individuals both reproduce and are produced and limited by the totality of which they are a part. This is the *principle of action*.
3   Recognize and treat a form of life as a totality of internal

relations. That which enables one to see phenomena as internally related, that which makes them into a self-moving being or totality, is the principle of *subjectivity*.

4   Recognize and treat a concrete form of life as contradictory. The contradictions are embodied in internal struggles of opposition. This is the *principle of growth*, hence of change.

The rest of this book will develop and illustrate these rules.

Summary

Dialectical phenomenology provides for a self-conscious or reflexive reading of Marx. This means that the reading and the text reciprocally produce each other. The reading formulates a problematic, a negation of some tradition, in light of which the text makes sense. Displaying this problematic through an analysis of the text constitutes the work of an animated reading. The problematic in terms of which I read Marx is the negation of unself-conscious production.

Dialectical phenomenology begins with objects that appear to be abstractions, independent of any subjectivity, and shows how the recognition of those objects, their sense, presupposes a subjectivity or purposive activity. Dialectical analysis reveals contradictions; phenomenology inquires into grounds. A dialectical phenomenology grounds its objects in a contradictory form of life, a divided subjectivity. The separation of subject and object makes dialectical phenomenology possible. The separation of subject and object is itself a contradictory mode of production. It is a production in which a subject fails to recognize that its object and itself are products of their relationship. It is production in which a subject does not know itself as producer or its object as product. Similarly, a subject does not know that it produces itself in its relation to its object.

A dialectical phenomenology shows how the ahistorical appearance of abstractions presupposes a contradictory form of life. The contradiction derives from the separation of subject and object by a mediation that is neither subject nor object, but replaces both. It is both subject and not-subject, object and not-object, of production. This contradictory subject-object is the commodity form

– the embodiment of an abstraction, exchange value, in a material thing.

Thus dialectical phenomenology recognizes its historical specificity as negation of the production of commodities (exchange value) or abstractions. The latter mode of production corresponds to a mode of theorizing that treats abstractions or objects as things in themselves and conceives of itself as the reflection of an objective reality (positivism). As a reading it presents itself as a literal reflection of 'objective facts.' It treats the text as an ahistorical thing. Its negation, dialectical phenomenology, inquires into the possibility of those facts, that text, their embeddedness in and, therefore, their specificity to an historical form of life, a relation of subject and object that makes them possible. That is, it treats the facts or the text as a display of their mode of production.

The tension between knowledge conceived as a (re)production and knowledge conceived as an 'objectivity' may be grasped in reading practices that distinguish a reflexive reading from a positivistic one. I present these reading practices as reading rules or rules of theorizing. Elaborating these rules with respect to Marx's *Grundrisse*, will constitute the remainder of this book, with the exception of the concluding chapter which shows how these rules and the reading it produces differ from other readings of Marx.

CHAPTER 2

From dialectical phenomenology to a re-reading of Marx

This chapter introduces each rule and its centrality to Marx's method: dialectical phenomenology. The four rules could be divided into two parts: the first two rules stressing the phenomenological aspect of theorizing and the second two rules stressing the dialectical basis. However, each rule presupposes the others; no rule or rules can stand apart from the others and still constitute dialectical phenomenology.

The first two rules emphasize the need to treat social phenomena as intelligible only in terms of a form of life. The form of life produces their intelligibility, hence their existence as intentional and understandable phenomena, objects of consciousness. Thus the first two rules establish social phenomena as products of something other than the individual, as products rather than self-sufficient, immediately or naturally intelligible things.

The second two rules reveal the dialectical aspect of the analysis. They show how products that are internal to a form of life appear to be external relations. When the internal relations are mediated by something external, they become external and indifferent to each other. The external mediation produces a contradictory form of life: a divided subjectivity in which one side negates the other side.

Together these four rules constitute a method of theorizing that is a critique of an unself-conscious form of life. As a way of reading Marx, it is a critique of readings that are either purely objective (positivist) or purely subjective (idealist), readings that fail to ground Marx's text in a subject-object unity, a mode of theorizing. I ground Marx's work in commitment to a self-conscious form of life.

Rule 1: treat concepts as grounded in an historically specific form of life

Because this rule provides the principle of analysis, the discussion of it will be much longer than the others. It is divided into two parts. First, I will discuss the concept as the point of departure in theorizing. Second, I will discuss what is meant by 'historically specific form of life' and its significance for theorizing. I will use the Introduction to the *Grundrisse* to illustrate.

In the 'Foreword' to his translation of the *Grundrisse*, Nicolaus relates that although Marx did not provide a comprehensive title to the seven notebooks that comprise the *Grundrisse*, in a letter to Lasalle (22 February 1858) Marx indicates that he had a title in mind, namely, 'Critique of the Economic Categories' (Nicolaus, 1973, p. 24). By economic categories, he refers to the basic concepts employed in political economy. The emphasis on categories is no insignificant aspect. Marx intended this major work to be a critique of certain concepts. This is not as strange as it sounds; Marx's entire analysis of capital proceeds as an analysis of the concept of capital. He states:

> The exact development of the concept of capital [is] necessary, since it [is] the fundamental concept of modern economics, just as capital itself, . . . [is] the foundation of bourgeois society (331).*

What is the difference between analyzing capital as a concept or as a thing in the world? For one thing, a concept, as opposed to an abstraction, refers to a relation; it is not merely a name for a thing. Analysis formulates what appears as a thing in terms of a relation and its presuppositions. 'The sharp formulation of the basic presuppositions of the relation [capital] must bring out all the contradictions of bourgeois production as well as the boundary where it drives beyond itself' (331).

Marx contrasts beginning an analysis with concrete things and beginning an analysis with concepts. He says that it seems to be correct to begin an analysis with the concrete. The concrete refers

---

* Page numbers in parentheses in the text refer to Karl Marx, *Grundrisse*, translated by Martin Nicolaus, Harmondsworth, Penguin Books, 1973 and (same text and pagination) New York, Random House, 1973. All italics in quotations, unless otherwise noted, are in the original.

to activities, things and people as they appear to the ordinary observer before analysis. However, he calls the concrete as it appears a 'chaotic conception of the whole.' For example, although it seems correct to begin in economics with the population, its geographical distribution and its particular activities, he claims that this proves false:

> The population is an abstraction if I leave out, for example, the classes of which it is composed. Those classes in turn are an empty phrase if I am not familiar with the elements on which they rest. E.g. wage labour, capital, etc. These latter in turn presuppose exchange, division of labour, prices, etc. (100).

Thus what appears to be concrete is really an empty abstraction. Rather than begin an analysis with what appears as concrete, one should begin with the concepts that express the 'elements on which they rest.' One cannot begin with the population, but would have to inquire into the relations and elements that are expressed by simpler concepts and which the concrete presupposes:

> Thus, if I were to begin with the population, this would be a chaotic conception (*Vorstellung*) of the whole, and I would then by means of further determinations, move analytically towards ever more simple concepts (*Begriff*), from the imagined concrete towards ever thinner abstractions until I had arrived at the simplest determinations (100).

The term 'imagined concrete' refers to the concrete before analysis, the concrete as it appears. It may be likened to an image without grounds, something that has no history; it simply appears. An 'imagined concrete' is given with speech; it is simply there, something that can be perceived or apprehended by the senses, something that can be observed and measured. Analysis, in contrast, moves from observation to the working up of observation into concepts. The concepts ground the concrete in relations and presuppositions. The analyzed concrete is 'a product of the working up of observation and conception into concepts' (101).

Analysis grounds objects by inquiring into the presuppositions necessary for knowing the object. It treats all objects as objects of knowledge. This rule may be understood as a critique of empiricism, which treats knowledge of an object as coming from the object alone which the theorist, then, discovers. The rule argues against such a purely objective (in the sense of coming from the object) knowledge. It treats an object as presupposing a relation of subject to object that gives it meaning. The subject-object relation presupposed in knowing an object constitutes the object's history or form of life. It is the totality in which the object is embedded.

Analysis reconceives the concrete as a totality of these presuppositions, a form of life. The totality arrived at in analysis is a totality of internal relations, a 'rich totality of many determinations and relations.' This contrasts with a concrete conception of a totality of external relations such as 'population, its distribution among classes, town, country, the coast, the different branches of production, export and import, annual production and consumption, commodity prices, etc.' which Marx eschews as a 'chaotic conception of the whole.'

To fail to analyze is to fail to produce a comprehensible totality, an ongoing history. According to Marx, what appears as concrete turns out to be 'empty abstractions.' His analysis of capital proceeds as an analysis of the concept of capital. This requires formulating it as a relation in terms of its presuppositions and their implications. This contrasts with treating capital as a concrete thing in the world that can be observed and measured.

The formulation of concepts in terms of relations and their presuppositions provides the foundations for the concrete. However, in the discussion of the 'Method of Political Economy,' Marx engages in a polemic with thinking that conceives of the concrete as only concepts that are independent of the human world:

> the concrete totality is . . . product of thinking and comprehending; but not in any way a product of the concept which thinks and generates itself outside or above observation and conception; a product, rather, of the working-up of observation and conception into concepts. The totality as it appears in the head, as a totality of thoughts, is a product of a thinking head, which appropriates the world in the only way it can, a way different from the artistic, religious, practical and mental appropriation of this world. The real subject retains its autonomous existence outside the head

just as before; namely as long as the head's conduct is
merely speculative, merely theoretical (101).

Concepts are the way in which we appropriate the world as a
totality. However, concepts are not the products of a mind that is
outside of or independent of the world. Although the world as a
totality is produced by analysis, the world and its relations do exist
concretely before analysis. Marx states that concepts 'can never
exist other than as an abstract one-sided relation within an already
given concrete living whole' (101).

Marx argues against the philosophy for which 'conceptual
thinking is the real human being,' for which the 'concrete totality is
a product of the concept which thinks and generates itself outside
or above observation and conception' (101). While it is easy to
ridicule the notion of a concept 'which thinks and generates itself,'
nevertheless Marx talks about the capitalist as the personification
of capital. Likewise, he talks about wage labor and abstract labor.
He does not talk about individuals.

Marx proceeds by analyzing the categories of political economy.
However, he makes it clear that the categories do not generate
themselves. This is a criticism of an idealist way of 'conceiving the
real as the product of thought concentrating itself.' However,
Marx's polemic with idealism is not the core of his theorizing.
Rather, I will show, he directed his theorizing toward bourgeois
political economy and its failure to be analytic. Marx's method
must be distinguished from both. It neither treats the concrete as
the product of concepts that generate themselves (idealism), nor
as knowledge that comes from the objects themselves (positivism).
Rather, the method of moving from the concept to the concrete is
only the way that thought appropriates and reproduces the concrete in the mind. It is the method of analysis. But this is not the
process by which the concrete itself comes into being (101).

If concepts merely reproduce the concrete, one might inquire,
'How does the concrete come into being?' An answer to this
question will help us to understand Marx's method of theorizing.
We have seen that the simple determinations of the concrete
according to Marx are relations. Concepts are the way in which
these relations are (re)produced theoretically (as distinguished
from artistically, for example). Marx states this explicitly in several
places: 'Relations can be expressed, of course, only in ideas' (164),

and again, 'the abstraction, or idea, however, is nothing more than the theoretical expression of those material relations' (164) and still again, 'relations can be established as existing only by being thought' (163).

The concrete is composed of relations and not independent individuals. Relations, however, can only be apprehended theoretically through concepts. Therefore, an analysis of the concrete must proceed as an analysis of concepts. The concrete that Marx analyzes is bourgeois society. Thus the concrete in this case comes into being with the relations that (are expressed by concepts and which) characterize bourgeois society: 'Society does not consist of individuals, but expresses the sum of interrelations, the relations within which these individuals stand' (265). The concrete is a totality of relations. In the sense in which I intend it, 'production' means any activity that is sensible or intelligible because of some reproducible method, a specific set of relations, rather than random or accidental behaviour.

In answer to the above question, the concrete comes into being through the relations (expressed by concepts) of productive activity. Marx analyzes concrete modern society as a mode of production. He concerns himself with the relations that constitute the process by which a society produces and reproduces itself as an historically specific form. In all forms of society there is one kind of production which predominates over the rest, 'whose relations thus assign rank and influence to the others. It is a general illumination which bathes all the other colours and modifies their particularity' (107).

Marx, therefore, conceives of bourgeois society as an historic organization of production, one that is the most developed and most complex. Its structure is comprehended through the concepts which express its relations. Thus Marx analyzes bourgeois society as an historical, social organization of production by examining its economic categories, the categories which express its relations. Marx stresses that, however, their subject, modern bourgeois society, is always what is given, in the head as well as in reality, and that these categories 'therefore express the forms of being, the characteristics of existence, and often only individual sides of this specific society, this subject' (106). Thus the categories may be one-sided. Marx's critique consists in showing the one-sidedness of such categories.

By conceiving a form of life as historical, the categories which express these relations must be seen as specific to that historical form. This means that these categories would mean something different or would be unintelligible in a different form of life. Marx gives the example of the economic category of labor. On the one hand, the notion of labor is a universal category that transcends particular forms of life. On the other hand, it is only within modern relations that the economic category of labor in the abstract is conceived as such, rather than as a specific productive activity such as sheep-raising which was known as producing a specific type of wealth.

The monetary system locates wealth as an external thing, money. The commercial or manufacturing system took a great step forward, according to Marx, by locating wealth not in a thing, but in activity, commercial and manufacturing activity conceived narrowly as money-making. In contrast to this system, that of the physiocrats posits a certain kind of labor – agriculture – as the creator of wealth and its object, the product of agriculture, the product of the earth (104).

Marx attributes the introduction of the economic category of labor in general as wealth-creating activity to Adam Smith. The concept of labor in general refers to human labor in the abstract rather than specific forms of labor. On the one hand, this only provides a more abstract conception of productive activity. On the other hand, Marx shows that the concept of abstract human labor or labor in general is produced by a form of society in which the production of wealth in general is not linked with any specific activity. Indifference toward specific labors corresponds to a form of society 'in which . . . the means of creating wealth in general . . . ceased to be organically linked with particular individuals in any specific form' (104).

This example of the economic category of labor is intended to show its historic specificity. This means that the category must be seen as a product of historically specific relations of production:

> Even the most abstract categories, despite their validity –
> precisely because of their abstractness . . . are . . . in the
> specific character of this abstraction, themselves . . . a
> product of historic relations, and possess their full validity
> only for and within these relations (105).

The validity of categories refers to grounds for their use. A valid category is one for which there are compelling reasons for it, reasons that show *how* the presence or absence of the category would make a difference. Therefore, we would expect that the absence of the category, labor, would not make a difference to other forms of life.

In one way this seems to be circular reasoning, for if it is produced by one form of life and not by another, then it was obviously not essential to the other form of life. But this is not what Marx is arguing. By saying that it was produced by a form of life, he is not saying that it first made its appearance in a given society, but that it was produced by certain *relations*. It is only 'for and within' those relations that the category is fully valid, particularly for and within a form of life in which those relations predominate. Therefore, analysis must formulate the category in terms of the relations that make it intelligible and valid.

The rule with which we began: 'Treat concepts as grounded in an historically specific form of life,' can now be understood to include the following:

1   The concrete is a totality of relations.
2   Relations are concepts.
3   The concrete is, therefore, a totality of concepts.
4   Concepts do not originate in consciousness. They presuppose a subject and its object.
5   A relation of subject and object is a production.
6   The concrete is the totality of a production, a form of life.
7   There are different modes of production, hence different forms of life.
8   The categories are historically specific to their mode of production.
9   Analysis reformulates objects of knowledge in terms of the historically specific mode of production that makes them possible.

History as production – a relation of subject and object
The question next arises as to the significance of the historical for Marx. What difference does it make to think in terms of the historical? What is Marx's conception of history and how is it related to concepts and analysis?

Marx considers certain concepts that are abstracted from historically specific forms of life as 'rational abstractions.' Such a one is 'production in general,' which 'brings out and fixes the common element and thus saves us repetition.' However, Marx claims that one must distinguish the relations and conditions that determine capital's specific mode of production from those relations and conditions which determine production in general. This is in order that 'their essential difference is not forgotten' (85).

In what sense can one speak of an 'essential difference?' The 'essential difference' between production in general and a specific mode of production makes for the difference between an ahistorical analysis and an historical one. Marx makes the point about focusing on the distinctive in examining other theorists' treatment of production. He noticed that they tended to preface their works with analyses of production in general. They would show how all production required objectified or stored-up past labor:

> No production without stored-up, past labour, even if it is only the facility gathered together and concentrated in the hand of the savage by repeated practice. Capital is, among other things, also an instrument of production, also objectified, past labour (85).

What difference does it make to treat capital as objectified labor? By conceiving of capital as objectified labor which is necessary for all forms of production, capital becomes 'a general eternal relation of nature; that is, if I leave out just the specific quality which alone makes "instrument of production" and "stored-up labor" into capital.'

What difference does it make to conceive of capital as a natural relation? We said earlier that production is the problematic for analysis. To be produced, corresponds to Marx's notion of history. Bourgeois economists treat capital as a natural instead of an historical product. This type of presentation eternalizes and, therefore, obliterates the historical, the specific social relations that produce it:

> The aim is, rather, to present production – see e.g. Mill – as distinct from distribution, etc., as encased in eternal natural laws independent of history, at which opportunity *bourgeois* relations are then quietly smuggled in as the inviolable natural laws on which society in the abstract is

founded. This is the more or less conscious purpose of the whole proceeding. In distribution, by contrast, humanity has allegedly permitted itself to be considerably more arbitrary (87).

These economists distinguish between production as encased in eternal, natural laws and distribution as subject to more arbitrary and problematic social arrangements. Marx suggests that they do this in order to indicate the possibility of human intervention in the distribution of wealth but not in its production. By implying that capital is a natural, eternal relation of production, and that bourgeois relations of production based on capital are, therefore, independent of history, they can then lead attention to distribution and away from production. Because they do not conceive of production as a history that includes distribution, they conceive of distribution only as problematic and that which is subject to intervention.

Marx's notion of history differs from a bourgeois conception. For the latter, history consists of changes in an abstract subject (culture or politics) or changes in external nature. In contrast to this, Marx includes nature in history; it is always a particular nature produced as such by its relation to particular human purposes, relations and activities. Thus history is an internal relation of a specific subject to its specific object. As a subject works on an object, the object changes and the subject transforms itself. Nature is internal to production; as an object of purposive action, it is an historical relation of production.

A bourgeois presentation of capitalist production as grounded in external, ahistorical nature, as essentially the same for all modes of production, as the 'inviolable natural laws on which society in the abstract is founded,' removes capitalist relations from history in the sense of human production. It treats capital as natural rather than historical. Marx's polemic with this thinking is made even sharper by his use of the phrase, 'inviolable natural laws,' with respect to their conception of bourgeois relations. Inviolable refers to that which is sacrosanct. If sacrosanct, they cannot be changed by human purpose or design. They are presented, therefore, as ahistorical in Marx's sense of the term. This means that the relations of production are seen not as grounded in social, historical purposive activity, but as natural.

By showing that they could just as easily present distribution as an eternal, natural relation, Marx supports his contention that their more or less conscious purpose is to present bourgeois relations of production as inviolable. Thus Marx wants to treat production and distribution historically rather than confounding or extinguishing all historic differences under general human laws (87).

Again it should be noted that Marx's notion of the historical differs from other possible conceptions, particularly that which might be attributed to bourgeois presentations. Bourgeois analyses treat what Marx considers essential differences as purely objective differences, differences in objective conditions, or as purely subjective differences, differences between subjects. For Marx, in contrast, differences are grounded in subject-object purposive relations. There is an essential difference between a conception of history that derives from concrete observation (concrete external changes) and a conception of history that derives from analysis (internal relations). This difference is essential for producing an analytic totality, an historically specific form of life.

If analysis concerns itself with history or grounds, then should an analysis of production proceed by examining the history of its relations as a historical sequence of categories? Does one begin with the earliest forms of production and trace their development? This would be a conception of history as temporal sequence. Marx makes a distinction between what I call concrete origins and analytic origins. An historical analysis of a category or form of life is not accomplished by tracing its changes in concrete appearance over time. Its analytic origins consist of its presuppositions: the relations by which it produces and reproduces itself.

One does not treat the categories in the order in which they first appear in order to understand the historical character of the relations that they express. Rather, one should treat them in terms of their relations within a particular form of life. Priority should not be given to those which are prior in time, but to those which predominate in the form of life under analysis. Marx argues it would be incorrect to let the economic categories follow one another in the same sequence in which they occurred over time (107).

Although those relations and categories which distinguish the modern from the other modes of production may have developed relatively late, analysis should begin with those. Thus Marx has a sense of historical that differs from that of temporal sequence. This sense of historical refers to predominant or determinant relations that constitute a specific form of life: its internal relations.

For the bourgeoisie, history is a record of observation (primary sources) or 'pseudo-observation' (secondary sources) from artifacts and documents. For Marx, history is a totality of internal relations produced by analysis. Instead of an inquiry into the temporal sequence according to which a category makes its appearance, analysis should inquire into the presuppositions of the category, the internal relations or form of life in which the category is grounded.

An historical analysis of a form of life either examines the presuppositions of its initial appearance or the presuppositions of the ongoing social processes and relations which reproduce it. Marx refers to the former approach as the 'history of its formation,' while he calls the latter approach its 'contemporary history' (459). He contrasts the two versions of historical analysis with respect to the history of capital by referring to the condition that the capitalist brings values into circulation, creates capital, with his own labor or some means other than by already available wage labor, as belonging to the historic presuppositions of capital, which as such, are past and gone, 'and hence belong to the history of its formation, but in no way to its *contemporary* history, i.e. not to the real system of the mode of production ruled by it' (459).

Marx claims that the historic presuppositions for the rise of capital presuppose precisely that it has not yet become. Once it has arisen, it posits its own conditions for its reproduction, these conditions being different from the original conditions for its arising. He uses the development of cities as an analogy. While the flight of serfs to the cities is an historic condition and presupposition of the emergence of urbanism, it is not a condition (moment) of the reality of developed cities. It is a condition that belongs to the presuppositions of their becoming which are suspended in their being. 'The conditions and presuppositions of the *becoming*, of the *arising*, of capital presuppose precisely that it is not yet in being but merely in becoming' (459).

Originally capitalists may have been formed by hoarding money received in exchange for products produced by their own labor. This may account for the history of capitalists' formation but not their contemporary history. Once they have developed into capitalists, with wage labor producing surplus value, there is no need for the capitalist to come into being through hoarding his wages. Although individual accumulations of capital may arise this way; they do not become capital, as distinct from money, until it is used to employ wage labor from whom surplus value is extracted:

> That is, individual capitals can continue to arise, e.g. by means of hoarding. But the hoard is transformed into capital only by means of the exploitation of labour. The bourgeois economists who regard capital as an external and *natural* (not historical) form of production then attempt at the same time to legitimize it again by formulating the conditions of its becoming as the conditions of its contemporary realization, i.e. presenting the moments in which the capitalist still appropriates as not-capitalist – because he is still becoming – as the very conditions in which he appropriates as *capitalist* (460).

Marx suggests starting from the contemporary history – the actual processes of realization – in order to provide an analysis of its foundation.

Marx states that in order to develop the laws of bourgeois economy, the relations necessary for the reproduction of capital, it is not necessary to write 'the *real history of the relations of production*' (460). That is, it is not necessary to analyze the historic conditions of its emergence or formation. But the analysis of its contemporary history, the laws of bourgeois economy as having themselves become in history, points to earlier historical modes of production.

Marx suggests that one understand the grounds of the present before investigating the past. In this way, one can grasp the past as a becoming of the present. This contrasts with the view of theorists who believe that one must know the past before one can understand the present. Marx implies that beginning with a study of the past without a grasp of the analytic foundations of the present, merely leads to seeing the past as different versions of the present (105). In addition to providing indications about the past, an analysis of its contemporary history, 'leads at the same time to the points at which the suspension of the present form of production relations gives signs of its becoming – foreshadowings of the future' (461). Just as the pre-bourgeois forms appear as suspended presuppositions, the contemporary conditions of production 'likewise appear as engaged in *suspending themselves* and hence in positing the *historic presuppositions* for a new state of society' (461).

That it is necessary to treat concepts as historical does not mean that one begins with its first appearance and then traces its developments over time. Nor does it mean that the presuppositions of its initial appearance are treated as its contemporary presuppositions. Rather, one analyzes the ongoing subject-object relation within which the concept is (re)produced, the relations which provide for the intelligibility of the concept, its contemporary history.

In order to treat concepts as grounded, analysis inquires into the form of life which provides the sense for and, therefore, produces them as categories of that form of life. This inquiry explicates history. And for categories it is history of sense. Analysis shows the contingency of categories by revealing their embeddedness. In this way, analysis calls attention to the reflexivity of language: concepts are only knowable in terms of a form of life and a form of life can only be expressed with concepts. Hence, the essential incompleteness of speech: it always presupposes a form of life – the experiences of the lived world.

Rule 2: treat individuals as grounded in an historically specific form of life

Grounding individuals accounts for action. According to this rule, one resists treating individuals' decisions, intentions or characteristics as the grounds of actions. Rather, one treats individuals' decisions, intentions and characteristics as grounded in, having sense in terms of, a form of life. This rule may be understood as a critique of psychologism, which treats all action, including knowing, as originating with individuals. The rule argues against such a purely subjective (in the sense of originating with a knowing or acting subject) version of action. It treats individual acts as made possible or intelligible by a form of life which they presuppose.

Wittgenstein identifies language with form of life: 'to imagine a language means to imagine a form of life' (1967, p. 8). Concepts derive from and express relations and purposive activity which constitute social production or form of life. Phenomenologists tend to consider language as the totality of social productions. Heidegger (1971, pp. 21–2), for example, refers to language as the 'house of Being.' For Marx, the totality is captured by the concept of production or mode of production.

Whereas 'form of life' refers to the totality of a language, Wittgenstein uses the term 'language-game' to refer to a limited aspect of a language. 'Here the term language game is meant to bring into prominence the fact that the speaking of language is part of an activity, or of a form of life' (*ibid.*), and again, 'A language game is part of a language, part of a form of life' (*ibid.*, p. 11).

I use Wittgenstein's term 'form of life' as equivalent to the Marxist terms, mode of production and social formation. I do so in order to: 1 stress the conceiving of a social totality as social activity or process; and 2 avoid a narrow economic connotation that the words production and mode of production have.

Wittgenstein and subsequent language theorists have developed the argument that there is no possibility of a language that is the product of a single, isolated individual. Marx makes the same assertion and similarly claims that production is not the result of the decisions and actions of single, isolated individuals:

> Production by an isolated individual outside society . . . is as much of an absurdity as is the development of language without individuals living *together* and talking to each other (84).

Emphasizing the point that the individual is not the starting-point for understanding production (i.e. a form of life in contrast with the making of a thing), he criticizes theorists Smith and Ricardo. Production is not to be conceived as the production of the 'individual and isolated hunter and fisherman, with whom Smith and Ricardo begin.' Instead, 'Individuals producing in society – hence socially determined individual production – is, of course, the point of departure' (83).

Marx argues that not only is production social, but the individual too only appears as a product of society. That is, one can only treat the acts of individuals as grounded in a particular type of society – as acts whose reasons are given in language. In other words, the recognizability and intelligibility of individuals' activities presupposes an historically specific form of life that makes the individual's acts sensible. 'The human being . . . is an animal which can individuate itself only in the midst of society' (84). Society as a concept and as a concrete presupposes relations: 'Society does not consist of individuals, but expresses the sum of interrelations, the relations within which these individuals stand' (265).

Although there are individuals, they are only individuals as such because of their relations. The unit for analysis, whether the focus is society or the individual, is the relation. But what is a relation? Marx gives an example of the slave and the citizen. He states that a person is a slave or a citizen in and through society:

> To be a slave, to be a citizen, are social characteristics, relations between human being A and B. Human being A, as such is not a slave. He is a slave in and through society (265).

All characteristics of individuals are relations between human beings. These characteristics are the way in which an individual is known. We can now better understand the following quotation:

> The human being is in the most literal sense a political animal, not merely a gregarious animal, but an animal which can individuate itself only in the midst of society (84).

The idea of society or what I call a 'form of life' originating with isolated and independent individuals was prevalent in the eighteenth century. Marx has an interesting way of explaining this thinking. Taking issue with a common interpretation, Marx writes that the thought of the eighteenth-century theorists 'in no way expresses merely a reaction against over-sophistication and a return to a misunderstood natural life, as cultural historians imagine' (83). Similarly, he argues that Rousseau's social contract, which refers to the coming together of *naturally* independent, autonomous subjects on the basis of a contract, does not rest on such a 'naturalism.'

He claims that the conception of isolated individuals is 'rather, the anticipation of "civil society," in preparation since the sixteenth century and making giant strides toward maturity in the eighteenth' (83). That is, there were particular historical developments that made that conception seem reasonable.

On the type of society that made such thinking possible, he writes:

> In this society of free competition, the individual appears
> detached from the natural bonds etc. which in earlier
> historical periods make him the accessory of a definite and
> limited human conglomerate (83).

Marx is arguing that the eighteenth-century conception of the natural human being as independent of community expressed the relations of the new type of society that was developing rather than, as the cultural historians claimed, that it expressed a reaction against modern sophistication.

For Marx, the conception of the natural individual was a product of the changes in society. For the eighteenth-century thinkers, on whose shoulders Smith and Ricardo stood, the individual was an ideal whose existence they projected into the past, not as an historical result which is Marx's position, but as history's point of departure. Marx argues that this eighteenth-century conception of the individual is a product of the dissolution of feudalism and the development of new forces of production:

> this eighteenth-century individual [is] the product on one
> side of the dissolution of the feudal forms of society, on the
> other side of the new forces of production developed since
> the sixteenth century (83).

Before that time, the individual appeared not as independent, but as dependent, not as isolated, but as belonging to a greater whole. It is only in the eighteenth century, in civil society, that social relations appear external to the individual, as mere means of accomplishing private aims, hence creating the appearance of a private individual (84).

Marx can be read as arguing that the notion of a natural, independent individual is grounded in particular historical societal developments, not in human nature or in mere reaction against modernity. There are two points here that are of particular interest for our thesis. One is Marx's insistence on the individual as part of a whole, whose production is 'socially determined.' He considers that which determines individual production to be the starting-point for analysis. His interest is not in supporting and elaborating

49

this view which he feels obvious, but in rebutting the individualistic perspective which was being reintroduced by several modern political economists of his time:

> The point could go entirely unmentioned if this twaddle, which had sense and reason for the eighteenth-century characters, had not been earnestly pulled back into the centre of the most modern economics by Bastiat, Carey, Proudhon, etc. (84).

The other point of interest is the way in which Marx engages in the critique. His criticism rests neither on charging and trying to prove that these theorists of the natural individual were unrealistic romantics, nor that they were just simple-minded or mistaken. Rather, he treats these eighteenth-century notions not as mistakes, but as products of a form of life, a form of life which reproduces the individual as an isolated individual and on which they report. The eighteenth-century theorists do not recognize their notions as being so grounded.

Marx does not simply try to prove that these theorists were wrong, but tries to account for *how* they could produce their ideas by showing in what sense they could be right. He does not point to possible individual motives or individual intellectual failure, but discusses how their conception, as an intelligible production, is possible, how their ideas are grounded in a form of life. Their theorizing is possible by taking for granted their own form of life as natural, rather than as a form of life – a socially produced form. They fail to analyze their own ideas, to inquire into their presuppositions. Hence it is not an analysis at all, but a projection of the concrete appearance of the individual in the bourgeois society of the eighteenth century on to the origins of history.

Thus Marx's polemic may be seen as illustrating the first rule: 'Treat concepts such as the natural individual as grounded in an historically specific form of life.' Rather than arguing the truth or falsity of a concept abstractly, he grounds it in the form of life that it presupposes. The concept is only valid for that form of life. The first and second rule display a phenomenological commitment to analyzing the foundations of social phenomena.

The second rule constitutes a critique of a bourgeois conception of the individual as the basis of society. The individual is seen as a product of society. 'Society does not consist of individuals, but expresses the sum of interrelations, the relations within which these individuals stand' (265). We should now examine how one arrives at the relations that constitute a totality, a form of life.

Rule 3: treat a form of life as a totality of internal relations

There are two aspects of this rule that need explaining. The first is the distinction between a form of life and a society or social group. The other is the distinction between a totality of internal relations and a totality of external relations. Both distinctions are aspects of the conception of a form of life. As aspects, they can only be understood in terms of each other or in terms of the whole that they constitute. In other words, the distinction between form of life and society is contingent on the distinction between internal relations and external relations and vice versa.

The concept of society implies a social grouping that has boundaries, a group that is distinguishable from other groups. However, the concept of society does not provide any particular means of distinguishing between societies, any differences can be used. Thus the specification of a society becomes arbitrary. One might designate a particular geographical area a society; a particular religious group a society; a particular language group a society; a politically autonomous area and all the people and activities that are included within that area; or all the features that characterize human life in a given historical period – modern society.

Unlike the generality of the concept, society, form of life is conceived more specifically as a dialectical process of social production, a process in which a subject produces itself as such in its production of objects. This means that subjects and objects reciprocally presuppose and produce each other. Together, they constitute a unity, a form of life.

As noted above, a form of life is a process of social production. It is not production in the limited economic sense, but more generally the process by which a particular type of act or type of experience is made possible. Thus a form of life refers to the conditions for producing an historical subject or object. Beginning with either subject or object, one could analyze its distinctive form of life by formulating a process by which it produces itself including its subjective and objective conditions. Hence, not only

51

can capital be analyzed in terms of its form of life, but such phenomena as bias in social science can also be analyzed in terms of the subject-object dialectic, the form of life that produces bias as a possibility (see McHugh *et al.*, 1974, pp. 47–9).

A form of life as a totality of internal relations, then, refers to the relations that are necessary for the production of the object that one studies. The relations are internal to its process of production. This differs from treating a social formation as everything that can be collected as existing within a particular historical period or within particular political boundaries. Thus the form of life that Marx analyzes is conceived as a totality of the subjective-objective conditions for producing capital – the relation of capital and wage labor. When he sketches an analysis of the form of life that characterized the Germanic tribes, he conceives of the totality as the self-sufficient family residence. In Marx's analysis the totality of the ancient Asiatic form of life included the relations of local communities to a higher unity, the despot. Thus religion was included in the subjective-objective condition for reproducing the Asiatic form. For Marx, therefore, a form of life is the totality of relations internal to the production of that form and not a totality of everything that can be observed in that time and place.

This contrasts with a conception of society as a totality of external relations. In this conception, an object is a thing that is given to the senses or given with speech and accounted for in terms of its external relations to other things. External relations such as cause and effect contrast with internal relations conceived as determinations. What is the distinction between the social-science notion of causality and Marx's notion of determinations? Causality treats of the observable or measurable relations between things, whereas determinations refer to the relations presupposed by the recognition of the thing. That is, in order to recognize an object as a particular kind of thing, certain relations are presumed.

According to Marx, nothing is what we know it to be outside of the relations and activities in which it is known. A typewriter, for instance, is only a typewriter for an observer who knows what typing is. A medicinal herb is a medicinal herb only within a form of life where medicinal herbs are known as such. Similarly, for all objects. Marx proceeds by making explicit the relations and presuppositions that are presumed by such recognition as the determinations that are internal to the knowledge of that object. The object is thereby treated as a human object or a social object produced by human relations and presuppositions.

These determinations differ from causal relations which are external to the object. Causality presumes that the object is immediately known as such. Its history as a human product, as an object mediated by human purposes and relations, is denied or covered over by treating it as a natural thing immediately known to the senses, something that is simply there which can be measured and shown to be related to other things. Analysis, then, is the attempt to recover the history of an object, its production as an intelligible and historically specific social phenomenon.

The notion of totality, as I use it, means that activities which may appear as indifferent to each other constitute a whole. This means that they are related to each other internally, that they require each other for their own possibility. According to Marx, they 'form the members of a totality, distinctions within a unity' (99).

On what basis can one claim that certain activities form a totality, a form of life? It is not enough to show that they always occur together, pointing out that each of these separate activities together form a process where each is contingent on the other, e.g. consumption presupposes distribution of the product, distribution presupposes production, and production presupposes consumption.

Analysis distinguishes a form of life from just any set of relations on the basis of its being self-moving. This means that it is a subjectivity or purposive action. This notion of purpose should not be confused with individuals' purposes or intentions. It is the purpose or end that is given with an already existing activity. Thus purpose does not originate with individuals' intentions, although it can be changed by individuals' intentions and actions. In analyzing a form of life, it is not enough to describe the internal relations in terms of objective conditions for its production – that which is used in accomplishing it. It is also necessary to describe the subjective conditions for its re-production – the particular purpose(s) that it accomplishes or realizes.

The subjective-objective conditions for its production and re-production constitute its grounds. They also constitute it as a form of life. To be a form of (human) life, is to have grounds. A form of life, then, is purpose and the conditions for realizing that purpose.

The relations between purpose and its conditions of realization are the internal relations that comprise a form of life.

Marx's object is the categories of political economy: production, consumption, distribution, exchange, etc. He reformulates them as a form of life, a totality of internal relations. In order to show it as such, he must establish a subjectivity or subject-object relation that unites the various categories in a self-moving process. Marx identifies production as the subjectivity that unites the categories and makes them into moments of a whole.

The political economy Marx was addressing had been criticized for treating production too much as an end in itself. It was argued that distribution was just as important a matter for political economy. However, Marx considers this criticism to be 'based precisely on the economic notion that the spheres of distribution and of production are independent, autonomous neighbours.' In other words, economists analyze production and distribution independently of each other. In this way, we noted earlier, problems of distribution could be treated independently of production which is 'inviolable,' based on natural laws.

The other criticism of political economy that Marx considered in the Introduction is that 'these moments were not grasped in their unity.' This seems to be a view that, given the quotation above, one would expect Marx to support. Yet he is not satisfied with this criticism either. He charges that this criticism essentially blames the separation of production and distribution on the failure of the theorists to recognize their unity.

He denounces this criticism because it implies that the problem is one of faulty conceptualizing whose remedy, therefore, is correct conceptualizing. His words, punctuated by an exclamation point, are:

> As if this rupture had made its way not from reality into
> the textbooks, but rather from the textbooks into reality,
> and as if the task were the dialectic balancing of concepts,
> and not the grasping of real relations! (90).

For Marx, the categories comprise a unity of production. This unity is belied or contradicted by the separation and apparent independence of its moments: the different processes that constitute the totality of production. Despite the unity which is uncovered in analysis, the various categories or moments of

54

production appear separate and independent of each other. This appearance is not a mistake or failure on the part of theorists. Rather, it reflects a real separation in time and space of the moments of production.

Marx must show how, despite an appearance of separation and externality, these categories constitute a totality, a subjectivity. Merely asserting that they constitute a unity, merely showing that they presuppose each other, is not enough. As Marx indicates, such an approach suggests that the problem is merely theoretical, a misconception. Rather, an analysis must show how a unity comes to be separated. It must show how the categories constitute a unity that comes to be separated in reality. By so doing, it provides for human intervention, for self-change. A subjectivity is capable of consciously changing itself. Instead of external, separate phenomena, the categories are conceived as aspects of a subjectivity. The predominant moment of this totality is production. Production determines the other moments.

It might seem that consumption and not production is the predominant relation, '(1) because a product becomes a real product only by being consumed. For example, a garment becomes a real garment only in the act of being worn.' The purposes to which it is put (its consumption) determines the type of product it is: 'a house where no one lives is in fact not a real house.' In addition it might seem that consumption is the predominant relation, '(2) because consumption creates the need for *new* production' (91). That is, it creates the motive for production in the form of an ideal, internally impelling cause for production.

As Marx indicates, 'No production without a need. But consumption reproduces the need' (91). Therefore, it would seem that consumption is the determinant moment. However, consumption reproduces the need that production produces. Marx enumerates three ways in which production creates consumption:

(1) furnishes the material and the object for consumption.
(2) Production . . . produces not only the object but also the manner of consumption, not only objectively but subjectively. Production thus creates the consumer . . . the object is not an object in general, but a specific object which must be consumed in a specific manner, to be mediated in its turn by production itself (92).

55

The example Marx offers is that of hunger. 'Hunger is hunger,' he states, 'but the hunger gratified by cooked meat eaten with a knife and fork is a different hunger from that which bolts down raw meat with the aid of hand, nail and tooth.' In addition to producing a material for the need, it also produces a need for the material:

> (3) . . . As soon as consumption emerges from its initial state of natural crudity and immediacy – and, if it remained at that stage, this would be because production itself had been arrested there – it becomes itself mediated as a drive by the object. The need which consumption feels for the object is created by the perception of it. The object of art – like every other product – creates a public which is sensitive to art and enjoys beauty (92).

Marx has been showing that just as consumption creates production, production also creates consumption. How is it that one can claim any predominance for one over the other? Marx states that:

> Not only is production immediately consumption and consumption immediately production, not only is production a means for consumption and consumption the aim of production, i.e. each supplies the other with its object (production supplying the external object of consumption, consumption the conceived object of production); but also, each of them, apart from being immediately the other, and apart from mediating the other, in addition to this creates the other in completing itself, and creates itself as the other (93).

According to Marx, this is the type of unity or identity that not only a Hegelian would find easy to posit, but so did 'socialist belletrists' and 'prosaic economists themselves.'

In spite of this identity, Marx claims that production and consumption are moments of one process, 'in which production is the real point of departure and hence also the predominant moment.' Marx claims that consumption is a moment of production. Why could one not similarly claim that production is an intrinsic moment of consumption? The only answer that Marx offers seems to beg the question:

The individual produces an object and, by consuming it, returns to himself, but returns as a productive and self-reproducing individual. Consumption thus appears as a moment of production (94).

If we examine that argument, Marx begins the process with production. One might have begun the process with consumption. While it is possible to talk about consumption or urges in the abstract as determining production, as soon as one talks of concrete consumption, urges with a specific realizable object, production is already presupposed. Whereas consumption may be the point of departure 'ideally,' in positing an 'ideal' for production to realize, consumption itself is only realized as a specific type of consumption, a consumption of specific objects, by the production of those objects. Hence a specific consumption presupposes a specific production.

Production is the starting-point because any intelligible activity is productive activity in that it produces and reproduces the actor as such. The human is a specific type of individual because of its activity. Even as consumer, the human is a specific type of consumer which is determined by its production. If one treated consumption as the starting-point, analysis would ask how consumption produces and reproduces itself. We have seen that as a specific type, it presupposes a specific object which in turn presupposes production. In other words, consumption is always consumption of a specific object. However, a specific object presupposes a specific relation to a subject, a specific mode of appropriation or production.

Marx similarly considers the possibility that distribution, rather than production, is predominant. He presents three possible reasons for this formulation. The first is that the distribution of social positions precedes production. For example, 'social distribution assigns the individual at birth to wage labour.' However, Marx replies that 'this situation of being assigned is itself a consequence of the existence of capital and landed property as independent agents of production' (96). In other words, a particular type of production results in the particular positions and their distribution.

There is a second basis for conceiving of distribution as preceding and determining production. The cases offered in support are: a conquering people divides the land among the conquerors, thus imposing a certain form and distribution of property in land, and thereby determining production. Or it enslaves the population that is conquered and makes slave labor the foundation of production. Or a people rises in revolution and smashes the great landed estates into small parcels, and hence, by this new distribution gives production a new character. Or a system of law assigns property in land to certain families in perpetuity, or distributes labor as a hereditary privilege and thus confines it within certain castes.

In all these cases, it seems that distribution is not structured and determined by production, but rather the opposite, production by distribution. However, according to Marx, these factors (of conquest, law, etc.)

> reduce themselves in the last instance to the role played by general-historical relations in production, and their relation to the movement of history generally. The question evidently belongs *within the treatment and investigation of production itself* (97).

How is it that the factors 'reduce themselves in the last instance' to the relations of production? The answer is: by carrying through an analysis of *how* distribution (e.g. after conquest) is possible, that is, by inquiring into the grounds of distribution, one then finds that production is always necessary.

He provides a brief example of how he feels such questions can be dealt with:

> In all cases of conquest, three things are possible. The conquering people subjugates the conquered under its own mode of production; or it leaves the old mode intact and contents itself with a tribute; or a reciprocal interaction takes place whereby something new, a synthesis, arises. . . . In all cases, the mode of production, whether that of the conquering people, that of the conquered, or that emerging from the fusion of both, is decisive for the new distribution which arises (97).

Thus he asserts it is not distribution that is predominant, but it is the mode of production which is decisive for distribution because it produces that which is distributed. One could change that which is distributed by changing production but not vice versa. For example, one might alter the distribution of products, of instruments of production or of people among wage labor and capital, but this would not change the mode of production. However, eliminating wage labor or capital would be decisive for the mode of production. It would change production and consumption and distribution. A change in the mode of production could change the type of consumption, and the nature of the distribution (that which is distributed).

The other moments cannot change their character and, therefore, cannot change production. A change in distribution cannot change that which is distributed; it can only change its concentration. A change in consumption cannot change production except ideally (as the desire for or idea of something else). Production, on the other hand, does determine distribution by determining the character of that which is distributed; likewise it does determine consumption by determining what is consumed.

Thus, if we want to analyze the totality as an historical form of life, as having a mode distinct from other totalities, as something vulnerable to intervention, then it is necessary to begin with production, for the distinctiveness of production determines the distinctiveness of the totality: 'A definite production thus determines a definite consumption, distribution and exchange as well as *definite relations between these different moments*' (99).

Why does Marx go to so much trouble eliminating other possibilities in favor of his stress on production? The notion of totality provides an answer. Marx recognizes a need to be able to grasp a totality as an ongoing and self-transforming subjectivity. In other words, one must be able to formulate a subject of history in order to conceive of participating in history. Otherwise, the subjects of history are conceived as objects moved about by external forces of the environment, and history becomes merely a record of such incidents and events. Marx formulates the subject of history as production or labor. One might be able to locate subjectivity with the other moments. For example, if capital is decisive for bourgeois economy, one might claim that capital arises with the desire for capital (consumption) or with the distribution of instruments of production or with exchange in which capital is realized. The need is to have some way of locating the core of a totality. Hence, production refers to the core of a totality not to a particular activity such as commerce or manufacture (which after all might exist in pre-capitalist formations as well which Marx acknowledges).

Production is both the total process of which the others are moments – a mode of production – and a set of particular activities called production. As the latter, it is also a moment of the totality. I take it that production as a set of particular activities is the antithetical definition to which Marx refers in the elliptical statement, 'Production dominates not only over itself, in the antithetical definition of production, but over the other moments as well' (99).

The antithetical definition is production in the sense of particular types of productive activities, the production of particular things. This notion of production is antithetical to the concept of production as a totality. We can now make sense of what might have seemed puzzling in relation to his earlier statement: 'Admittedly, however, in its one-sided form, production is itself determined by the other moments' (99).

That is, production is determined by the other moments if one does not treat production as the totality – a mode of production – but treats it only one-sidedly as particular activities. He illustrates how the other moments might determine production (its one-sided form) by explaining that in the sphere of exchange, the expansion of the market causes production to grow in quantity. In the sphere of distribution, changes such as concentration of capital or different distribution of the population between town and country, etc. can also change the specific activities of production. Similarly, the needs of consumption also determine the specific activities of production. He concludes, 'mutual interaction takes place between the different moments. This is the case with every organic whole' (100). However, his whole is not an interaction of externals. Rather, these moments are internal relations, internal to a mode of production.

They are not autonomous or merely interdependent, but they are themselves determined (in the sense of made possible or intelligible as particular types) by the predominant moment of the process which is the point of departure and the point of return – the ground in the sense of totality as process.

A key word, 'moments,' comes from the word 'movement,' which as we shall see is the way Marx conceives of the totality. The totality is not just a circular process, a mere repetition, but this process is itself a movement. This means that the totality itself is changing. Hence, its categories are not elements or parts in a stable structure, but are sides or aspects of a totality, 'moments' in a movement. Marx explicitly states that the determinations (moments) are constantly changing, that they may appear to be natural but are historical products:

> if they appear to one epoch as natural presuppositions of production, they were its historic product for another. Within production itself, they are constantly being changed. The application of machinery, for example, changed the distribution of instruments of production as well as products (99–100).

Marx's conception of the whole is that it is a process of production that is moving or changing, on the one hand, because it is composed of moments or determinations that are constantly changing. On the other hand, it is moving because the predominant moment cannot sustain itself. Therefore, the totality, the mode of production which is determined by the predominant moment, cannot sustain itself.

The next question to be addressed is why a particular mode of production cannot be sustained. The answer takes the form of an analysis showing how its predominant moment is self-contradictory, how its conditions for realizing itself contradict its conditions for reproducing itself. Hence, one side of the relation is trying to suspend another side of the relation.

Rule 4: treat a concrete form of life as contradictory

This rule constitutes the principle of growth. We have seen that grounding the individual in a form of life accounts for individual action. We have also seen that treating a form of life as a totality of internal relations united by purpose constitutes a subjectivity which accounts for self-movement. Growth is different from action and self-movement. Growth is development that is transcendence, a going beyond what is, a becoming more than or other than what is. Growth, for a subjectivity, is learning. The resolution of contradiction is a learning. The movement of a contradictory form

61

of life may be thought of as a process of learning, one that provides for its own growth, its own supersession. A concrete form of life treats phenomena as discrete things that are related to other things. This contrasts with an analytic form of life which treats phenomena as grounded objects, internal relations of a totality. A concrete form of life does not know grounds; it does not know subjectivity. To be a form of life, however, is to have grounds. A form of life that forgets grounds denies itself as such. It is self-contradictory.

Concrete theorizing is a display of unself-conscious theorizing. Analytic theorizing is a display of self-conscious theorizing. By way of an analysis of the concrete, analytic theorizing displays its own possibility – the possibility of a self-conscious form of life. It does this by showing how its repression, i.e. a concrete form of life, is accomplished. In other words, it grounds its own possibility as a form of life in the overcoming of its repression, the over-coming of a concrete form of life. Hence it must show how its repression is accomplished, the conditions that produce repression. Marx grounds the repression in contradiction. He shows how a concrete form of life is a result of a self-contradictory movement, a subjectivity that is divided into opposing moments.

An analytic form of life is a production that remembers grounds, an internal relation of production to grounds. This means that an object is posited in terms of purposes that it realizes. The object is not divorced from purpose. Conversely, the purpose of a pro-duction is posited in terms of an object to be mastered. The purpose of production is not divorced from the object of pro-duction. The unity of purpose and object is realized in labor.

Furthermore, purpose is not just natural urgencies but a sub-jectivity, a knowing or self-consciousness that is able to posit its own aims. This means that production as a unity of purpose and object is a unity of subject and object. The object is only sensible as an object in terms of a subject for which it has meaning.

This seems to be a simple formulation: an analytic form of life is the intentional production of meaningful objects. Without qualifying or elaborating this formulation, I will contrast it with an equally simple and familiar one, that of a concrete form of life. A concrete form of life is a production that does not recognize itself as a unity. Rather, it understands itself only in terms of subject *or* object. As subject, it is divorced from objects to be mastered; it is pure purpose, planning that does not actively contend with the resistance of objects. On the other hand, conceived in terms of objects, it is activity as adaptation to objective conditions, a struggle with external objects of nature in which the character of the subject is irrelevant or conceived in a general way as survival.

In contrast to an analytic form of life, a concrete form is conceived in terms of external relations, cause and effect, rather than internal relations of purpose and the conditions for realizing that purpose. An external relation is one in which purpose is not realized in the activity itself. For instance, the aim of making money as such is indifferent to the specific labor involved. The aim is not realized in specific activity. This distinction is sometimes understood simply as the difference between intrinsically meaningful and extrinsically meaningful activity.

The difference between extrinsic and intrinsic, concrete and analytic, is not a difference attributable to individuals. It is not a moral choice that is decided by individual will. It is not that a concrete form of life or activity which is extrinsically meaningful reveals moral weakness, whereas an analytic form of life or activity which is intrinsically meaningful reveals moral integrity. Such a formulation is not analytic because it fails to account for the choice as possibility. It treats the choice in terms of pure subjectivity divorced from its objective conditions. In other words, it fails to account for its own possibility. For analysis, the possibility of extrinsic meaning and external relations is grounded in a historically specific form of life. In other words, a concrete form of life must be seen as a history and not simply individuals' choice.

Analysis shows the history of activity that is only extrinsically meaningful, a concrete form of life, in the separation of labor from its objective conditions. In contrast to the separation that analysis describes is the unity which analysis knows, the unity of an analytic form of life. I formulated this unity earlier as the realizing of purpose in a material object.

A form of life that denies itself as a form of life is one in which purpose is separated from the conditions for its realization. This separation of subject and object makes for a divided subjectivity. Instead of a single subject, there is a divided or dual one. Marx analyzes political economy by showing how this dual or divided subjectivity is accomplished. The subject-object of bourgeois political economy is the production of wealth in the form of

63

the commodity – capital. The commodity is a dual object. It is exchange value and use value.

A contradiction occurs when a term means two mutually exclusive things, A and not-A. A contradictory form of life is a totality of opposing moments, moments that negate each other. This is the case with the commodity in the form of capital.

A commodity is distinguished from any object by having exchange value. Exchange value refers to an object's abstract exchangeability with other objects. This means that objects must be identical in some quality such that the only difference between them is quantitative. Hence, three units of one item, for example, may be equivalent to five units of another item. This exchange value is an abstraction, a purely formal quality, because it is independent of any relation to a subject. It is independent of the natural substance of the commodity. A commodity has a calculable exchange value regardless of the demand or need for its specific substance, i.e. regardless of any use value. In calculating exchange value, all consideration of use value is excluded.

On the other hand, in order to realize its exchange value, the commodity must have use value. But use value is not a purely objective calculation as is exchange value. On the contrary, use value refers to a commodity for which there is a subject for whom it realizes purpose – a buyer. Exchange value cannot exist as a real thing rather than an abstract calculation without use value. In other words, exchange value presupposes use value. On the one hand, it is an abstraction independent of use value. On the other hand, it only realizes itself in, and hence presupposes, use value. It is self-contradictory because it presupposes on the one side that which it excludes on the other.

The commodity is this contradictory relation, a totality of opposing moments: production of exchange value which excludes use value and the realization of exchange value which requires use value. It is both use value and not-use value. This contradiction is realized only in capital. In simple circulation, as opposed to the circulation of capital, 'whose highest perfection is money' not capital, exchange value is not both a specific commodity and money in the same form: 'money loses its value quality when it is exchanged for a particular commodity' (270).

However, as capital, exchange value and use value remain united in the commodity form. In simple circulation, exchange value and use value are separated, taking the form of money or specific commodity but never both in the same form. In its money form, it loses its quality as value when it exchanges for a commodity which it consumes. In its form as capital, it does not lose its quality as value when it consumes a commodity. Capital is the unity of commodity and money: 'Exchange value posited as the unity of commodity and money is *capital*, and this positing itself appears as the circulation of capital' (266). The only use value in exchange with which capital does not lose its value quality is labor power. The employment of labor power reproduces and increases value. Marx develops the contradictory relation of capital and labor in which capital presupposes labor as use value – the production of value – while it treats labor exclusively as exchange value – a cost of production. The accumulation of capital requires contradictory conditions. It requires suspending its conditions of reproduction (labor as use value) in order to realize its purpose (increase in exchange value). Therefore, it cannot see itself as a totality. It must forget one side. When remembering one relation, it must forget the other.

Thus capital must see the commodity either as pure exchange value – a commodity whose worth is determined by exchange relations. Or it must see the commodity as pure use value – a product that is itself the realizing of purpose. It justifies itself by remembering that it is the production of use values. In actual production, however, it must forget this as its *raison d'être* and remember that its purpose is the production of exchange value. Is there any essential difference between use value and exchange value that makes the above assertion sensible?

If a commodity is both use value and exchange value, then are not the two identical, just different sides of the same relation? Isn't the monetary (exchange) value of a product identical with the product itself such that having a product is also having a certain exchange value (potentially or ideally)? Likewise, isn't having a certain exchange value in the form of money, also having (potentially or ideally) any product that is an equivalent exchange value? If identity were the case, then the purpose of producing exchange value would be identical with the purpose of producing use value. There would be no 'real' difference between the (purposive) relations of production (production of exchange value) and the means of production (the production of use value).

65

They would form a unity, a form of life.

Treating the two as different would merely be a mistake due to the failure to see the totality, a failure to analyze. With analysis and the recognition of the mistake, the two would be one and production would directly and immediately realize both purposes. The opposition between use value and exchange value would cease. This means that there would no longer be speculation, stockpiling or overproduction. Each of these activities presumes that exchange value and use value are not identical. Each is made possible by a disunity of use value and exchange value. Each case presumes that a commodity's exchange value may change while its use value remains the same, and conversely that its use value may change while its exchange value remains the same. These variations in one or the other aspect of value account for the fluctuation of price.

For a form of life in which opposition is only an appearance, analysis (self-consciousness) would dissolve the difference by revealing the identity. It would show that exchange value is only possible through commodities and that commodities as use value are only possible through the production of exchange value, hence that the two are an identity. It would show that the struggle between them, such as in stockpiling or overproduction, is due to the lack of recognition on the part of exchangers and producers that commodities and exchange value are identical.

The treatment of exchange value and use value as identical is idealist theorizing. Idealism assumes that the movement of consciousness from apparent opposition of subject and object, from apparent separation of purpose and that which realizes purpose, to the realization of their unity, produces the movement of concrete social phenomena. According to my reading of Marx, the failure to analyze, the failure to recognize their identity is due to a real difference between exchange value and use value (a difference that is internal to the commodity form). It is a real difference (not an ideal one in consciousness) that prevents recognition of identity.

In a self-conscious form of life the subject (purpose) and the object (the realization of that purpose) together would constitute an identity – aspects of a unity. In the commodity form as capital, the aim is production of exchange value (wealth) and the means is the production of use values. Exchange value and its agents do not recognize use value and its agents as identical with itself (different aspects of a unity) because the difference between them is not an ideal difference. It is not a product of cognition. Remembering origins in this case is not remembering a unity in which the two sides produce themselves as subject and object for each other. It is a remembering of the subject's origins in disunity. The movement of categories is not an ideal movement from an appearance of difference to the reality of identity. To quote Marx,

> Therefore, to the kind of consciousness – and this is characteristic of the philosophical consciousness – for which conceptual thinking is the real human being, and for which the conceptual world as such is thus the only reality, the movement of the categories appears as the real act of production – which only, unfortunately, receives a jolt from the outside – whose product is the world (101).

The jolt that idealism receives from the outside comes from the movement of reality. The latter conflicts with its own movement: a movement from apparent difference to recognition of identity. This seems to be the import of the note he makes to himself to remember: 'Dialectic of the concepts productive force (means of production) and relation of production, a dialectic whose boundaries are to be determined and which does not suspend the real difference' (109).

Thus the dialectic of the concepts cannot be determined as if it were a dialectic of consciousness. Within the latter, the difference between a concept and its other (subject and object) is suspended through the development of consciousness as it comes to recognize the oneness of what had appeared to be external relations, the recognition that the object is the subject in objectified form. Analyzing the dialectic of its moments, showing the grounds of their apparent difference, does not suspend the real difference of the moments of capitalist production.

A concrete form of life does not remember grounds. This is not to say that it is a forgetting in the usual sense, contingent on other things such as distraction or lack of interest. Rather, it is like repression because it is a necessary forgetting. Grounds *cannot* be remembered; the totality *cannot* be conceived as a totality of internal relations – a subjectivity. This is because the means (objective conditions) for realizing and reproducing that subjectivity are contradictory. It is impossible to remember and proceed. Remembering would be the recognition that in realizing its purposes, the conditions for its reproduction are being violated. Remembering would be recalling its internal violence, hence an impossibility. The conditions for realizing and increasing wealth as exchange value contradict the conditions for producing and increasing wealth as use value.

Capital cannot know itself as a totality of use value and exchange value or it would know itself to be a contradiction. Hence, it sees itself sometimes as one, sometimes as the other, but it cannot reconcile these different sides of itself. In its exchange with labor, capital must see its product as exchange value only not as use value. It exchanges with labor only to the extent that the latter produces exchange values. It restricts employment and production when exchange value cannot be realized. Capital cannot see its product as use value in its exchange with labor. To do so would be to recognize that it restricts the production of use values in the face of its aim (and claim) to increase the wealth produced.

Similarly, capital cannot treat labor itself as use value – as having value for capital. For labor's use value to capital would be identical with the exchange value of its product. If capital treated labor as use value, it would exchange with labor an equivalent of the exchange value that labor produces. That is, labor's use value for capital. If it did this, capital would cease to exist as such. Hence, capital cannot recognize labor as use value. Yet as we have seen, it presupposes labor as use value.

If it did recognize labor as use value but insisted on treating it as exchange value, it would then have to confront the contradiction between what it knows and what it does. It would have to recognize itself as theft, exploitation and oppression rather than exchange, freedom and equality. Yet it justifies its own existence in terms of the freedom and equality among exchangers that it presupposes and makes possible.

On the one hand, we have seen that capital must see the commodity as exchange value in order to produce it and in order to employ labor. On the other hand, capital must see the commodity that is produced as a use value both in order to sell it and in order to justify its existence. It attributes to itself the production of use values: 'Without capital, there is no production – no products for consumption.' Thus at one time it must see commodities and labor as exchange values exclusively (when it comes to employment and production). At another time it must see commodities as use values both in order to sell them and in order to justify its existence.

Forgetting (repression) allows a contradictory form to persist, but it does not eliminate the contradictions. It is a tense form because the side that is repressed is in conflict with its other side. It is a tense form because it is a coerced unity – there is a suppression of one side in order to allow its other side to realize itself. The suppressed side could not be acknowledged without dissolving the subjectivity, the purpose that distinguishes it as a totality.

Acknowledgment would be the recognition that the subject is divided. It is divided between the purpose of producing use value (production) and realizing exchange value (circulation). The recognition of a divided subject makes for class consciousness: the recognition that the production of exchange value is not identical with the production of use value, that the purpose of the agents of exchange value (capitalists, sellers) are not identical with the agents of use value (workers, buyers), that the realization of one purpose is not the realization of the other purpose.

Just as the object of production, the commodity, is a divided form, so is the subject. The division between labor and capital is reflected in class conflict, in the struggle of labor to realize itself as use value against the struggle of capital to realize itself as exchange value. This conflict is internal to the production of capital. It provides for learning and growth – the development of a self-conscious, socialized proletariat.

CHAPTER 3

Concepts: grounded versus subjective or objective

Since political economics is the concern with the production of wealth, a logical starting-point for analysis is the concept of wealth. Marx formulates the concept of wealth as a *relation* between a product and the particular need which it satisfies. This contrasts with a conception of wealth as an objective thing:

> Every particular commodity . . . in so far as it is realized not as price, but in its natural property, is a moment of wealth by way of its relation to a particular need which it satisfies; and in this relation expresses (1) only the wealth of uses (2) only a quite particular facet of this wealth (218).

Marx distinguishes wealth in the form of money from wealth that is not money. He shows the differences in forms of life that they presuppose and the types of poverty to which they are related. I will illustrate the rule of this chapter, to treat concepts as grounded, by describing Marx's analysis of wealth. I begin with the distinction between wealth as money and wealth that is not money.

Wealth as money

In the quotation above, wealth, in the form of a particular commodity 'in its natural property' – that is, not as exchange value, but as use value – is a relation to particular uses or needs. In contrast, money as wealth is a relation to any need: Money is general wealth because it can be used to satisfy any need in so far as the object of the need is available for exchange. Money is not only the form that general wealth takes, but it is the content itself.

70

There is no such possibility as general wealth where money has not developed. 'The concept of wealth, so to speak, is realized, *individualized* in a particular object' (218).

In being the general form of wealth, money is distinguished from all other commodities. The substance of money is the totality of all commodities in their exchangeability, their relation to each other. A product that is posited as an exchange value is no longer a 'simple thing' but a relation:

> A product posited as exchange value . . . is posited as a *relation*, more precisely as a relation in general, not to one commodity but to every commodity, to every possible product. It expresses, therefore, a general relation (205).

Exchange value is wealth. It is also the substance of money. It is wealth 'in its totality in abstraction from its particular modes of existence' (221). Exchange value is both the totality of all commodities and the abstraction from all particular commodities. As itself a commodity, it is therefore 'the god among commodities':

> Thus, in the first role, money is wealth itself; in the other, it is the *general material representative of wealth*. This totality exists in money itself as the comprehensive representation of commodities. Thus, wealth (exchange value as totality as well as abstraction) exists, individualized as such, to the exclusion of all other commodities, as a singular, tangible object, in gold and silver. Money is therefore the god among commodities (221).

The analogy to a god suggests what Marx's analysis of a god might be, an analysis similar to Durkheim's (1961). On the one hand, a god is the totality of all lives and the abstraction from all particular lives. On the other hand, a god is a concrete representation of life, existing in an individualized and singular form to the exclusion of all other forms of life. Thus, on the one hand, it is all embracing and, on the other hand, it is intolerant and exclusive. Individuals cease to be god-like except in so far as they live the specific form of life represented by the god.

In money, wealth has ceased being particular products in their relation to particular needs. Instead wealth exists as exchange value, to the exclusion of all other commodities, in money.

Commodities cease to be wealth except in so far as they can be exchanged for money.

Particular wealth and its form of life

The importance of Marx's identification of general wealth with money is not simply to achieve the kind of understanding one gets from a lexical definition. In order to understand the significance of his identifying general wealth and money, money must be treated as historical. Marx does this by showing the difference in form of life (social relations) that general wealth presupposes as compared with wealth in particular things where money is not involved. Particular kinds of wealth presuppose an

> *essential relation* between the individual and the objects, in which the individual in one of his aspects objectifies (*vergegenstandlicht*) himself in the thing, so that his posses-sion of the thing appears at the same time as a certain development of his individuality: wealth in sheep, the development of the individual as shepherd, wealth in grain, his development as agriculturist, etc. (222).

In the last cited passage, Marx states that the possession of the thing appears as a certain development of his individuality, e.g. wealth in sheep, the development of the individual as shepherd. This is particularly relevant with respect to the *accumulation* of wealth. The accumulation of wealth in the form of capital does not imply any specific development of the individual. This differs from the accumulation of wealth in specific forms. 'Accumulating sheep does not make one into a shepherd' (233). To be a shepherd presupposes specific relations to a specific object.

Similarly, the accumulating of slaves or land, which might not seem to involve the development of a particular capacity on the part of the individual, does require relations of domination and subordination (233). Accumulating particular wealth as distinct from general wealth or money involves more than a simple increase in wealth. Wealth in the form of the accumulation of *particular* things presupposes a *particular form of life*.

Furthermore, if the possessors of the particular kinds of wealth want to realize other kinds of wealth from it, they have to trade with the particular commodity accumulated. 'I have to be a grain merchant, cattle merchant, etc.' (233).

In other words, the accumulation of particular wealth (as distinct from general wealth or money) presupposes a particular mode of existence, involving the relation of a producer to the product (i.e. the development of his productive ability or talent), the relation of a possessor to others (e.g. domination or subordination) and the relation of an individual to a particular type of exchange activity (e.g. grain merchant, cattle merchant). In each case, the particular wealth presupposes a particular set of relations which is not the case for the possession of general wealth or money.

General wealth and its form of life

The concept and phenomenon of general wealth also presupposes a form of life. However, the concept of wealth presupposes and (re)produces a very different mode of existence, one in which the possession of it in no way implies the development of any essential aspects of the possessor's individuality:

> Money . . . does not at all presuppose an individual relation to its owner; possession of it is not the development of any particular essential aspect of his individuality; but rather possession of what lacks individuality, since this social (relation) exists at the same time as a sensuous, external object which can be mechanically seized, and lost in the same manner (222).

Marx explains that, since it is a tangible object, money or wealth may be searched for, found, stolen, or discovered. The individual's relation to it 'appears as a purely accidental one having no connection with his individuality.' It gives him at the same time, however,

> a *general power* over society, over the whole world of gratifications, labours, etc. It is exactly as if, for example, the chance discovery of a stone gave me mastery over all the sciences, regardless of my individuality. The possession of money places me in exactly the same relationship

towards wealth (social) as the philosopher's stone would
towards the sciences (222).

Marx is making the analogy between the individual who, through
an external thing independent of any talents or abilities, is able to
be the master of all the sciences, and the individual who, without
any particularly developed talents or abilities, is able to have
influence over other people's social activities and things, over all of
society. In his identifying wealth with the social, we may infer that
the wealth is social because it is produced socially, and power over
the wealth is, therefore, power over other people's activity or
work.

Marx accomplishes a phenomenological analysis of money as
general wealth. By phenomenological analysis, I mean that he
treats the notion itself as problematic – inquiring into the relations
(i.e. the relation of the producer to production, to others, and to
society) that are presupposed by and (re)produced by it. These
social relations are the grounds of the notion; they provide for the
intelligibility of the category. This is in distinction to a concrete
analysis which treats money (as wealth) positionally, as a thing
whose only source of interest is its external relations or position,
e.g. relation of (or effect of) scarcity or plenitude to crises or
prosperity.

Universal venality and corruption

In addition to contrasting the form of life presupposed by money
as general wealth and that presupposed by wealth in particular
things, Marx analyzes activities and character types to show how
they presuppose the specific form of life of money as general
wealth. In contrast with a type of theorizing for which concepts
such as universal venality and corruption would represent
'natural,' ahistorical phenomena, Marx shows the analytic history
of such notions, their internal relation to a form of life. Marx
attributes these phenomena to 'the exchangeability of all products,
activities and relations with a third, *objective* entity which can be
re-exchanged for everything *without distinction*' (163).

Since people can exchange their particular activity for any other
activity or product, people can prostitute themselves; they can

perform for money that which they might not ordinarily perform without money. These activities and products are not valued by the producer for their distinction but for their exchangeability, their equation with anything else, hence the corruption of the distinctive. According to Marx, this form of life, performing for the sake of money, is important in the development of the social character of personal talents and abilities:

> Universal prostitution appears as a necessary phase in the development of the social character of personal talents, capacities, abilities, activities. . . . The equation of the incompatible, as Shakespeare nicely defined money (163).

Regardless of the distinctiveness of an activity or product, it can be equated with every other. Through exchange value, personal talents, abilities, activities are seen as social; that is, their relation to others is recognized. However, the social is not seen in the origins of the activities, that is, in their grounding in social life, but in their exchangeability. People may work to develop their abilities because of their social value but only through the mediation of money, only as exchange value.

Marx shows how wealth in general, as distinct from wealth in particular products, originates in the quality of money as general exchangeability embodied in a particular, material thing (gold and silver). Money, as the material representative of general wealth, generates the possibility of universal venality and corruption because now people can perform solely in order to realize exchange value or general wealth.

Greed

Similarly, instead of conceiving of greed as a universal category, natural to human affairs, Marx grounds the notion of greed in money. Without money, the desire for accumulation and accumulation itself is restricted, on the one hand, by needs and, on the other hand, by the restricted nature of the products which might not allow for accumulation beyond a certain amount without other problems emerging, e.g. storage, deterioration, etc.

Marx distinguishes between greed, as mania for unrestricted accumulation, and cravings for a particular kind of wealth, e.g.

75

wealth in weapons, jewelry, women, wine. 'Greed . . . is possible only when general wealth, wealth as such, has become individualized in a particular thing' (222). The distinction between greed and cravings for particular things presupposes the difference between a way of life where one may possess wealth in general (i.e. the wherewithal to realize all desires through unrestricted accumulation of a particular thing – money) and a way of life where there are only particular things or particular kinds of wealth. Greed as such is indifferent to particular uses.

Marx develops the relation of money and greed by stating that money is not only *an* object, but is *the* object of greed, and not only the object but also the fountainhead of greed. By showing that greed presupposes money, Marx shows greed to be an historical as opposed to a natural phenomenon. This is not to say that greed is unnatural or deviant, but that its possibility derives not from an ahistorical human nature but from an historical, social development. Marx begins from the notion of greed as a phenomenon that we already know, that is, as an object of knowledge, and then analyzes what is presupposed in that knowledge. In this way, he shows how the phenomenon, as we know it, is socially produced:

> The mania for possessions is possible without money; but greed itself is the product of a definite social development, not *natural* as opposed to *historical*. Hence the wailing of the ancients about money as the source of all evil (222).

Money, with the greed that it makes possible, is destructive of whatever the ancients considered sacred; it is destructive of the form of life to which they were committed. It is capable of destroying all commitment, hence the source of all evil.

General industriousness

For Marx, as we have noted, wealth is the totality of the products of human activity which correspond to social needs. The source of wealth, of these products, is human activity. Industriousness refers to that human activity when it is accomplished with perseverance and zeal. Money as the representative of general wealth makes possible not only greed, but general industriousness, industriousness that is not specific to a particular activity or product. By making possible general industriousness, money also makes possible the reproduction of general wealth. It may sound confusing to state that money, the representative of general wealth, makes possible the production of general wealth. Marx explains:

> Greed, as the urge of all, in so far as everyone wants to make money, is only created by general wealth (money). Only through working for money, i.e. wage labour, can the general mania for money become the wellspring of general, self-reproducing wealth. When labour is wage labour, and its direct aim is money, then general wealth is posited as its aim and object. (In this regard, talk about the context of the military system of antiquity when it became a mercenary system). Money as aim here becomes the means of general industriousness. General wealth is produced in order to seize hold of its representative. In this way the real sources of wealth are opened up (224).

General industriousness is distinguished from industriousness based on the desire for producing a particular thing which satisfies particular uses and needs.

When the aim of labor is money, it is indifferent to the particular activity or product that is being produced and will be performed in any form in order to make money. The crucial or essential element in general industriousness is that money is the aim of labor:

> General industriousness is possible only where every act of labour produces general wealth, not a particular form of it; where, therefore, the individual's reward, too, is money. Otherwise, only particular forms of industry are possible. Direct labour which produces exchange value as such is, therefore, wage labour (224).

Where the individual's reward is not money which represents general wealth, there would not be general industriousness. This means that general wealth is the foundation of general industriousness. Thus, the industriousness which Weber attributes to the protestant ethic, as a desire to work and be productive in general, Marx would see as a product of a form of life in which activity is rewarded in money. 'In antiquity, one could buy labour, a slave, directly; but the slave could not buy money with his labour' (224).

The implication is that one cannot have general industriousness on the part of slaves or on the part of any groups who do not labor for money. General industriousness, industriousness that is not limited to particular activities that relate to particular needs, becomes possible only with labor for money. On the other side, the destruction of leisurely forms of life also seems to be made possible and with that the concept of idleness as a denigration of the state of being unoccupied.

Hedonism and miserliness

In addition to discussing the relationship between greed and industriousness, Marx indicates the two forms that greed for general wealth can take. One is hedonism; the other is miserliness.

With money, it is possible for all pleasures to be available to the possessor without any special achievements or work on his or her part. Once *all* forms of pleasure are potentially available, it becomes possible to treat life in those terms – as the ongoing attempt to realize all pleasures. In this way, 'Abstract hedonism realizes that function of money in which it is the material representative of wealth' (222). This is because money, in its function as material representative of wealth, makes all pleasures available.

Abstract hedonism appears to have nothing in common with miserliness. Whereas hedonism attempts to satisfy every sensual desire, miserliness attempts to limit consumption in order to retain the representative of wealth. However, analysis shows miserliness to have the same origins as hedonism: the development of money as the general form of wealth. 'Miserliness [realizes that aspect of money in which it] . . . is only the general form of wealth as against its particular substances, the commodities' (222).

That is, miserliness is the treatment of money – its possession and accumulation – as wealth in itself without having to exchange it for particular commodities. In order to maintain money as the general form of wealth, all relationships to the objects of particular needs must be sacrificed, hence general abstinence.

The notion of abstinence is suggestive of the related concept of asceticism. In the following passage, Marx anticipates Weber's famous thesis on the relation of the protestant ethic to the spirit of capitalism, but with different emphasis and perspective:

One sees how the piling up of gold and silver gained its true stimulus with the conception of it as the material representative and general form of wealth. The cult of money has its asceticism, its self-denial, its self-sacrifice – economy and frugality, contempt for mundanes, the temporal and fleeting pleasures; the chase after the eternal treasure. Hence the connection between English Puritanism or also Dutch Protestantism and money making (232).

The curious connection between money-making and consumption is attributed to the possibility of acquiring general wealth. By spending gold and silver, general wealth is lost. Abstinence becomes a way of holding on to general wealth. However, abstinence contradicts the meaning of general wealth – its exchangeability for particular commodities. Like Weber, Marx explicitly notes the connection between asceticism, versions of protestantism and money-making.

The orientation to abstinence was not just stressed by the puritan and protestant religions. Marx quotes a writer of the beginning of the seventeenth century as expressing the matter 'quite unselfconsciously' when he writes:

We consume among us too great an excess of wines from Spain, . . . silkenware of Italy, the sugar and tobacco of the West Indies, [etc.]; all this is not necessary for us, but is paid for in *hard* money . . . . If less of the foreign and more of the domestic product were gold, then the difference would have to come to us in the form of gold and silver, as treasure (232).

Weber's thesis describes the anxiety that seems to be the motivating force in the Calvinist tradition. Marx's analysis of money reveals a relationship to anxiety. With respect to the above quotation, Marx states:

The modern economists naturally make merry at the expense of this sort of notion in the general section of books on economics. But when one considers the anxiety involved in the doctrine of money in particular, and the feverish fear with which, in practice, the inflow and outflow of gold and silver are watched in times of crisis, then it is evident that the aspect of money which the followers of the

Monetary and Mercantilist System conceived in an artless one-sidedness is still to be taken seriously, not only in the mind, but as a real economic category (232).

In addition to the anxiety, Marx attributes an 'absolute' division of labor to money:

Money provides the possibility of an absolute division of labour, because of independence of labour from its specific product, from the immediate use value of its product for it (200).

In other words, the independence of labor from the immediate use value of its product means that the product has no use value, is not valued by labor because of its use. The only value it has for labor is the money received. Because the product, its final form or qualities, is not the reason for labor (money is), it is possible for labor to be accomplished without any commitment or attachment to its product or activity; there is a complete divorce between labor's purpose and its performance. One section of the labor process can do its work without interest, concern or knowledge of other sections. In this way, 'money provides the possibility of an absolute division of labor' (200).

In this sense division of labor refers not to the co-operation and specialization of labor, but to the separation among the different aspects of the production. Absolute division of labor means a separation in which the people at one job have no knowledge of the other types of jobs involved in the production. Such an absolute division of labor is made possible when people work for wages that are paid on the basis of particular types of work. In contrast to this system of working for wages would be one in which people work in order to provide products for the community which includes themselves. The people would organize the work themselves, therefore the separation between jobs could not be absolute. Thus Marx distinguishes a division of labor from an organization of labor.

Exchange value as historical

The totality of Marx's work in the *Grundrisse* and in *Capital* can be read as an analysis of exchange value. Here I will show how Marx conceives of exchange value in its developed forms of money and capital as an historical relation – as grounded in a historically specific form of life. This is in contrast to a concrete treatment that conceives of it as a natural ahistorical relation (outside of social relations).

We have already seen how the difference between wealth in general and wealth in particular things stems from the embodiment of exchange value in a form that is separate from the product. Thus the notion of wealth (in general, as money) derives from exchange value. Value, in the sense of exchange value, refers to the comparability of products on the basis of their costs of production – the amount of labor time it takes on the average to produce them. The notion of value, treating products in terms of their comparability or generality with all other products, pre-supposes and reproduces the process of exchange. This treatment contrasts with a treatment of products in terms of their relation to particular needs, hence as having particular value (use value) not value in general. Particular (use) value corresponds to a unity of purpose and production.

The notion of value in general as distinct from specific value (use value) is produced by a particular mode of production – production for exchange – where particular purpose or need is separated from production and can be realized only in exchange:

> The existence of value in its purity and generality pre-supposes a mode of production in which the individual product has ceased to exist for the producer in general and even more for the individual worker, and where nothing exists unless it is realized through circulation (252).

The notion of value in the abstract as opposed to particular types of value is, therefore, historical in that it presupposes an historically specific mode of production for its possibility. In this mode of production, the producer does not relate to production or to the product as a particular activity or particular product realizing particular purposes or needs.

Even the work of the individual, regardless of its products, would be nothing, of no value, if it could not realize exchange value. The positing of exchange value is not only a matter of the form that value takes; it is also a matter of substance. For the individual whose work is only an infinitesimal part of a final product, the substance of that work is meaningless except as an exchange value. If the 'person who creates an infinitesimal part of a yard of cotton . . . had not created an exchange value, money, he would have created nothing at all' (252).

We have seen how value as an abstraction, value in general, presupposes money. This leads to the development of capital which becomes a dominant form of production:

> It has become apparent in the course of our presentation that value, which appeared as an abstraction, is possible only as such an abstraction, as soon as money is posited; this circulation of money in turn leads to capital, hence can be fully developed only on the foundation of capital, just as, generally, only on this foundation can circulation seize hold of all moments of production (776).

Therefore, it seems that the notion of value in general depends on the development of circulation and money which is only fully developed in capital. The analysis of value thus calls attention to ('makes visible'): the historic character of social forms such as capital; the historic foundation (grounds) of the category, value; and the historical changes which certain categories, e.g. money, undergo:

> This development, therefore, not only makes visible the historic character of forms, such as capital, which belong to a specific epoch of history; but also (in its course) categories such as value, which appear as purely abstract, show the historic foundation from which they are abstracted, and on whose basis alone they can appear, therefore, in this abstraction; and categories which belong more or less to all epochs, such as e.g. money, show the historic modifications which they undergo (776).

Because the concept of value depends on the development of circulation and money which are only fully developed in capital, which itself presupposes value, the concept of value is, therefore, specific to capital and its production process:

> The economic concept of value does not occur in antiquity. Value distinguished only juridically from pretium, against fraud, etc. The concept of value is entirely peculiar to the

most modern economy, since it is the most abstract expression of capital itself and of the production resting on it. In the concept of value, its secret betrayed (776).

An analysis of value, therefore, reveals the specific historical character of capital which other economists overlook. By failing to treat capital as exchange value, they conceive of it only as objectified labor used as a means of production:

> When it is said that capital 'is accumulated (realized) labour (property, objectified [*vergegenständlichte*] labour), which serves as the means for new labour (production),' then this refers to the simple material of capital, without regard to the formal character without which it is not capital. This means nothing more than capital is – an instrument of production, for, in the broadest sense, every object, including those furnished purely by nature, e.g., a stone, must first be appropriated by some sort of activity before it can function as an instrument, as means of production (257).

Marx is claiming that this definition is too general and ahistorical. If capital is anything produced by labor and used in production, then it has existed in all societies without distinction. He argues that even where the limbs of the body are the instruments of production, they too would have to be considered capital according to this definition because they have to be developed (produced) through human activity and they must be reproduced – nourished – in order to function.

In addition, Marx criticizes the formulation for being abstract in that the particular material of which the products are composed (e.g. material that requires gathering, husbandry, or mining; material from the bodies of animals that require domestication or hunting; material that requires certain processes of preparation before it can be used, etc.) is not considered. Similarly, the product is treated in abstraction from the particular purpose for which the making of this product is intended to serve as means and merely production in general is posited as purpose.

Marx states that such abstraction seems to be merely the work of providing a definition that will lead the analysis further than would be the case without it. However, one result of such abstracting is that it is then possible to conceive of capital as an ahistorical thing, as something that is necessary for all production. The proof that it is necessary for all human production is accomplished by abstracting capital 'from the specific aspects which make it the moment of a specifically developed historic stage of human production' (258).

This means that instead of conceiving of capital as expressing certain historical, social relations required for its production, capital is treated as an ahistorical thing. Just as we have seen that money as representative of general wealth presupposes and reproduces a form of life that is different from the one given with wealth in particular things, we will see that capital presupposes and reproduces its own distinctive form of life. The bourgeois political economists miss this by treating capital merely as a thing: objectified labor:

> The catch is that if all capital is objectified labour which serves as means for new production, it is not the case that all objectified labour which serves as means for new production is capital. *Capital is conceived as a thing, not as a relation* (258).

Bourgeois political economists treat capital as a thing rather than an historically specific set of social relations necessary for its possibility as exchange value. Therefore, they cannot understand the historically unique social significance of capital as a form of life.

Equality and freedom

In so far as labor is conceived as a commodity having exchange value and the relation in which commodities are exchanged is conceived of as the exchange of exchange values, then the individuals are conceived of only as exchangers. In their formal character of exchangers, there is no distinction between them. As subjects of exchange, each has the same social relation toward the other that the other has toward him. The nature of the relation, then, is one of equality. Such a relation characterizes simple exchange, the exchange of one commodity (exchange value) for another. This aspect of equality provides a refuge for bourgeois democracy to 'construct apologetics for the existing economic relations' (241). Considering only the formal character of exchange, there are only three moments each of which is a relation of equality:

> the subjects of the relation, *the exchangers;* the objects of their exchange, exchange values, *equivalents*, which not only are equal, but are expressly supposed to be equal, and are posited as equal; and finally the act of exchange itself, the mediation by which the subjects are posited as exchangers, equals, and their objects as equivalents, equal (241).

Thus equality is posited by and presupposed by exchange.

Not only the relation of equality, but that of freedom is made possible by simple exchange. The exchange only takes place because the exchange values, while formally equal, are also commodities that as use values are substantially different. These differences satisfy the differences among the exchangers' needs. They obtain the use values they desire through exchange. In the exchange relation, appropriation does not take place by force, but voluntarily through reciprocity. Exchangers recognize each other as proprietors and the commodities as their private property. This recognition means that their relations are not those of force, but of freedom.

That exchangers are stipulated for each other as equals can be understood against a relation where inequality of position or individual distinctions pervade relationships. Similarly, the relation of freedom is understood against a relation of force. Because exchange presupposes the recognition of each by the other as proprietors, the process of exchange grounds the juridical relation of the person to the commodity (243). That is, if exchange is only possible if one recognizes proprietorship, then the juridical person, the legal rights of the individual with respect to commodities (as well as the freedom 'contained' in this relation), is consequently also recognized. This means that 'No one seizes hold of another's property by force. Each divests himself of his property voluntarily' (243).

Freedom which is contained in the legal rights of individuals with respect to their property is presupposed and posited by the exchange relation. This means that exchange requires these moments (the juridical moment of the person and freedom) and that these moments are reproduced in exchange. They constitute internal relations of exchange.

Freedom of the individual is posited in exchange also in that the individual acts only according to self-interest, not external compulsion. 'Each arrives at his end only in so far as he serves the other as means; . . . each becomes means for the other (being for another) only as end in himself (being for self)' (243–4). This reciprocity is presupposed as natural precondition of exchange. However, 'it is irrelevant to each of the two subjects in exchange. . . . [It] proceeds, as it were, behind the back . . . of one individual's interest in opposition to that of the other' (244).

Equality and freedom, which are based on the exchange relation, become developed and expressed in juridical, political and social relations:

> Equality and freedom are thus not only respected in exchange based on exchange values but, also, the exchange of exchange values is the productive, real basis of all *equality* and *freedom*. As pure ideas they are merely the idealized expression of this basis; as developed in juridical, political, social relations, they are merely this basis to a higher power (245).

In the phrase, 'the real basis of all *equality* and *freedom*,' I do not read Marx as meaning the basis of every type of equality and freedom, but rather equality and freedom in general as abstractions as opposed to particular, limited forms of equality and freedom. Without exchange, a particular limited form of equality or freedom may have existed, but our notions of equality and freedom in general would not have been known. Only with exchange do we have a form of life based on equality and freedom. Only with exchange does equality and freedom as we know them become conceivable.

The notions of freedom and equality would have different meaning, would correspond to a different form of life, within the ancient world, the Middle Ages and modern society:

> Equality and freedom as developed to this extent [in juridical, political and social relations] are exactly the opposite of the freedom and equality in the world of antiquity, where developed exchange value was not their

basis, but, where, rather the development of that basis destroyed them. Equality and freedom presuppose relations of production as yet unrealized in the ancient world and in the Middle Ages. Direct forced labour is the foundation of the ancient world; the community rests on this as its foundation (245).

He contrasts this direct forced labor as the foundation of the ancient world with the foundation of the Middle Ages and the foundation of the modern world: 'Labour itself as a "privilege", as still particularized, not yet generally producing exchange values is the basis of the world of the Middle Ages' (245).

In the modern world, 'Labour is neither forced labour; nor as in the second case, does it take place with respect to a common higher unit (the guild)' (245). Thus the notions of freedom and equality as we know them presuppose specific relations of production where labor is neither forced nor a privilege granted by a higher unit.

Marx similarly discusses the relation of Roman law to the exchange relation showing the difference between the situation there and the situation of modern society. 'In Roman law, the servus is, therefore, correctly defined as one who may not enter into the exchange for the purpose of acquiring anything for himself' (245). In other words, the definition of *servus* (slave), which is the antithesis of the free individual, is the lack of freedom to enter into the exchange for one's own self-interest. This is completely different from the modern legal situation. Marx explains how Roman law anticipates the legal relations of industrial society. But the development of the legal right 'which bourgeois society had necessarily to assert against medieval society' and its relations of privilege, coincides with the dissolution of the Roman community:

It is, consequently, equally clear that although this legal system corresponds to a social state in which exchange was by no means developed, nevertheless, in so far as it was developed in a limited sphere, it was able to develop the *attributes of the juridical person, precisely of the individual engaged in exchange*, and thus anticipate (in its basic aspects) the legal relations of industrial society, and in particular the right which rising bourgeois society had necessarily to assert against medieval society. But the development of this right coincides completely with the dissolution of the Roman community (246).

Marx's analysis can be compared with Weber's. In testing his hypothesis that the rationalization of worldly activities together with the necessary economic preconditions were required for the development of capitalism, Weber stressed the availability of a rational legal system developed by the Romans as being of crucial importance in the development of capitalism. Weber's research led him to conclude that a rational legal system as well as a rational system of book-keeping, free wage labor, etc. were important preconditions of the development of capitalism. However, Weber treats the relation as an external one, stressing the crucial significance of the prior development of Roman law on the subsequent development of capitalist relations.

Weber does not inquire into the social grounds of the Roman legal system and of the modern system, but explains the modern in terms of its concrete development from the Roman system. Marx, on the contrary, inquires into the presuppositions of the legal system to show how it is related to exchange and how this relation in the modern industrial society which presupposes and posits the freedom of the individual differs from that in ancient Roman society where it applies to the *servus*, who is not free to enter into exchange for his own interest.

Simple circulation versus complex circulation

Marx accounts for relations of freedom and equality, ideas of freedom and equality, and legal relations reflecting and protecting the basis of freedom and equality, in terms of their grounds in the system of exchange based on exchange values. However, he goes on to argue that equality and liberty are grounded in the *simple circulation* of exchange values, the exchange of commodity for money and then for a different commodity (C.M.C.). In the complex circulation of industrial capital, the exchange of money for commodity and commodity for even more money (M.C.M.'), the simple relations of circulation are only the surface process. The equality and freedom of these relations are only surface appearances.

By conceiving of relations in terms of simple circulation, the essential differences between the relations of simple circulation and those that correspond to another, more developed process of industrial capital, are disregarded:

> If this way of conceiving the matter (in terms of the relations of simple circulation) is not advanced *in its historic context*, but is instead raised as a refutation of the more developed economic relations *in which individuals relate to one another no longer merely as exchangers or as buyers and sellers,* but in specific relations, no longer all of the same character [e.g., labour and owners of capital], then it is the same as if it were asserted that there is no difference, to say nothing of antithesis and contradiction, between natural bodies, because all of them are equal . . . because all of them occupy three dimensions (247).

Marx is referring to the use of the relations of simple exchange in which people relate as buyers and sellers of equivalent exchange values, hence as free and equal individuals, as a way of counteracting the critique of the relations of wage labor and capital. 'Exchange value itself is here similarly seized upon in its simple character, as the antithesis to its more developed, contradictory forms' (247).

Rather than treating exchange value in terms of its latest and most complete development in industrial society, in talking of freedom and exchange, people are referring to exchange in its simple character. This simple character is contradicted by its later form. The appearance of freedom and equality which correspond to simple exchange is treated by Marx as a surface process in modern industrial society.

Marx conceives of the depths as the process of production which is based on the relation of capital to labor in which the 'apparent individual equality and liberty disappear.' Marx makes that statement by analyzing how exchange value as the basis of production already implies compulsion over the individual. Compulsion is implied because the product is not a product for the individual who produces it, but only becomes such in the social process of exchange. The product must take on the form of exchange value. Furthermore, 'the individual has an existence only as a producer of exchange value, hence . . . the whole negation of his natural

existence is already implied . . . he is, therefore, entirely determined by society' (248).

Marx shows that it only appears that the individual is completely
free; in 'reality,' that is, in analysis, the individual's acts of
self-interest are *social* acts; the realization of self-interest requires
exchange. As a producer of exchange value, the individual is no
longer merely a 'natural' being because the production of
exchange values is not a relation outside of social relations, but is a
relation within social relations.

Marx uses the expression 'natural existence' in the sense of
external to social relations. This was the way the theorists that he
criticized used it. For Marx, on the contrary, we have seen that
there is no such possibility. Nature, for Marx, is always a particular
nature understood as such in relation to a particular subject.
Nature is not nature in the abstract external to social relations of
production. Similarly, the individual's existence is not natural, but
always formed by social relations. Therefore, the individual is not
free, but is 'entirely determined by society.' This is not to say that
the performance of particular acts is determined, but that the
'types' of acts, the sense of the acts, is so determined. The
production of exchange values also presupposes relations other
than those of exchange – those of production:

> this further presupposes a division of labour, etc., in which
> the individual is already posited in relations other than that
> of mere *exchanger*, etc. That therefore this presupposition
> by no means arises either out of the individual's will or out
> of the immediate nature of the individual, but that it is,
> rather, *historical*, and posits the individual as already *deter-
> mined* by society. . . . What is overlooked, finally, is that
> already the simple forms of exchange value and of money
> latently contain the opposition between labour and capital,
> etc. (248).

Marx states that the legitimizing of modern society with the
concepts of freedom and equality is based on abstracting the
relations of simple exchange from the totality in which they are
grounded. Thus Marx does not treat the matter subjectively, as
differences in opinion, stating that he disagrees with the identification of modern society with relations of freedom and equality
pointing out ways in which this is not the case. Neither does Marx

90

treat the matter as one of objectivity, claiming that the association
of modern society with freedom and equality is based on incorrect
observation. Rather, he deals with the claim analytically, inquiring
into the grounds for that claim, the subject-object totality which it
presupposes:

> Thus, what all this wisdom comes down to is the attempt to
> stick fast at the simplest economic relations, which, con-
> ceived by themselves, are pure abstractions (248).

The exchange relation, freedom and equality, is only one side of
the totality of bourgeois relations; the production of exchange
value, the relation of capital to wage labor, is its other side, its
antithesis.

In explicating the grounds of freedom and equality in the
exchange relation, Marx shows the 'foolishness' of those socialists
who 'want to depict socialism as the realization of the ideals of
bourgeois society articulated by the French revolution' (248). This
is a critical statement, critical from the standpoint of comprehend-
ing the difference between the grounds of Marx's critique of
capitalism and those of other socialists. Marx criticizes those
theorists

> who demonstrate that exchange and exchange value, etc.,
> are *originally* (in time) or *essentially* (in their adequate
> form) a system of universal freedom and equality, but that
> they have been perverted by money, capital, etc. Or, also,
> that history has so far failed in every attempt to implement
> them in their true manner, but that they have now, like
> Proudhon, discovered, e.g., the real Jacob, and intend now
> to supply the genuine history of those relations in place of
> the fake (248).

For Marx also exchange and exchange value correspond to
equality and freedom, but money and capital are the developed
system of exchange and exchange value:

> The proper reply to them is: that exchange value or, more
> precisely, the money system is in fact the system of equality
> and freedom, and that the disturbances which they
> encounter in the further development of the system are
> disturbances inherent in it, are merely the realization of

91

equality and freedom, which prove to be inequality and unfreedom (249).

Therefore, Marx argues that the critique of capital should not be grounded in the desire to realize the ideals of equality and freedom of the exchange relation because as such these are bourgeois ideals, bourgeois relations in the form of ideas. By bourgeois relations, Marx means relations of exchange. Marx claims that whereas the 'bourgeois apologists' identify these ideals with the relations of exchange and use them for purposes of legitimizing those relations, the socialists are utopian in being unable to 'grasp the necessary difference between the real and the ideal form of bourgeois society, which is the cause of their desire to undertake the superfluous business of realizing the ideal expression again, which is in fact only the inverted projection [*Lichtbild*] of this reality' (249).

Both the bourgeois economists and the socialist critics abstract from bourgeois relations of exchange. For both, 'everything [is] reduced to the undeveloped relation of commodity exchange' (249) either in its ideal form for the utopian socialists, or in its material form for the bourgeois apologists. Marx, on the other hand, has a notion of freedom and equality which is not grounded in bourgeois relations of exchange; it is the notion of the free social individual. Neither the apologists, nor the utopian socialists *analyze exchange value* which would enable them to see the internal contradiction between its relation of freedom and equality and its relation of unfreedom and inequality.

The pauper and overpopulation

I began this chapter with 'general wealth' as the object of production. I showed how Marx analyzed it as a historically specific relation. I will conclude this chapter on grounding concepts in a historically specific form of life with Marx's treatment of the negation of wealth – his analysis of pauperism. I distinguish pauperism meaning destitute of *all* means from the poverty of wage labor which I discuss in chapter 5.

Marx claims that the concept of free labor implicitly contains that of pauperism. This is because free labor can only attain necessaries if it exchanges labor with necessaries. Its relation to the means of production depends on circumstances external to itself, conditions that are accidental for it and indifferent to its availability and willingness to work. This means that the ability to produce its necessities is not due to conditions that are internal to labor – e.g. its own incapacity, technology, conditions of land, weather and materials but conditions which are external and accidental for labor such as changes in market conditions. If individuals must sell their labor capacity for wages, if they cannot simply apply themselves to the production of necessaries but must find a buyer for their labor power, then the individuals are virtual paupers:

> It is already contained in the concept of the *free labourer* that he is a pauper; virtual pauper . . . if the capitalist has no use for his surplus labour, then the worker may not perform his necessary labour; not produce his necessaries. Then he cannot obtain them through exchange; rather if he does obtain them, it is only because alms are thrown to him from revenue. He can live as a worker only in so far as he exchanges his labour capacity for that part of capital which forms the labour fund. This exchange is tied to conditions which are accidental *for him*, and indifferent to his *organic* presence. He is thus virtual pauper (604).

Capitalism is based on trying to increase surplus value which can be conceived as surplus labor. As more surplus value is produced, more necessary labor can be eliminated. For example, if the workers can produce more value over and beyond the value necessary to keep them alive than they had previously been able to produce (through working longer hours, working more intensively, introducing new machinery or new techniques, etc.), then fewer workers can be employed to produce the same amount of surplus value as before. Those workers who are laid-off will have lost the opportunity of exchanging their labor power for money. If they cannot get other employment, they must become paupers:

> Since it is further the condition of production based on capital that he produces, ever more surplus labour, it follows that ever more *necessary labour* is set free. Thus the chances of his pauperism increase. To the development of

surplus labour corresponds that of surplus population. . . . Only in the mode of production based on capital does pauperism appear as the result of labour itself, of the development of the productive forces of labour (604).

The condition of overpopulation, surplus labor and pauperism varies for different modes of social production. Each mode of production is based on a particular relation of the people to the conditions of their reproduction. The society is reproduced or continued through the members reproducing the relation to conditions of production that characterize the society. If the relation of an individual or part of a population to these conditions is dissolved, if a portion of the population is deprived of any relation to the conditions of production, then that individual or segment of the population is placed outside of the conditions for reproducing the society, hence may be considered overpopulation which is identical with pauperism:

> In different modes of social production, there are different laws of the increase of population and of overpopulation; the latter identical with pauperism. These different laws can simply be reduced to the different modes of relating to the conditions of reproduction, or, in respect to the living individual, the conditions of his reproduction as a member of society, since he labours and appropriates only in society. The dissolution of these relations in regard to the single individual, or to part of the population, places them outside the reproductive conditions of this specific basis, and hence posits them as overpopulation, and not only lacking in means but incapable of appropriating the necessaries through labour, hence as paupers (604).

Because the specific relation to specific conditions of production differs for different periods, the nature of overpopulation may be different for different societies and the character of this over-population (or surplus population, a term Marx favors) may be different. Marx gives the illustration of the colonies of antiquity which were people deprived of the relation to the conditions of production that characterized the society. Although overpopulation, they could not be considered paupers:

> Thus, what may be overpopulation in one stage of social

production may not be so in another, and their effect may be different. E.g. the colonies sent out in antiquity were overpopulation, i.e. their members could not continue to live in the same space with the material basis of property, i.e. conditions of production. The number may appear very small compared with the modern conditions of production. They were, nevertheless, very far from being paupers. Such was, however, the Roman plebs with its bread and circuses. The overpopulation which leads to the great migrations presupposes different conditions again (604).

Unlike capitalism, where the continual development of the forces of production is the basis of the production of wealth, all previous forms of production are based on a specific, restricted relation to the conditions of production which is merely supposed to be reproduced not changed. That is, the form of property (relation to the conditions of production) includes among its conditions, the reproduction of the forces of production as already developed – not something to be further developed. Just as the development of the forces of production is restricted in this way, the development of population which is also a force of production, is similarly restricted. This is because the conditions of a community, its mode of production, is 'consistent only with a specific amount of population' (605).

So far, we have discussed only the limits on the size of the population posited by the conditions for reproducing the community with its given property relations. However, if the conditions of production change, then the barriers to population likewise change.

The rate of population increase changes with changes in the conditions of production that constrain population. There is a certain amount of population which is consistent with (allows for) the reproduction of the community on the basis of the already given relation to the conditions of production. The notion of overpopulation as indicated above, refers to a part of the population that cannot reproduce itself on the basis of the established relation to the conditions of production. Therefore, the community cannot reproduce itself through the production of these individuals. The latter, therefore, comprise the excess population, but excess only for that type of society, for the particular relation to the conditions of production (i.e. the property relations which characterize a society):

> The amount of overpopulation posited on the basis of a specific production is thus just as determinate as the adequate population. Overpopulation and population, taken together, are *the* population which a specific production basis can create. The extent to which it goes beyond its barrier is given by the barrier itself, or rather by the same base which posits the barrier (605).

Marx then goes on to a critique of Malthus's treatment of overpopulation. He faults Malthus's theorizing for failing to conceive of overpopulation in terms of the specific historical conditions of production which produce historically specific types of overpopulation:

> His conception is altogether false and childish because he regards *overpopulation* as being *of the same kind* in all different historical phases of economic development; does not understand their specific difference, and hence stupidly reduces these very complicated and varying relations to a single relation, two equations, in which the natural reproduction of humanity appears on the one side, and the natural reproduction of edible plants (or means of sub-sistence) on the other, as two natural series, the former geometric and the latter arithmetic in production. In this way he transforms the historically distinct relations into an abstract numerical relation, which he has fished purely out of thin air, and which rests neither on natural nor on historical laws (606).

Marx argues that overpopulation is determined by the historically specific subjective and objective conditions for reproducing the particular form of life. It is not determined by a numerical relation of human reproduction to the reproduction of edibles abstracted from a specific mode of production. For Marx, unlike Malthus, overpopulation is a historically determined relation, determined not by abstract numbers or absolute limits on the rate of pro-duction, limits that are the same for all modes of production, but 'by limits posited . . . by *specific conditions of production*. As well as restricted numerically' (606).

The limit to population that is posited by particular conditions of production is in numerical terms. The restriction to population in numerical terms means that the size of 'overpopulation' is limited by (or determined by) the type of society: 'How small do the numbers which meant overpopulation for the Athenians appear to us' (606).

The character of surplus population

In addition to the notion of overpopulation and the size of the overpopulation being historically determined by the specific conditions of production, the particular character of the overpopulation is likewise determined by the type of society (its specific conditions of production):

> An overpopulation of free Athenians who become transformed into colonists is significantly different from an overpopulation of workers who become transformed into workhouse inmates. Similarly the begging overpopulation which consumes the surplus produce of a monastery is different from that which forms in a factory (606).

Marx presents and elaborates Ricardo's response to Malthus which was that the quantity of grain available for consumption was not the issue for the worker who was unemployed, but rather it was the means of employment and, more generally than Ricardo had formulated it, the conditions of production that made him part of the surplus population.

Marx illustrates his point about the *relation* to the conditions of production being the key factor with the case of the surplus population of antiquity. The surplus population there did not consist of the slaves, but of non-workers:

> There was no barrier to the reproduction of the Athenian slave other than the producible necessaries. And we never hear that there were surplus slaves in antiquity. The call for them increased, rather. There was, however, a surplus population of non-workers (in the immediate sense), who were not too many in relation to the necessaries available,

but who had lost the conditions under which they could appropriate them (607).

Similarly the case of the workers under capital and the beggars at the monasteries were products of particular conditions of production:

> The invention of surplus labourers, i.e. of propertyless people who work, belongs to the period of capital. The beggars who fastened themselves to the monasteries and helped them eat up their surplus product are in the same class as feudal retainers and this shows that the surplus produced could not be eaten up by the small number of its owners (607).

A final example that Marx uses before going on to discuss overpopulation based on capital is the case of hunting people (607). He argues that the existence of overpopulation among them, which shows itself in the warfare between tribes, does not prove that the earth with its natural production rate of edibles could not provide subsistence for their small-sized population, which would be the conclusion based on Malthus's theory, but rather that the *condition of their reproduction*, i.e. reproduction of the same relation to the conditions of production, involved a large amount of land for the relatively few people.

Thus Marx concludes that overpopulation is not a relation to an absolute quantity of means of subsistence, but is the result of a specific relation to production, a specific subject-object totality. Instead of a relation to an absolute mass of means of subsistence, overpopulation is a relation to the specific conditions of producing those means. A surplus population, therefore, would not necessarily be a surplus in a different mode of production:

> Never a relation to a non-existent absolute mass of means of subsistence, but rather relation to the conditions of reproduction, of the production of these means including likewise the conditions of reproduction of human beings, of the total population, of relative surplus population. This surplus purely relative; in no way related to the means of subsistence as such, but rather to the mode of producing them. Hence also only a surplus at this state of development (607–8).

Marx shows the relation of overpopulation to the conditions of (re)producing capital. We briefly indicated earlier the two ways in which surplus population is produced by capital. First, that in order to be able to produce at all, labor must be able to produce surplus value that can be realized by capital. If the surplus labor cannot be realized as value by the capitalist, then labor capacity will not be employed, will not be allowed to produce. It stands outside of the conditions of its reproduction – employment (609).

Second, necessary labor time, the equivalence in labor time necessary to produce the necessaries required to reproduce the worker, is only utilized to the extent that the worker also produces surplus value that is appropriated and realized by the capitalist. Thus, from the standpoint of the capitalist whose only interest is the surplus value, necessary labor, the time for which the worker must be paid appears as superfluous – something to be reduced as much as possible. The capitalist realizes nothing from necessary labor time (609).

Under this point it should be remembered that the condition of production under capital involves the tendency to increase the surplus labor and reduce necessary labor. Thus Marx's use of 'necessary' labor reveals the contradictory character of capital: necessary labor is both necessary and superfluous. As more relative surplus labor is produced while using less necessary labor, the released labor potential now exists as surplus labor capacity or overpopulation. In this way production based on capital, and the continual movement toward increasing surplus value, produces a particular type of overpopulation – that which stems from the inherent tendency of capital to continually develop the forces of production in order to produce more surplus value relative to necessary labor:

> Since the necessary development of the productive forces as
> posited by capital consists in increasing the relation of
> surplus labour to necessary labour, or in decreasing the
> portion of necessary labour required for a given amount of
> surplus labour, then, if a definite amount of labour capacity
> is given, the relation of a necessary labour needed by
> capital must necessarily continue to decline, i.e. part of
> these labour capacities must become superfluous, since a
> portion of them suffices to perform the quantity of surplus

labour for which the whole amount was required previously (609).

The superfluous population that is produced through reducing the amount of necessary labor needed to produce the same amount of surplus value as before, may be supported by others, rather than supported by its own labor. This is the condition of being dependent on the mercy of others; hence the tramp and pauper. The surplus working class is maintained by other parts of the society for later use by capital. The capitalist 'shifts a part of the reproduction costs of the working class off his own shoulders and thus pauperizes a part of the remaining population for his own profit' (609–10).

The implication that the surplus labor is supported by others for the benefit of the capitalist refers to the subsequent need of capital for additional workers. This is due to the tendency of capital to reproduce itself in an increasing quantity. With the growth of surplus capital, a part of the surplus population that was set free may again be required to produce in the new branch(es) of production that the surplus capital now opens up (610).

Just as Marx claims that it is misleading to talk of production in general, he makes the same point with regard to overpopulation. The notion of surplus population depends on the particular society. The surplus population differs qualitatively as well as quantitatively according to the type of society. In this analysis Marx does not treat surplus population as a given, observable, natural thing, but as a social phenomenon grounded in and produced by a *particular*, historical form of life. Moreover, just as Marx claims that the form of life presupposed and posited by money is historical and not 'natural,' he makes the assertion that a different form of life – communism – is also not attributable to nature, but to history:

> Universally developed individuals, whose social relations, as their own communal (*gemeinschaftlich*) relations, are hence also subordinated to their own communal control, are no product of nature but of history (162).

Marx's treatment of forms of life and notions such as greed and industriousness may be contrasted with the usual treatment of such social phenomena. The usual treatment may be thought of as the debate over human nature and the nature of society. The opposing positions within these debates tend to underlie much of the theorizing in sociology, psychology and religion. Are people essentially aggressive, individualistic, self-interested or sinful? Are people essentially peaceable, loving, communal or good? Must society constrain the individual's unruly and destructive passions? Is society the means for the individual's self-realization? Is society oppressive? Is society essentially conflictual or consensual?

Marx's work may be read as claiming that none of these characteristics should be conceived as natural. Instead of claiming one or the other, one should inquire into how such claims are possible. What are the social grounds for a particular claim? Marx insists on the need to treat concepts and social phenomena as grounded in specific historical social conditions. This is different from treating those versions of humankind or society as given, natural or universal.

Marx's method, therefore, differs from treating concepts either as objective reflections of real things external to a knowing subject or as ideas representing particular interests of particular subjects. Marx's method of grounding, the principle of analysis, inquires into the social activities and relations presupposed by the concept, the activities or subject-object relations (language in Wittgenstein's sense of form of life) that make the concept intelligible or possible as such.

CHAPTER 4

The individual: historical versus natural

We have seen how characteristics attributed to individuals such as greed, industriousness, asceticism, even pauperism, do not originate with the individual, but with a form of life that makes them possible or intelligible as such. This is not to say that an individual could not evince similar traits in another form of life, but only that they would be understood differently; they would have different meanings. In Marx's theorizing, the individual's acts and intentions do not originate with the individual. They are possibilities given with a form of life.

Conceiving of individuals in terms of a form of life must be understood against the conception of individuals' acts as either natural or purely subjective. A natural individual refers to the individual abstracted from social life. Conceiving of individuals' acts in terms of nature means that purposes are reduced to natural impulses, instincts, drives, outside of particular social formations. For Marx, human nature takes form within social life.

The human as species being may have certain traits that distinguish it from other species but these are not the object of analysis, for analysis is concerned with history. This version of human nature parallels the discussion of production in general. Marx would argue that the human is an historical being, one that produces its own conditions of existence and, therefore, its own life. This means that the individual is always historically specific. In fact, Marx states that 'human beings become individuals only through the process of history. . . . Exchange itself is a chief means of this individuation' (496). Originally, the human being appears as a species being, a clan being, a herd animal. Exchange dissolves this herd-like existence by making possible individuation.

Similar to the conception of a natural individual is the subjective individual, one whose particular desires and needs have no origins other than the individual. This means that purposes are only accounted for as personal desires, needs, goals understood in terms of the unique situation or biography of an individual, the individual as author of his acts. Given this conception, social life would be a conglomeration of private purposes. With society reduced to the activities of subjective individuals, there would be no way of determining activity or regulating social life, hence the Hobbesian problem of order. Given this conception of individual behavior, social order can only be understood as a social contract among the individuals or as social controls by domination. These theories of social life are logical conclusions from conceiving of the individual as pure subjectivity.

Both of these conceptions of the individual – as natural and as subjective being – differ from Marx's notion of the objective individual, the individual defined as Roman, Greek, etc. For Marx, individuals' purposes always presuppose a form of life:

> The point is rather that private interest is itself already a socially determined interest which can be achieved only within the conditions laid down by society and with the means provided by society; hence it is bound to the reproduction of these conditions and means. It is the interest of private persons; but its content, as well as the form and means of its realization, is given by social conditions independent of all (156).

For analysis there are no private purposes, if by this is meant purposes that originate with an individual outside of social life. The concept of a private person might refer to persons who are not conscious of their purposes as socially determined, that is, as purposes that presuppose social origins. Unself-conscious individuals who appear as private persons are themselves products of a particular form of life, a form of life in which history is repressed.

Analysis only knows individuals as types given with a form of life. This means that the relations of a form of life determine the types or categories of purposes and acts that distinguish individuals. However, to say that the individual's acts as they are known are determined by the form of life within which they occur is not to say that the individual has no choice, no will of his own, no opportunity to be creative or spontaneous or deviant. It is that social conditions and relations constrain and make possible the individual's acts and purposes. Thus the possibility of types of acts does not originate with the individual, but with the relations and conditions within which the individual acts. Within these constraints, the individual may be creative and spontaneous.

However, it is not the spontaneous, creative individual and his or her personal situation or personal biography that is the subject of analysis. Rather, it is the individual as personification of a form of life. Analysis does not begin with the individual, but with what makes a type of act and, therefore, a type of individual possible. It concerns itself with the origin of types of acts not with the concrete biographical origins of the acts of particular human beings. Of course, this is not to deny the personal individual or the species being. It is to say that the historical individual only is the object of analysis.

I will illustrate the notion of an historical individual, the individual as known from within a form of life, with Marx's analysis of three pre-capitalist forms of life: Asia, antiquity and the early Germanic form. Before proceeding, it is necessary to note that they are considered pre-capitalist forms. This means that they are analyzed in terms of the capitalist form. Their history is understood as the pre-history of capitalism. This is to say not merely that capitalism developed from them, but that their history is known in terms of the disunity of capitalism, the separation of subject from object, of labor from its material presuppositions. Hence, from this standpoint, pre-capitalist forms are stages in history. Analysis describes them in terms of that which must be suspended in the development of capitalism.

Marx does not do an empirical history, but using empirical illustrations, he formulates the possibility of capital in terms of possible forms that are *analytically* prior to the form of capitalism – unity as analytically prior to separation. Thus the stages are not empirical events in history, but analytic formulations.

Marx formulates these pre-capitalist forms as forms of landed property. The next question to be addressed is why these forms of life are treated as property relations. Forms of life are conceived in terms of unity, the unity of production, the unity of purpose with the objective conditions for realizing the purpose. This unity is conceived as a property relation to the extent that it is recognized by others, i.e. secured by the community. In forms of landed property, 'the individual relates to himself as proprietor, as master of the conditions of his reality' (471).

In these pre-capitalist forms, 'the purpose of the work is the sustenance of the individual proprietor and of his family, as well as of the total community.' Thus, the individuals relate 'not as workers but as proprietors – and members of a community, who at the same time work' (472). In other words, the aim of work is not the creation of value such that the individual becomes merely a worker, a producer of something that has calculable value without relevance for the sustenance of the individual, his family or community. 'The positing of the individual as a *worker*, in this nakedness, is itself a product of history' (472). Capitalism pre-supposes and (re)produces the separation of labor from its purpose. Instead of labor being the means for reproducing the individual and the community, it becomes a means for (re)pro-ducing something that is separate from the individual, exchange value.

The natural community and landed property

In examining pre-capitalist forms of life from the perspective of unity, Marx begins with the migratory form. In this form of production, where the community 'grazes off what it finds,' the community appears as the presupposition for the temporary appropriation and utilization of the land. In this form of life, the community is not a result of anything. It is not the result of history as struggle; it is a natural community, not a self-conscious one.

Conceiving of the community as naturally existing ('the natural community') rather than as a result of individual appropriation and utilization of the land, points out that there is nothing prior that produces community. Community is not a result of the coming together of 'natural' individuals. The 'natural community' of blood, language, customs is not external to production; it is neither external cause nor external result of the production of individuals. Rather, the 'natural community' is a presupposition of that production, just as that production reproduces the language, blood, customs that constitute the 'natural community' (472).

The natural community is the first presupposition of the individual's activity. Through this activity, individuals reproduce themselves and their community. The community's and hence the individual's character is determined in the sense of made possible by its relation to its specific object just as the character of the object for the subject is determined by the subject's relation to it. To illustrate, the character of the subject, a community of tillers, is determined by its object – land and tools for tilling. Reciprocally, the character of the land as soil for tilling is determined by its subject – the community's knowledge and goal of tilling.

Although the 'same' material may exist in two different forms of life, within those forms they may not be the same object. In one, cattle may be an object of production, consumption and exchange as well as a symbol of wealth. In the other, cattle may be a sacred being which is allowed to eat up the produce of the land, thereby contributing to material poverty. Thus the mere presence of material elements does not determine production. Objective conditions although necessary are never sufficient. Production cannot be reduced to one or the other. Production must be treated as a subject-object totality.

Production is not related externally to community (cause or effect), but is an internal relation, a unity in which the conditions of community are conditions of production and the conditions of production are conditions of community. As such, the conditions of production are conceived as the community's, the earth as the property of the community that appropriates it:

> They relate naïvely to it (the earth) as the property of the community, of the community producing and reproducing itself in living labour . . . . Each individual conducts himself only as a link, as a member of this community as proprietor or possessor. The real appropriation through the labour process happens under these presuppositions, which are not themselves the *product* of labour, but appear as its natural or *divine* presuppositions (472).

The naïveté consists in not recognizing that their labor appropriates the land, that they (re)produce the community. The individual members and workers do not constitute a self-conscious community. This is because the community (re)produces itself in living labor; it is presupposed to labor. Because the community is not produced by labor, but is presupposed to it, the community is natural or divine. The conditions for reproducing this natural or divine community are also the conditions for the individuals' activities, the conditions for production.

Durkheim elaborates on this theme. In the *Elementary Forms of the Religious Life*, he theorized that religion is the recreation of community and community is the presupposition of human life and individual activity. As such we may understand community not as the particular living human beings, but the community as a metaphysical force in the lives of people, in the literal sense of more than mere physical presence. It is awe in the face of this metaphysical force that constitutes the sense of the sacred as we may understand it in Durkheim's analysis.

Durkheim analyzes religion as an abstract universal. He formulates religion as the recreation and strengthening of the individual's relation to the natural, metaphysical community. In doing so, he eternalizes the natural community as the presupposition of human activity and treats all community as prior to the individuals and divine as such.

Marx does not treat the relation of individual to community abstractly, but analyzes the relation historically by showing the presuppositions of the relation, the conditions for its reproduction and showing how this relation changes and produces different historical forms of life. In the early forms of production, the natural community is presupposed. The individuals relate to their individual production as members of a community, where the community is the proprietor of that which they appropriate.

This means that individuals as members do not see their community as produced by themselves. This is because the community is not a product of labor, but is presupposed to labor. The individuals see themselves as 'mere accidents' or 'natural component parts' of the community. Marx recognizes that this form of life with the same land relation as its foundation can realize itself in very different ways:

> in most of the *Asiatic* land-forms, the *comprehensive unity* standing above all these little communities appears as the higher *proprietor* or as the *sole proprietor*; the real communities hence only as hereditary possessors (472–3).

In other words, the unity that is the comprehensive unity of all the

107

smaller communities is the real proprietor. This unity can appear as a particular entity above the real particular communities. In such a case, the individual is propertyless or property appears mediated for him through a cession by the total unity – a unity realized in the form of the despot, the father of the many communities – to the individual, through the mediation of the particular commune (473).

Landed property may take other forms. Marx uses empirical illustrations to show analytic possibilities of landed property. However, the empirical accuracy of the illustrations is not the point. Rather, it is the illustration of the possibilities for and restrictions on development that are given with this type of landed property that is the point of the analysis. Hence, he can speak of communes vegetating. He can also show the possibility of the development of serfdom (villeinage) from this type of unity. A certain amount of labor may be appropriated for communal reserves to meet the expenses of the community such as for war or religion. Marx calls this the first occurrence of the 'lordly dominium,' a realm above the individuals that can command their labor. This makes possible the transition to 'villeinage,' the situation where a human lord commands labor for his own ends. Communality make take different forms. The clans may represent their unity in a clan chief which makes for a relatively despotic form. Or they may represent their unity as a relation among the patriarchs, thereby making for a relatively democratic form (473).

Asiatic landed property

In the Asiatic form of landed property, where a 'comprehensive unity' standing above the individual communities appears as the sole proprietor in the form of a person, the surplus product belongs to this 'higher unity.' According to Marx, this relation which he calls oriental despotism does not contradict the notion of communal property. Rather, the latter is the foundation for it:

> Amidst oriental despotism and the propertylessness which seems legally to exist, there, this clan or communal property exists in fact as the foundation. . . . A part of their surplus labour belongs to the higher community, which exists ultimately as a person, and this surplus labour takes the

form of tribute, etc., as well as of common labour for the exaltation of the unity, partly of the real despot, partly of the imagined clan-being, the god (473).

Because the integrity of the 'little communities' and their immediate relation to nature is not destroyed, the uniting of these communities does not create a new community, but is a surrender or devotion to a higher unity, an externally imposed unity; hence, the despot. Within the Asiatic form, aqueducts were very important. The building of aqueducts unites the 'little communities.' The products of this unity such as the means of communication appear as the work of the higher unity, 'of the despotic régime hovering over the little communities' (473).

Given a particular form of production, e.g. the Asiatic, analysis inquires into the form of unity that is presupposed, the relation of individual to the conditions of production. Furthermore, analysis might ask what other possible forms such a relation might take; what limits if any such a relation might impose with regard to production and its development. Analysis of Asiatic production leads to a consideration of religion. In the ancient Asiatic form of life, religion is not one institution while production is another. Rather, where production is accomplished by a natural, hence divine, community, religion is the way in which members acknowledge that divinity. The relation of individuals to their community, devotion or religion, is internal to their mode of production. It is not externally related as a separate institution. Or rather, one might say that their production is internal to their community, hence internal to religion. Community, expressed as religion, is a presupposition, 'the first presupposition' of production.

In my reading of Marx, religion is not the superstructure merely reflecting an economic base, but a relation of individuals to their unity. Religion is the relation to the unity as a natural or divine presupposition of individual production and hence individual life. The negation of religion, secularism, then, might be reformulated as the separation of individual activity from this unity which comes with the historic transformation of the unity from a natural and, therefore, divine presupposition to an historic community conceived as the result of individual labor (and exchange).

Private property of antiquity

The second form of landed property that Marx considers as an historic development from the natural community and the natural unity of worker and the earth as workshop is that of antiquity. Like the first form, it undergoes essential modifications brought about not by some immutable law of history, but by the 'fates and modifications' of the original clans. This form also 'assumes the community as its first presupposition, but not, as in the first case, as the substance of which the individuals are mere accidents, or of which they form purely natural component parts' (474). Rather, it presupposes the town as the created foundation of community. This means that the community is no longer a purely natural presupposition but a partly historic one.

In the first form of landed property where the natural community is a presupposition of production, as in the case of Asia, the property of the individual is directly communal property and the individual is merely its possessor as distinguished from proprietor (Marx's distinction). In this form, communal labor, e.g. the building of aqueducts, was a presupposition of individual production. The communal labor required by irrigation presupposed the natural community.

In the second form of landed property that Marx considers, communal labor (for irrigation) and the natural community are not presuppositions for the individual. This means that without the need for communal labor and with the breaking up of the 'purely naturally arisen, spontaneous character of the clan' by historic movement, migration and with the occupation of alien ground, the clan enters into new conditions of labor and develops the energy of the individual more, and the common character of the community appears more as a negative unity toward the outside. Given all of this, the more 'are the conditions given under which the individual can become a private proprietor of land and soil – of a particular plot – whose particular cultivation falls to him and his family' (475).

However, private property in land presupposes membership (citizenship) in the community (Rome) and membership in the community requires private property. The community is no longer natural but is the result of struggle to occupy land or to protect the land against alien occupation: war becomes the basis of the unity of antiquity.

The relation to the earth remains one of unity regardless of the obstacles it may place in the way of working it. It is related to as the 'inorganic nature of the living individual, as his workshop, as the means and object of labour and the means of life for the subject' (474). The difficulties which the commune encounters can arise only from other communes, which have either previously occupied the land and soil, or which disturb the commune in its own occupation. 'War is therefore the great comprehensive task, the great communal labour which is required either to occupy the objective conditions of being there alive, or to protect and perpetuate the occupation' (474).

Thus the unity of the community is no longer a natural pre-supposition of individual productive activity. Instead, the unity is an historic presupposition, a unity that is produced by the struggle against the outside and the 'protection of the *ager publicus* for communal needs and communal glory, etc.' However, although antiquity, unlike the first form, is characterized by private property in land, this private property still presupposes membership in the commune as a necessary condition. The individual relates to the land and soil as his private property, but he relates to 'his being as commune member; and his own sustenance as such is likewise the sustenance of the commune, and conversely, etc.' (475).

Because membership (citizenship) is the presupposition and not the product of individual productive activity, this relation to the land as private property, therefore, presupposes the commune as a divine presence. This is in spite of the fact that the commune is a product of history here, not only in fact but also known as such, and therefore *possessing an origin*' (475). However, because membership in the commune is either given or not, independently of individuals' activity, and because membership is a presup-position of property in land and soil and hence of the individual as a private proprietor, membership is a 'presupposition regarded as divine' (475).

Just as the individuals as private proprietors relate to their beings as commune members – citizens of a (city) state – and the sustenance of the commune (e.g. its protection and glorification) as their own sustenance, the sustenance of the individual as private proprietor is conversely the sustenance of the commune. Hence, Marx describes the conditions for (the reproduction or survival of)

111

the form of life of antiquity in terms of the preservation of its members as free, self-sustaining peasants:

> The survival of the commune is the reproduction of all of its members as self-sustaining peasants, whose surplus time belongs precisely to the commune, the work of war, etc. (476).

Thus the leaders of antiquity were concerned about the provision of landed property for the community members in order to preserve the community:

> When the auguries, Niebuhr says, had assured Numa of the divine sanction of his election, the pious king's first concern was not worship at the temple, but a human one. He divided the lands which Romulus had won in war and given over to occupation; he endowed the order of Terminus. All the law-givers of antiquity, Moses above all, founded their success in commanding virtue, integrity and proper custom on landed property, or at least on secured, hereditary possession of land, for the greatest possible number of citizens (476).

The unity of the community is reproduced as a conscious struggle to maintain or occupy land as the private property of the members. The reproduction of this community, however, presupposes the unity as divine, as other than the activity of the members themselves. The divine unity is represented by the city. This differs from the German form.

Germanic private property

The third form of landownership that Marx delineates is that of the German tribes in which community members live long distances apart and the community appears as a coming together for periodic gatherings:

> Among the German tribes, where the individual family chiefs settled in the forests, long distances apart, the commune exists, already from *outward* observation, only in the periodic gathering-together (*Vereinigung*) of the com-

mune members, although their unity-in-itself is posited in their ancestry, language, common past and history, etc. (483).

Marx is making the distinction between unity-in-itself and unity-for-itself. Unity-for-itself in this case is not the unity as an already given natural fact of human life, or as an already given accomplishment which now forms the basis of individual property and protection against the outside – the state. Rather, unity for itself is the unification of independent or separate individuals, that is, the active self-conscious commitment of individuals to forming the community by their own decision to do so:

> The *commune* thus appears as a coming together (*Vereinigung*), not as a *being-together* (*Overein*); as a unification made up of independent subjects, landed proprietors, and not as a unity. . . . For the commune to come into real existence, the free landed proprietors have to hold a meeting, whereas e.g. in Rome it *exists* even apart from these assemblies in the existence of the *city itself* and of the officials presiding over it, etc. (483).

The distinction between the Germanic form of landed property and the two previously discussed forms is that in the Germanic, the relation of the individual as landowner to the land does not appear to be a relation within community. 'Individual property does not appear mediated by the commune; rather the existence of the commune and of communal property appear as mediated by, i.e. as a relation of, the individual subjects to one another' (484).

These three different forms of life as modes of producing and reproducing community are forms of appropriation, property relations. The Germanic offers the most extreme form of precapitalist community that Marx analyzes, for here the commune does not appear as a presupposition of individual activity. It is the absence of community as presupposition except in terms of ancestry and language:

> The economic totality is, at bottom, contained in each individual household, which forms an independent centre of production for itself (manufactures purely as domestic secondary task for women, etc.). In the world of antiquity, the city with its territory is the economic totality; in the Germanic world, the totality is the individual residence,

which itself appears as only a small dot on the land belonging to it, and which is not a concentration of many proprietors, but the family as independent unit (484).

The Germanic form of production does not presuppose a relation to community. Hence, the totality of production is the family unit of the proprietor. In this case, Weber's thesis that the communal is not necessarily the 'original' form of property seems to hold.

Weber describes the concrete origins of seven types of property in land and their consequences with respect to relations of domination, relations between nobility and taxable dependents, between citizens and non-citizens (1950, p. 53). Weber provides this concrete history in order to show that agrarian communism is not necessarily the original form of social life, the opposite claim being a particular interpretation of Marx's theorizing. Weber shows how private property in land originates with either military leadership and relations of production, conquest and booty, or clan leadership with authority to regulate a community's trade.

However, according to Marx's analysis, the private proprietorship that results from these historic transformations does not mean that community is not presupposed. It is presupposed as a 'communality of language, blood, etc.' The difference is that with the Germanic form, the commune does not appear as a presupposed entity separate from the individual proprietors as it does in the Asiatic form in which the individual appears as mere accident, nor does it appear in the existence of the city of antiquity and its 'civic needs as distinct from those of the individual':

> rather, the commune, on the one side, is presupposed in-itself prior to the individual proprietors as a communality of language, blood, etc., but it exists as a presence, on the other hand, only in its *real assembly* for communal purposes (485).

The consequence of the commune not appearing as a separate entity apart from the members themselves, a form of alienated life, is that the individual *proprietors* are free from the domination of an alien presence, the domination of their community as a presence separate from themselves. Their freedom to be individual proprietors is

guaranteed by the bond with other such family residences

of the same tribe, and by their occasional coming together
(*Zusammenkommen*) to pledge each other allegiance in
war, religion, adjudication, etc. . . . . The commune exists
only in the interrelations among these individual landed
proprietors as such (484).

In other words, the community still exists but only in these
relations, not as an ideal entity alongside the real relations of
individual proprietors. Instead the community is recognized as
these relations. Thus Weber's problematic – the empirical origins
of property is not Marx's. The problem is not an empirical one of
seeing if the earliest forms of property were communal or private.
According to my reading of Marx, the aim is not to prove that
agrarian communism is the original form of property and hence
natural. Rather, it is to show the consequence of different forms of
community on individual productive activity, the individual's form
of life as made possible by the community's property relations.

These are treated as pre-capitalist forms; the purpose of discussing them is as a contrast with the individual's productive
activity that characterizes the property relations and form of life of
capital:

> In all these forms – in which landed property and agriculture
> form the basis of the economic order, and where the
> economic aim is hence the production of use values, i.e. the
> *reproduction of the individual* within the specific relation to
> the commune in which is its basis – there is to be found:
> . . . . Appropriation not through labour, but presupposed
> to labour; appropriation of the natural conditions of labour,
> of *earth* as the original instrument of labour as well as its
> workshop and repository of raw materials (485).

This is an important quotation as it indicates what all of these
forms have in common that make them 'pre-capitalist' and not just
different forms.

In contrast to the worker of the capitalist form of life, the
worker in the pre-capitalist forms is in unity with the objective
conditions for reproducing himself. The worker possesses these
conditions. This form of life contrasts with the capitalist form of
life characterized by a separation of subject and object. In the pre-
capitalist forms,

> The individual relates simply to the objective conditions of
> labour as being his; [relates] to them as the inorganic
> nature of his subjectivity, in which the latter realizes itself;
> the chief objective condition of labour does not itself
> appear as a *product* of labour, but is already there as
> *nature*; on one side the living individual, on the other the
> earth, as the objective condition of his reproduction (485).

In pre-capitalist forms, the individual has an objective mode of
existence presupposed to him with his ownership of the land. This
contrasts with the laboring individual of capital whose existence is
simply that of abstract labor, an individual who appears to be
purely subjective existence, purpose or desire or need separated
from any objective conditions for realizing itself, hence pure
subjectivity divorced from any objectivity:

> The labouring individual . . . thus appears from the outset not
> merely as labouring individual, in this abstraction, but who
> has an *objective mode of existence* in his ownership of the
> land, an existence *presupposed* to his activity, and not
> merely as a result of it, a presupposition of his activity just
> like his skin, his sense organs, which of course he also
> reproduces and develops, etc. in the life process, but which
> are nevertheless presuppositions of this process of his repro-
> duction (485).

The individual does not first have to work in order to know himself
as an individual; rather, it is through work that he *reproduces*
himself as an individual.

Property as membership

Within pre-capitalist forms, the relation between individuals and
the objective conditions for realizing themselves as such is not
mediated by exchange value. The individual does not first have to
work in order to produce himself as an individual. Rather, the
relation is a unity of subject and object, an inner unity in which the
individual's subjective existence (as member) includes its objective
conditions (the land) as 'the inorganic nature of his subjectivity':

> He actually does not relate to his conditions of production,

but rather has a double existence, both subjectively as he himself, and objectively in these natural non-organic conditions of his existence (491).

This inner unity, the unity of subject and object in these pre-capitalist forms, is a property relation. As such it is mediated by membership in a community, 'is instantly mediated by the naturally arisen, spontaneous, more or less historically developed and modified presence of the individual as *member of a commune*' (485).

In Marx's analysis property means belonging to a community:

An isolated individual could no more have property in land and soil than he could speak. He could, of course, live off it as a substance, as do the animals. The relation to the earth as property is always mediated through the occupation of the land and soil, peacefully or violently, by the tribe, the commune, in some more or less naturally arisen or already historically developed form (485).

The distinction that Marx is drawing between property and substance that an individual could live off seems to be based on the recognition and realization of rights by others. These rights and their realization constitute the subjective and objective existence of the individual as such:

Property therefore means *belonging to a clan* (*community*) (have subjective-objective existence in it); and by means of the relation of this community to the land and soil, [relating] to the earth as the individual's inorganic body; his relation to land and soil, to the external primary condition of production . . . as to a presupposition belonging to his individuality, as modes of his presence. *We reduce this property to the relation to the conditions of production* (492).

As members, individuals' activities, their property relations, their speech are public activities as opposed to private ones. This means that they do not originate with an individual, but with life in a community, membership. Individual activity is typical, a system of typifications. The individual is a type of individual and is not an individual otherwise. Individuation occurs through typification within society, within social relations. The individual is not that which is external to or hidden from society as in the notion of a private individual. Rather, the individual's recognition of himself in that which is his, including his speech (acts), presupposes membership in a community:

> As regards the individual, it is clear e.g. that he relates even to language itself *as his own* only as the natural member of a human community. Language as the property of an individual is an impossibility. But the same holds for property.
> Language itself is the product of a community, just as it is in another respect itself the presence [*Dasein*] of the community, a presence which goes without saying (490).

Property relations, the relations of an individual to the objective conditions of his existence including the relation to intelligible speech as his own, which are given with membership, are 'modes of his presence.' Without the property that is given with language and membership, with social relations, the individual would be unable to separate himself from his acts. The acts would not be his; they would be him. He would be unable to reflect and determine his acts self-consciously. Hence, he would not be an individual to himself; he would not recognize himself or know himself as an individual, but only as a species being, a being that is one with its natural impulses.

The identification of property relations with 'modes of his presence' does not seem to correspond to the usual understanding of an individual's property. The usual understanding of property is either of two formulations. In one, property is everything potentially, the character of property inheres in its thingness – its objectivity. This character is realized, that is, things become property in actuality, in being appropriated by an individual. Hence, property is an object that is appropriated by an individual.

The other formulation is that property is a set of rights and obligations (guaranteed by law). As such, property is a mental relation among individuals – a purely subjective relation. Neither of these seems to refer to modes of an individual's presence. We have seen that, for Marx, property presupposes membership, relations within a community. This seems to correspond to the second interpretation, a set of rights and obligations. However, according to Marx, this mental relation is a relation to the conditions of production.

Why does Marx reduce this property to the relation to the conditions of production? Why not a relation to the conditions of consumption? How do either refer to a mode of presence? The property relation, as a set of rights and obligations of an individual to an object, is only realized, that is, made real instead of remaining mental, by an active relation of the individual to the thing. This active relation is production. Consumption itself always presupposes production including the production of certain capacities on the part of the subject:

> Property, in so far as it is only the conscious relation – and posited in regard to the individual by the community, and proclaimed and guaranteed as law – to the conditions of production as *his own*, so that the producer's being appears also in the objective conditions *belonging to him* – is only realized by production itself. The real appropriation takes place not in the mental but in the real, active relation to these conditions – in their real positing as the conditions of his subjective activity (493).

Property is a conscious relation to the conditions of production as his own. This conscious relation is only made real in an active relation. By active, I do not read Marx as meaning a mere exertion of energy or force on to a thing as might happen when one falls against something, but active in the sense of purposive – intending some end or object as product of the exertion which in turn transforms the thing into an object of a subject. Thus active means a purpose that is being enacted; hence, a production. Therefore, in stating that property is only realized by an active relation to objective conditions, Marx is saying that property is only realized by production.

A specific property relation that is presupposed by a particular productive activity is not only identical with a specific relation within which individuals stand, but with types of individuals as well. A property relation not only defines and distinguishes societies, but also defines and distinguishes individuals, their modes of presence. The individuals' objective presence may be as the property of a person who embodies the communal unity or as citizens of the city or as independent proprietors of land or of instruments of production (craftspeople), any of which is realized in the activity and relations of individuals. This is what Marx means by the objective individual, the individual as Roman, Greek, etc.

The individuals only realize themselves as such, (re)produce their particular mode of presence and recognize themselves as individuals, by their particular active relation within a totality, by the realization of a property relation, a production as a form of life, that is given with membership in a community of landed property.

In all these forms in which landed property and agriculture form the basis of the economy, 'the economic aim is the production of use values, i.e., the *reproduction of the individual* within the specific relation to the commune in which he is its basis' (485). This contrasts with the production of exchange values as economic aim of capital which is the reproduction of capital. Capital is produced by labor in general – wage labor, rather than a particular specific relation such as landowner.

Property relations provide the conditions for (re)production but, at the same time, these conditions restrict the development of production; production is restricted to the reproduction of these property relations. In Marx's analysis, the restriction of production is identical with the restriction of the individual's development. Because Marx treats individuals as social actors (not simply as members of the human species) and social activity as production, restriction of production is identical with the restriction of the individual's development. We have already seen that production is not limited to the economic notion of buying and selling, that any purposive activity is a production and that any production presupposes a particular subject-object relation, a property relation. Therefore, a restriction of production is a restriction of individual purposive activity, hence of individual development.

Marx said of the Roman form, 'But there can be no conception here of a free and full development either of the individual or of the society, since such development stands in contradiction to the original relation' (487). He then asks if in antiquity there was no inquiry into which form of landed property is the most productive, creates the greatest wealth, and answers that in antiquity the question is always which mode of property creates the best citizens. According to my reading of Marx, this means that the production of wealth was limited by the property relations that characterized Roman citizenship. Roman citizenship was based on landed property. The free and full development of the individual and the society was not compatible with the reproduction of the Roman form of community, its particular property relations. Marx states that these property relations allowed for the development of wealth and of the individual (the Roman individual) and society up to a point, but then restricted further development. This raises the issue of identifying the development of wealth with the development of the individual and society.

Wealth and the individual

The identification of the development of wealth with the free and full development of the individual is significant for clearing up a serious problem in readings of Marx. According to Weber, for instance, positing the production of wealth as the aim of individuals and societies is disturbing as well as historically erroneous. Weber seemed to stress that 'people do not live by bread alone,' a certain culture is always presupposed by any mode of production and, furthermore, such cultures exert restrictive or supportive influence on the development of the economy – the production of material wealth. Weber expressed concern over the intent to organize society as if it were one large business enterprise, the aim of which is the production of material wealth. He saw this as reducing the human being, its culture, its freedom and its creativity. Therefore, it will be helpful to understand the seemingly questionable identification of wealth as the object of human activity and the development of wealth as the free and full development of the individual. Marx states,

> Thus the old view, in which the human being appears as the aim of production, regardless of his limited national, religious, political character, seems to be very lofty when contrasted to the modern world, where production appears as the aim of mankind and wealth as the aim of production (488).

However, Marx goes on to inquire what wealth is. He asks if, when the limited bourgeois form is stripped away, wealth is none other than the

universality of individual needs, capacities, pleasures, productive forces, etc., created through universal exchange?
The full development of human mastery over the forces of
nature, those of so-called nature as well as of humanity's
own nature? The absolute working-out of his creative
potentialities, with no presupposition other than the
previous historic development, whch makes this totality of
development, i.e. the development of all human powers as
such the end in itself, not as measured on a *predetermined*
yardstick? Where he does not reproduce himself in one
specificity, but produces his totality? Strives not to remain
something he has become, but is in the absolute movement
of becoming? (488).

This striking passage is noteworthy for the identification of wealth
as the unrestricted development of the individual. Wealth is not
the production of particular objects, not even money.

This passage reveals a view of wealth as a mode of being where
there are no limits imposed on the individual's development
except for the limits of previous historic development which the
individual strives to transcend. The wealthy individual, then, is
one whose needs and abilities, created through universal exchange,
are developed in every direction ('universality of needs, capacities,'
etc.), whose life is the movement of becoming all of which it is
capable. However, for such an individual to be possible requires a
certain type of society, where the conditions of production do not
limit the development of the individual. In pre-capitalist forms,
the conditions of production did limit the development of the
individual.

Capital dissolves the limitations imposed by the old conditions
of production, and in doing so opens up the possibility of the
universal development of the individual. However, the relation
which dissolves the old form and makes this one conceivable at the
same time prevents this development, because capital is based on
the separation of labor from its objective conditions.

The presupposition of the capitalist form of society is wealth in
the form of a thing (capital), rather than the free and universal
development of the individual which should be the presupposition
of society. Although capital posits the production of wealth
independent of particular relations, it substitutes a general relation

of production that is also restrictive, the relation of labor to capital. Whereas there is no longer a predetermined yardstick for the development of human powers – the individual as Roman, for example – the modern aim of producing wealth in the form of money appears as the sacrifice of the human end-in-itself to an entirely external end:

> In bourgeois economics – and in the epoch of production to which it corresponds – this complete working-out of the human content appears as a complete emptying-out, this universal objectification as total alienation, and the tearing-down of all limited, one-sided aims as sacrifice of the human end-in-itself to an entirely external end. This is why the childish world of antiquity appears on one side as loftier. On the other side, it really is loftier in all matters where closed shapes, forms and given limits are sought for. It is satisfaction from a limited standpoint; while the modern gives no satisfaction; or, where it appears satisfied with itself, it is vulgar (488).

Whereas the world of antiquity is satisfaction from a limited standpoint (from within certain constraints), the modern gives no satisfaction. The line, 'where it appears satisfied with itself, it is vulgar,' is interesting. How can satisfaction be vulgar? I take it Marx means 'lacking in cultivation, perception, or taste.' In other words, the satisfaction that the modern world provides is the satisfaction of realizing wealth in the form of money. We have seen that money, as general wealth, presupposes no particular activity, skill or ability. Hence, being satisfied with money is being satisfied without the satisfaction deriving from some particular achievement other than the achievement of money-making.

This is precisely what Weber seemed to despise and reject, the reason for his polemic with what he considers Marxist theorizing. Unlike Marx, however, Weber did not treat wealth as having grounds, as presupposing a particular, historical form of life. Rather, Weber treated wealth as a thing externally related to other social phenomena such as religion or culture. To give pre-eminence to the thing is certainly to reduce the human as cultural being. However, for Marx, the appearance of wealth as a thing corresponds to particular forms of life. With the dissolution of these forms, wealth as the free and full development of the individual becomes possible.

Wealth and needs are dialectically related. The needs of sustenance, as the subjective aspect, lead to production which makes wealth, the objective aspect, possible. But the act of production which includes social interaction and the products themselves, i.e. wealth, creates new needs:

> needs are produced just as are products and the different kinds of work skills. . . . The greater the extent to which historic needs – needs created by production itself, social needs – needs which are themselves the offspring of social production and intercourse, are posited as *necessary*, the higher the level to which real wealth has become developed. Regarded materially, wealth consists only in the manifold variety of needs (527).

Thus needs, which seem to be a characteristic of the individual, are seen by Marx as historical and social, products of social activity. If the individual is identifiable on the basis of his needs as well as his acts, then, we again see Marx grounding the individual in an historically specific form of life. It is not just production that creates the individual, but production which includes consumption:

> consumption reproduces the individual himself in a specific mode of being, not only in his immediate quality of being alive, and in specific social relations. So that the ultimate appropriation by individuals taking place in the consumption process reproduces them in their social being, and hence reproduces their social being – society – which appears as much the subject as the result of this great total process (717).

While wealth is ordinarily attributed to possession of things, Marx formulates it as the development of the individual's potentials; similarly while great need is ordinarily associated with lack of wealth, Marx shows that the greater the extent and variety of social needs, needs which are treated as necessary, the higher the level of wealth.

The mode of production based on capital is production for the sake of wealth, although wealth posited in a limited way as capital. Thus, this mode of production whose aim is wealth is not limited to reproducing forces of production merely in order to reproduce a given relation to a given set of objective conditions. It rather tries to continually develop the forces of production. However, it does so only as a means for some other end – increase in capital – which at the same time limits the development of the forces of production. Therefore, the mode of production based on capital provides the basis for a new mode of production, where the development of the forces of production is not limited as it is by the pre-capitalist forms nor as it is by capital. Capital posits the production of wealth itself, 'and hence the universal development of the productive forces, the constant overthrow of its prevailing presuppositions as the presupposition of its reproduction' (541).

This is the fundamental difference between capital and all previous modes. Capital requires 'no particular kind of consumption, etc., of intercourse, etc. as absolute condition; and likewise every degree of the development of the social forces of production, of intercourse, of knowledge, etc. appears to it only as a barrier which it strives to overpower' (541). Contrasted with capital, we saw Marx's formulation of pre-capitalist forms where:

> property in the conditions of production was posited as identical with a limited, definite form of the community; hence of the individual with the characteristics – limited characteristics and limited development of his productive forces – required to form such a community. This presupposition was itself in turn the result of a limited historic stage of the development of the productive forces; of wealth as well as of the mode of creating it (541).

In the pre-capitalist forms, the purpose of the community 'is the reproduction of these specific conditions of production and of the individuals . . . and relations – as living carriers of these conditions' (541). Capital changes that purpose of the community to one where specific conditions of production or specific types of individuals and relations are not required, but rather the constant overthrow of all previous conditions is required.

The reason that capital is not the ultimate form of production and social life is that there is an inherent limit presupposed by capital:

> The barrier to *capital* is that this entire development

proceeds . . . in such a way that the working individual *alienates* himself; but this antithetical form is itself fleeting, and produces the real conditions of its own suspension. The result is . . . the basis (for) the possibility of the universal development of the individual, the universality of his real and ideal relations (541).

The new mode of production which corresponds to the dissolution of capital will posit the universal development of the forces of production as the presupposition of the society:

Although limited by its very nature, it (capital) strives towards the universal development of the forces of production, and thus becomes the presupposition of a new mode of production which is founded not on the development of the forces of production for the purpose of reproduction or at most expanding a given condition, but where the free, unobstructed, progressive and universal development of the forces of production is itself the presupposition of society and hence of its reproduction; where advance beyond the point of departure is the only presupposition (540).

The new mode of production presupposes 'advance beyond the point of departure.' In other words, continual change is the presupposition of that society, continual change through developing the forces of production. Thus, wealth in terms of the development of the forces of production, which is also the development of labor, is the aim and presupposition of this new type of society. In the past, 'societies foundered on the development of wealth.' This is because the aim of all previous societies was to reproduce the specific social relations and conditions which constituted the society. In early societies, where the form of life is based on agriculture and the relation to the land, the development of the individuals was limited by that relation. However, as more wealth was produced on that basis, the basis itself – the conditions of those social relations – changed:

The feudal system for its part foundered on urban industry, trade, modern agriculture (even as a result of individual inventions like gunpowder and the printing press). With the development of wealth – and hence also new powers and

expanded intercourse on the part of individuals – the
economic conditions on which the community rested were
dissolved, along with the political relations of the various
constituents of the community which corresponded to those
conditions: religion, in which it was viewed in idealized
form (and both [religion and political relations] rested in
turn on a given relation to nature, into which all productive
force resolves itself); the character, outlook etc. of the
individuals (540).

In the above passage, Marx puts forth a theory of social change
which includes changes in the political relations, in religion, even
in the character and outlook of individuals. He attributes such
revolutionary changes in these aspects of society to the development of the forces of production. These changes in the forces of
production constitute the development of wealth. Changes in
wealth, the development of the forces of production, change the
relation to the objective conditions, which entails change in the
political and religious spheres as well as changes in the character of
the individual. Thus, history is conceived as changes in the
relations to the objective conditions, a subject-object dialectic.
This conception of history contrasts with the version of it as
changes in the objective conditions (development of the forces of
production) or changes in the subjective conditions (changes in
needs, leaders, purposes).

The universal individual as analytic possibility

For Marx, the overriding interest is the development of the
individual. The basis for this development is the development of
the forces of production – of wealth. A form of life based on the
development of the individual would consist of a constant suspension of barriers to that development:

The basis [of the new mode of life] as the possibility of the
universal development of the individual, and the real
development of the individuals from this basis as a constant
suspension of its *barrier*, which is recognized as a barrier,
not taken for a *sacred limit* (542).

Marx's notion of the third stage of history which is characterized

127

by the universal development of the individual is an analytic possibility. It is the analytic result of negating the conditions that produce the disunity and restrictiveness of capital. This analytic notion is made possible by dissolving the disunity presupposed and produced by capital, the disunity of production as a subject-object or property relation, the disunity of production formulated as a division of labor. I mean by this a division between the purpose of realizing exchange value and the activity of production, in other words, a division within labor (production), a separation of purpose and activity, the division of capital and labor. This disunity restricts the development of labor, limits production to accord with the property relations – the exchange relations of a market economy. The third stage is the analytic resolution of this conflict between the relations of production and the forces of production.

Marx's notion of the third stage is a form of life in which the possibility of the universally developed individual becomes the basis for production, the basis for the real development of the individual. The possibility of the universally developed individual is the product of the dissolution of all relations that restrict that development. All previous modes of production were based on property relations, relations to the objective conditions of self-realization, that restricted development. The final stage of history will be characterized by property relations that have been generalized, in other words, a relation of subject to objective conditions, including social relations as its own to be reappropriated and mastered, as barriers to be suspended, limits to be overcome, a unity of purpose and activity presupposed to and posited in labor.

The difference between the new form of life and earlier ones may be conceptualized as the difference between pre-history and history (self-conscious history) or between history (changes in property relations) and the end of history, or between private property and social property, property recognized and treated as objective conditions to be used and transformed for the development of the social being.

The production of wealth, the universal or all-sided development of the individual, was not the basis of production in the pre-capitalist forms of life. Instead, the individual and the community were defined by specific property relations. Development and production was always production within these relations. Hence, the individual was restricted. In pre-capitalist forms without a greatly developed system of exchange such as exists with capitalism, the individuals are 'imprisoned within a certain definition, as feudal lord and vassal, landlord and serf, etc., or as members of a caste etc. or as members of an estate, etc.' (163). He states that the individuals are 'imprisoned' within certain definitions although their relations appear to be more personal.

Marx seems to be opposing imprisonment with personal relations, suggesting that if the relations were 'really' personal instead of just appearing that way, imprisonment would not be possible. This raises the question of the relation between personal relations and freedom. What is the relation between personal ties and freedom (as the antithesis of imprisonment)? It seems that, where there are personal ties of dependence as in feudal relations, individuals have less freedom than in the impersonal relations of exchange in a market economy. Weber, for example, makes reference to this difference in his mention of the preference expressed by serfs for becoming urban wage-workers even when it was clear that remaining in the patriarchal relation of serfdom was economically more advantageous. Marx compares the two forms of life with respect to individual freedom:

> In the money relation, in the developed system of exchange
> (and this semblance seduces the democrats) the ties of
> personal dependence, of distinction of blood, education,
> etc. are in fact exploded, ripped up (at least, personal ties
> all appear as personal relations); and individuals *seem*
> independent (this is an independence which is at bottom
> merely an illusion, and it is more correctly called indif-
> ference), free to collide with one another and to engage
> in exchange within this freedom; but they appear thus only
> for someone who abstracts from the *conditions*, the *con-
> ditions of existence* within which these individuals enter into
> contact (and these conditions, in turn are independent of
> the individuals, although created by society, appear as if
> they were natural conditions, not controllable by individuals)
> (164).

With both the personal ties of feudalism and the impersonal relations of the market, the individual is restricted. In the first case, the individual appears to be restricted by personal relations. In the second case, he is restricted by relations that are independent of him, and 'sufficient' unto themselves, not controllable by individuals. 'Since the single individual cannot strip away his personal definition, but may very well overcome and master external relations, his freedom *seems* to be greater in case 2' (164). In spite of the possibility that a single individual may overcome these external relations by amassing enough wealth to get on top of these relations, 'the mass of those under their rule cannot, since their mere existence expresses subordination, the necessary subordination of the mass of individuals' (164). These external relations of subordination are the elaboration of the general foundation of relations of personal dependence. The foundation is the property relation which consists of a division into property owners and non-property owners. Although the external relations of the market appear to be the abolition of relations of dependence, they are rather these relations of dependence dissolved into a general form (164).

Marx had stated that although their relations appear to be more personal, the relations of individuals in pre-capitalist forms were 'imprisoned' within certain definitions. However, even with the external relations of a market economy, the relations of individuals are still determined but in this case by abstractions:

> Here also individuals come into connection with one
> another only in determined ways. These *objective* depen-
> dency relations also appear, in antithesis to those of
> *personal* dependence (the objective dependency relation is
> nothing more than social relations which have become
> independent individuals; i.e. the reciprocal relations of
> production separated from and autonomous of individuals)
> in such a way that individuals are now ruled by *abstractions*,
> whereas earlier they depended on one another (164).

This brings us to the interesting question of the connection between personal relations and independence. Where individuals relate within market conditions as agents of the abstraction, exchange value, their relations are abstracted from themselves as persons with histories. As agents of exchange value, all personal distinctions are dissolved, yet dependency on externalities still exists. Hence, the 'independence' of individuals within the impersonal relations of the market is an illusion. On the other hand, we have seen that the 'personal' relations of the precapitalist societies are also not characterized by independence. However, Marx claims that the personal relations of feudal times were also an illusion:

> As regards the illusion of the 'purely personal relations' in feudal times, etc., it is of course not to be forgotten for a moment (1) that these relations, in a certain phase, also took on an objective character within their own sphere, as for example the development of landed proprietorship out of purely military relations of subordination; but (2) the objective relation on which they founder has still a limited, primitive character and therefore *seems* personal, while, in the modern world, personal relations flow purely out of relations of production and exchange (165).

Neither the pre-capitalist, nor the capitalist worlds are characterized by true personal relations. The personal relations have an 'objective character' in both cases. I take it this means that the relations are external to and presupposed to individuals. In other words, true personal relations would be those relations that are not determined externally to the individuals. This means that the relations within which individuals stand would be treated as a barrier to be overcome and not as a 'sacred limit.' Thus the individuals would not relate within a specific, externally determined relation such as landowner and serf, nor within an abstract, externally determined relation such as buyer and seller. The individuals would not be limited and known by the relations within which they stand, such as Roman citizenship, nor by the relations of producing abstract exchange value. Rather, individuals would be understood historically. In other words, individuals' acts and relations by which they are known would be understood as presupposing relations and conditions within which they were developed and which individuals in turn transform or suspend.

The individual within a market economy

Instead of independence and impersonality, Marx formulates the relations of individuals in a market economy as those of dependence and indifference. The individual is dependent on other individuals each of whom is indifferent to the other. The dependency that forms their social bond takes the form of money. The individual is dependent on the production of exchange value and its realization in money:

> The reciprocal and all-sided dependence of individuals who are indifferent to one another forms their social connection. This social bond is expressed in *exchange value*, by means of which alone each individual's own activity or his product becomes an activity and a product for him; he must produce a general product – exchange value, or the latter isolated for itself and individualized – money (157).

Just as each is dependent on money, each individual has power in money. If the individual has money, he can satisfy his needs without having to do so through his own activity. With money, his dependence is not recognized as the product of a history in which individuals are mutually dependent, a history characterized by personal dependence, mutual dependence reproduced and realized in personal relations. Instead of personal dependence, the individual with money possesses power over others to whom he relates with indifference without recognizing their history as one of mutual dependence. Instead of mutual personal dependence, there is personal indifference made possible with the power of money which mediates social relations. Money is the individual's bond with society enabling him to have power over others' productive activity (157).

With exchange value, the individuality and peculiarity of the product and the activity that produced it are extinguished. This means that 'activity, regardless of its individual manifestation, and the product of activity, regardless of its particular make-up, are always exchange value' (157). Exchange value is a generality, in which all individuality is extinguished. The condition of producing exchange value, then, is very different from that of production in which the individual member's 'activity and his share in production are bound to a specific form of labour and of product, which determine his relation to others in just that specific way' (157).

The relation of the individual to his activity as the production of exchange value is one of alienation. The individual does not realize himself as a subject with a specific purpose in his activity.

He does not engage in the activity in order to realize a purpose that is his own, but in order to produce exchange value, an abstract or general aim and hence an abstract or generalized activity that is independent of his specific needs and purposes. Similarly, the relation of the individual to others is one of alienation in that the exchange of activities and products which has become a vital condition for each individual, appears, not as a recognition of mutual personal dependence, an exchange of purposes and abilities realized in products, but as 'their subordination to relations which subsist independently of them and which arise out of collisions between mutually indifferent individuals.' Exchange appears as something alien to them, autonomous, as a thing. 'In exchange value, the social connection between persons is transformed into a social relation between things; personal capacity into objective wealth' (157).

Marx's analysis of the individual, the relations of a market economy, and even of pre-capitalist forms of life, is in terms of alienation. This is not to say that alienation is simply one concern among others. Some theorists have claimed that the concern with alienation characterized Marx's earlier 'philosophical' work and that his later 'scientific' analysis of capital eschews it. The issue is not a concrete one of whether Marx did or did not retain a concern for alienation. Pointing to passages in the *Grundrisse* to support the contention is not the point of my analysis. Rather, my aim is to show how alienation is internal to Marx's method of analyzing forms of life, particularly capital.

By formulating a form of life as a mode of production, a subject-object unity, the disunity (alienation) of capitalism becomes the problematic. The form of life where the production of wealth is identical with and realized directly as the development of the forces of production (including the individual) contrasts with alienated forms of life in which the individuals relate to their social relations and products, their conditions of existence, as objective relations alienated from themselves.

Marx characterizes capitalism in terms of its universality and its alienation:

> The degree and the universality of the development of wealth where *this* individuality becomes possible supposes production on the basis of exchange values as a prior

133

condition, whose universality produces not only the alienation of the individual from himself and from others, but also the universality and the comprehensiveness of his relations and capacities (162).

Compared to the universal development of the individual that is made possible (but not realized) by exchange value and the production of exchange value, and even compared to the limited development of the individual in pre-capitalist forms, the development of the individual as producer of exchange value appears as a 'complete emptiness.' Yet he argues against comparing this situation to earlier stages of development in which the individual seems to be developed more fully. He says that the individual only seems to be more fully developed, because 'he has not yet worked out his relationships in their fullness, or erected them as independent social powers and relations opposite himself.' Marx states that it is just as ridiculous to yearn for a return to that original fullness as it is 'to believe that with this complete emptiness history has come to a standstill.' He claims that the bourgeois viewpoint 'has never advanced beyond this antithesis between itself and this romantic viewpoint' (162). Unlike the bourgeois viewpoint, Marx goes on to contrast the alienation of labor with the possibility of non-alienated labor without relying on an image from earlier stages of development.

Non-alienated labor: work as mastery

A mode of existence in which individual production is *directly* social and general production, in which the development of the individual is, therefore, also directly the development of the society and known as such, in which the production of wealth is the production of universally developed individuals is a self-conscious form of life. As such it is the opposite of an alienated form of life in which individual production is separated from social wealth such that labor does not realize itself as wealth.

The mode of existence in which the universal development of the individual and the continual development of the forces of production (wealth) are presupposed and posited as aim by the society may be summed up by the phrase, 'self-conscious mastery.'

This mastery includes human knowledge of the processes of nature. In this form of life, wealth means scientific knowledge which includes understanding one's own history as a process. A self-conscious form of life would, therefore, include the development of science as an essential element in the development of the forces of production:

> Hence also the grasping of his own history as a *process*,
> and the recognition of nature (equally present as practical
> power over nature) as his real body. The process of
> development itself posited and known as the presupposition
> of the same (542).

A self-conscious form of life which, for Marx, is a scientific form of life would be one that recognizes the process of development and posits it as presupposition of this development, hence a form of life in unity with its own process of development.

Marx contrasts his notion of work as self-conscious mastery over the conditions of life with Adam Smith's conception of work as a sacrifice, a sacrifice of the tranquillity of not working. Adam Smith's formulation of work corresponds with work under capital, or as Marx cogently puts it, 'Adam Smith, by the way, has only the slaves of capital in mind.' The conception of labor as self-sacrifice is made possible by a form of life in which labor does not posit the conditions of work, in which 'labor has not yet created the subjective and objective conditions for itself . . . in which labor becomes attractive work, the individual's self-realization' (611).

In most pre-capitalist forms of production, the objective conditions of labor – land and agriculture – are property of the community as an external being not the property of labor itself. Hence, labor is self-sacrifice; in order to exist as labor, as having a right to its objective conditions, labor must surrender itself to the *external* being and aims of the community.

In the capitalist form of production, although the objective conditions of labor are produced by labor, the subjective conditions of labor, the purpose of labor, is not posited by labor itself, but by capital and the market as an external condition. Hence, labor is again self-sacrifice, surrendering of the self to an external, abstract being.

Thus it is not that Adam Smith's conception of work as sacrifice is not true; it is true within historically specific modes of production. Marx, however, describes the conditions in which a different conception of work would be possible. Adam Smith's conception is true within a form of life but false as a general assertion about work. Adam Smith treats work abstractly, failing to treat it as grounded in an historically specific form of life:

> But Smith has no inkling whatever that this overcoming of obstacles [work] is in itself a liberating activity – and that, further, the external aims become stripped of merely external natural urgencies, and become posited as aims which the individual himself posits – hence as self-realization, objectification of the subject, hence real freedom, whose action is, precisely, labour (611).

Thus real freedom in action, self-realization, is the positing of aims by the self (rather than merely trying to satisfy natural urgencies), whose action is labor. Self-realization as the positing and producing of an object as the object or aim of the active subject is the unity of labor. Marx specifies two conditions for the unity of labor as self-realization:

> Really free working, e.g. composing, is at the same time precisely the most damned seriousness, the most intense exertion. The work of material production can achieve this character only (1) when its social character is posited, (2) when it is of a scientific and at the same time general character, not merely human exertion as a specifically harnessed natural force, but exertion as subject, which appears in the production process not in a merely natural, spontaneous form, but as an activity regulating all the forces of nature (612).

These two conditions deserve some explication. First, the condition of positing the work as social. I take this to mean that one conceives of the work as social in the sense that the individual recognizes that his characteristics, intentions and actions are possibilities given with a form of life, that his individuality presupposes the history of that form of life. Thus the unity of individual and society as the unity of subject, of purpose. Furthermore, the individual assumes that that history, that form of life, is a process of continual change.

In addition to the individual's intentions and actions, the

individual's products and the objective conditions for his activity would be social products. This means that they would presuppose and reproduce the changing conditions and purposes of the society and the individual living within it. Hence, the individual as purpose and as product would be recognized as immediately social – the purpose and product of social life.

Second, the condition of being scientific and at the same time general should be explicated. Marx means mastery of the forces of nature, rather than mere exertion of natural force in accomplishing a particular aim. For example, in attempting to get water, rather than simply exerting oneself by traveling to a spring for water, which is a particular aim, one could try to figure out a way of getting the water by regulating or subjecting the forces of nature to one's aim. This would be a more general aim (e.g. developing a system of aqueducts). It would entail the development of scientific knowledge which by its nature is general and which presupposes history – the previous labor of society. Marx identifies science with a condition 'where labour in which a human being does what a thing could do has ceased' (325). Thus, in his discussion of how the development of wealth has resulted in the dissolution of previous modes of existence, Marx can include science as a form of wealth – i.e. science as the development of the individual's potential which is also a development of the human forces of production:

> The *development of science alone* – i.e. the most solid form of wealth, both its product and its producer – was sufficient to dissolve these communities. But the *development of science*, this ideal and at the same time practical wealth, is only one aspect, one form in which the *development of the human productive forces*, i.e. of wealth, appears (540).

In this chapter, I have shown how the objective individual is produced by the analysis of forms of life. The analysis itself proceeds from the standpoint of a unity that is a solution to the problem of the disunity of capital. I have traced the objective individual within the specific relations of a restricted landed property economy whose production is characterized by the subject-object unity of agriculture. I then sketched the objective individual within the abstract relations of an unrestricted market economy whose production is characterized by the division of capital and labor. Finally, I described the possibility of the individual within the personal and general relations of an unrestricted economy whose production is achieved by the unity of labor. Labor would take the form of scientific mastery of the processes of nature, including its own process – labor as a self-conscious history whose process is understood as presupposition and as product. I will now show how Marx analyzes the labor process within a market economy, the history of capital as a totality of internal relations.

CHAPTER 5

Form of life: internal relations versus external relations

In this chapter, I reformulate Marx's analysis of money and capital as a history. This conception of history does not involve the tracing of sequence that causes or results in the initial formation of capital, i.e. history as external relations such as cause and effect. Rather, it is analysis of the relations and conditions that are presupposed and produced by the (re)production of capital – its internal relations.

As a form of life, its movement or development does not depend on external forces as does an inanimate object or thing. The history of capital is the totality of its internal relations. The internal movement by which it reproduces itself constitutes its analytic history. An analysis of capital inquires into the pre-suppositions that make capital possible, the totality of internal relations necessary for reproducing it:

> While in the completed bourgeois system every economic relation presupposes every other in its bourgeois economic form, and everything posited is thus also a presupposition, this is the case with every organic system. This organic system itself, as a totality, has its presuppositions, and its development to its totality consists precisely in subordinating all elements of society to itself (278).

If Marx is correct in asserting that the development of capital consists in subordinating all elements of society to itself, then an analysis of any element of capitalist society should implicate capital in some way. An analysis, however, is not the same as employing Marx's conclusions and categories as explanation. Such a rigid one-sided method of theorizing is not unlike the one that Marx negates. In other words, one cannot simply use Marx's categories or assert *a priori*, as an explanation of some phenomenon, that it expresses, reproduces or is caused by capital or capitalist relations. Such an assertion or use of a category presumes a prior analysis. One cannot simply 'prove' the assertion or the category by documenting it the way that positivists assert reality by pointing to it. Rather, one inquires into the presuppositions for reproducing whatever one is analyzing: the necessary subjective and objective conditions.

Marx does not begin with some *a priori* totality, such as capitalism or economics, with which he then explains everything. Rather, he begins with capital as a given object of knowledge and through an inquiry into its presuppositions he arrives at its totality, that which grounds it. The same procedure for arriving at a totality should apply to the analysis of any object; by inquiring into its presuppositions, one arrives at a historically specific totality and its categories, i.e. concepts that can be used to grasp and convey those presuppositions.

The totality arrived at through the analysis refers to a relation of subject to its object, a relation formulated as production. Marx conceives of the totality of subject and object as a property relation. When Marx refers to the relationship of private property (1963, p. 137), he does not mean the relationship of private property to something else, something external to private property. Rather, the relationship of private property refers to the relations that are internal to or presupposed by the (re)production of private property, 'the relation of private property includes within itself, the relation of private property as labour, the relation of private property as capital, and the mutual influence of these two' (1963, p. 139).

We can understand the relation of private property to mean a subject-object relation, a mode of production. Thus the subject-object relation of private property is a mode of production in which the subject (re)produces and relates to itself as labor, 'the abstract existence of man as a mere working man,' and (re)produces and relates to its object as capital 'in which every natural and social character of the object is dissolved' (*ibid.*). Thus Marx does not analyze capitalism as made up of external relations among separate institutions, but analyzes it in terms of its internal relations, its presuppositions as a mode of production: the relations of subject and object.

140

Internal relations of pre-capitalist forms

Marx formulates capital's form of life in terms of the separation of productive activity from its objective conditions, subject from object. He formulates capitalism's pre-history in terms of unity. In the various pre-capitalist forms of life characterized by unity of subject and object, of producer and means of production, the community mediates that unity. The act of production presumes a secure property relation, one that is secured by the community in which the producer is member. However, the community is a restricted and restrictive form; it reproduces itself as a specific relation of subject and object, a specific and limited development of the forces of production and hence of the individual.

Marx analyzes the past in terms of the relations and conditions that are suspended and transformed in the relations and conditions of capital. Similarly, he analyzes the present in terms of those conditions the suspension of which would make possible a new form of life. From the perspective of a future possibility, socialism, Marx analyzes the present conditions of production as suspending themselves:

> Just as on one side the pre-bourgeois phases appear as
> merely historical, i.e., suspended presuppositions, so do the
> contemporary conditions of production likewise appear as
> engaged in *suspending themselves* and hence in positing the
> *historic presuppositions* for a new state of society (461).

For Marx, the pre-bourgeois phases are 'merely historical,' in that they are presuppositions for the emergence of capitalism that are then suspended once capitalism develops. They are not the pre-suppositions of capital's contemporary history.

I see Marx making reference to pre-capitalist forms for two analytic reasons. One is to show the relations of capital as an historical, as opposed to natural, separation by showing its pre-history as a unity. The second reason for the reference is to show the consciousness of pre-capitalist forms in terms of membership. Membership in a community is the self-consciousness of pre-capitalist forms; it is the consciousness of the individual's relation to his community as that which makes the individual possible. This contrasts with the consciousness of capital which sees the individual as original, as pursuing his own private interests:

The main point here is this: In all these forms – in which
landed property and agriculture form the basis of the
economic order . . . there is to be found: (1) Appropriation
not through labour, but presupposed to labour. . . . The
individual relates simply to the objective conditions of
labour as being his, [relates] to them as the inorganic
nature of his subjectivity, in which the latter realizes itself
. . . (2) but this *relation* to land and soil . . . is instantly
mediated by . . . his naturally arisen presence as member of
a commune (485).

Given this reading, questions about the empirical validity or
accuracy of Marx's descriptions are not relevant. If one were to do
an empirical reading (as opposed to a phenomenological or
analytic one), such questions would of course be relevant. An
empirical reading of Marx's discussion of pre-capitalism might ask
how there came to be different forms of landed property or how
capitalism differs from other forms of society. The questions
presume that difference is given and can be explained by some
external principle, such as economic conditions, environmental
influences or natural temperament.

Unlike an empirical reading, dialectical phenomenology formulates difference analytically as answering to a problem of analysis,
'early' forms being used to show the historic character or analytic
possibility of 'later' forms. An empirical reading begins with
difference as an already given problem. Instead of showing how
difference is a product of analysis, instead of asking how difference
can be seen as a problem to be addressed, how difference comes to
be as such, an empirical theorist asks how a particular difference
comes to be. One might read Marx as doing this, as asking
empirically how pre-capitalist forms come to be. Consider the
following:

these different forms . . . depend partly on the natural
inclinations of the tribe, and partly on the economic conditions in which it relates as proprietor to the land and soil
in reality, i.e., in which it appropriates its fruits through
labour, and the latter will itself depend on climate, physical
make-up of the land and soil, the physically determined
mode of its exploitation, the relation with hostile tribes or

neighbour tribes, and the modifications which migrations, historic experiences, etc. introduce (486).

One could, of course, develop such a history of a particular society. However, I would distinguish that from an analytic history. The above passage reveals Marx's awareness of the complexity of empirical history. Although Marx does not develop an elaborate empirical history, he does make what appear to be empirical descriptions of pre-capitalist forms. Further, I see him addressing the question of social change and history. However, rather than an empirical history, I reformulate his description of social change in terms of the restrictive conditions of 'early' forms and their suspension in 'later' forms.

The restrictiveness of the early forms is known retrospectively in terms of their conditions of existence which must be suspended in the development of later forms. Early and late are not empirical categories of time. They refer to analytic possibilities. That is, they are made possible by Marx's problematic. The restrictiveness of early forms and its overcoming is one analytic problem to which Marx's discussion of pre-capitalism orients.

One might inquire into the transition from early to late. If a form of life is a relation to objective conditions, that is, not reducible to the purposes and acts of individuals prior to, or outside of some society, then how does this relation change? If the relations within which individuals stand are given with the individual, then how do these relations change? How do pre-capitalist conditions of production come to suspend themselves?

For Marx, the property relation which presumes membership in a community is a presupposition of pre-capitalist production. Production is the way that the property relation and the community reproduce themselves. However, production changes the objective conditions the relation to which constitutes the practical life of the community. Thus changes in the conditions of production are also changes in the practical life of the community.

Since the reproduction of the community's form of life is the reproduction of the relation to objective conditions, changes in the objective conditions that result in the destruction of those conditions bring with them the destruction of the community and the property relations on which it was based. This is not to say that aspects of the community do not remain such as religion or music

143

or food preferences and taboos. However, these do not constitute a vital part of the community. Thus the vitality of the community can be said to decline and the community to decay. Either that, or the other aspects of the community may be absorbed in a new form of life, a new relation to objective conditions, in which case one could say that the community's form of life has changed, although certain features have remained. The important point is that reproduction changes the relation to objective conditions, the property relation, and destroys the community that is known in terms of that relation:

> The survival of the commune as such in the old mode requires the reproduction of its members in the presupposed objective conditions. Production itself, the advance of poulation (this too belongs with production) necessarily suspends these conditions little by little; destroys them instead of reproducing them etc., and with that, the communal system declines and falls, together with the property relations on which it was based (486).

Marx is not saying that the advance of population in itself necessarily suspends these conditions. It is only because the size of the population is a condition of production based on landed property that its advance suspends the conditions of production. The form of life which presupposes a certain size population as a condition of production declines.

If the conditions for reproduction, a particular form of life, include a certain amount of land for each producer, then an increase in the population of producers will change the internal conditions of that form of life. The impoverishment which might result would contribute to suspending the old conditions of production, particularly through the development of warfare and conquest:

> If the individual changes his relation to the commune, he thereby changes and acts destructively upon the commune; as on its economic presupposition; on the other side, the alteration of this economic presupposition brought about by its own dialectic – impoverishment, etc. In particular, the influence of warfare and of conquest, which e.g. in Rome belonged to the essential conditions of the commune itself, suspends the real bond on which it rests (487).

The 'real bond' on which an historical community rests, as distinct from an ideal bond which would be consciousness of a relation, is its production. Production is the activity that presupposes and reproduces community as a specific relation of the individual to the conditions of his existence, including his co-workers. The reproduction of these relations is the foundation of social and economic development, the development of production:

> In all these forms, the *reproduction of presupposed* relations
> – more or less naturally arisen or historic as well, but
> become traditional – of the individual to his commune,
> together with a *specific, objective* existence, *predetermined*
> for the individual, of his relations both to the conditions of
> labour and to his co-workers, fellow tribesmen, etc. – are
> the foundation of development, which is therefore from the
> outset *restricted*, but which signifies decay, decline and fall
> once this barrier is suspended (487).

Reproduction of the presupposed relations of individual to commune, to the conditions of labor, to co-workers, fellow tribesmen, provides for the development of the community and the individual. However, that development is restricted to those specific relations. Once the restriction or barrier to further development is suspended, the community declines and falls because it fails to reproduce itself as the community that knows itself in terms of those conditions. Thus production entails the realization and reproduction of the conditions of a form of life and also the changes in those conditions and the destruction of that form of life:

> It is thereby also clear that *these conditions change.* Only
> when tribes hunt upon it does a region of the earth become
> a hunting domain; only cultivation of the soil posits the
> land as the individual's extended body. After the *city of*
> *Rome* had been built and the surrounding countryside
> cultivated by its citizens, the conditions of the community
> were different from what they had been before (493).

The aim of communities is survival, according to Marx, but not survival in general. The aim is not to provide for the needs of individuals where those needs are conceived in an abstract, general form so that they are universally attributable to all societies. Rather, survival is the reproduction of particular relations among members that constitute a particular society:

> The aim of all these communities is survival, i.e. repro-
> duction of the individuals who compose it as proprietors,
> i.e. in the same objective mode of existence as forms the
> relations among the members and at the same time there-
> fore the commune itself. This reproduction, however, is at
> the same time necessarily new production and destruction
> of the old form (493).

In other words, the very attempt to preserve the mode of existence
based on a particular form of property relations, through the
activities of production, introduces new conditions and forces that
ultimately change the original conditions and the property relations
that correspond to them. Marx refers to this as 'the alteration of this
economic presupposition brought about by its own dialectic –
impoverishment, etc.' (487). Marx gives the example of a form of
life for which a given number of acres of land per individual is
required:

> For example, where each of the individuals is supposed to
> possess a given number of acres of land, the advance of
> population is already under way. If this is to be corrected,
> then colonization, and that in turn requires wars of con-
> quest. With that slavery, etc. . . . Thus the preservation of
> the old community includes the destruction of the con-
> ditions on which it rests, turns into its opposite (494).

In addition to the changes in the objective aspects of existence,
the subjective mode of existence changes too. That is, the producers
themselves change as they actively go about reproducing themselves and their property relations:

> Not only do the objective conditions change in the act of
> reproduction, e.g. the village becomes a town, the wilder-
> ness a cleared field, etc., but the producers change too, in
> that they bring out new qualities in themselves, develop
> themselves in production, transform themselves, develop
> new powers and ideas, new modes of intercourse, new
> needs and new language (494).

Marx emphasizes the restrictiveness of pre-capitalist forms and
attributes it to the specificity of the relation to objective conditions.

This means that the form of life specifies the reproduction of these objective conditions and the relation to them. According to Marx, the restrictiveness and specificity of these forms of life correspond to a relatively limited development of production which is necessarily limited:

> All forms (more or less naturally arisen, spontaneous, all at the same time however results of a historic process) in which the community presupposes its subjects in a specific objective unity with their conditions of production, or in which a specific subjective mode of being presupposes the communities themselves as conditions of production, necessarily correspond to a development of the forces of production which is only limited, and indeed limited in principle (496).

The above quotation should be read with the emphasis on the word 'specific': the community presupposes a *specific* objective unity between the subjects and their conditions of production or a *specific* mode of being presupposes a specific form of community as a condition of production. This condition limits the development of production. The specificity of the conditions of existence, however, is only specific against the changes which suspend those conditions. In other words, the conditions of landed property are only possible as conditions when other conditions are possible. They are only known as specific and restrictive retrospectively. It is only from the perspective of later developments that they are specific and restrictive.

The specificity of these conditions is only known as such in terms of the generality of the conditions for the reproduction of capital's form of life – labor in general. It is against the generality of labor, 'labor in general,' that the specificity of labor in pre-capitalist forms is known as such. The community that knows itself in terms of a specific relation to objective conditions cannot know itself in terms of labor, because the community there is not a product of labor. It is a community that is presupposed to labor but not produced by labor. Therefore, it can only know itself in terms of the specific relation to objective conditions in which it reproduces itself. Thus it is not a mistake or morally inferior *choice* for these communities to identify themselves with a specific relation to objective conditions. Rather, the community can only know itself in that specific relation.

147

It is only with capital that the community ceases to know itself in terms of a specific relation to objective conditions which must be reproduced as such. With capital, the community knows itself in the exchange of products. Hence, money becomes the community. It is with the generality of labor that the freedom of socialism is possible as opposed to the restrictiveness of pre-capitalist and capitalist forms. Pre-capitalist forms restrict development to a specific objective mode of existence. The capitalist form restricts development to pure subjectivity. 'In bourgeois society, the worker, e.g. stands there purely without objectivity, subjectively; but the thing which stands opposite him has now become the *true community*' (496). By positing labor as general immediately without having to be realized in exchange value, the restrictiveness of capital is suspended and the freedom of socialism made possible.

Social change and the relation to objective conditions

From the perspective of their suspension in the relations of capital, which in turn provides the possibility of socialism, Marx formulates pre-capitalist forms as *specific relations to objective conditions*. Thus social change is seen in terms of a *relation* to objective conditions. This is different from an explanation in terms of changes in a subject – new purposes or needs – or changes in objective conditions. Conditions are only known as such in terms of that for which they are the conditions. An object is only known as such in terms of a subject for which it is an object.

Other readings of Marx interpret him as attributing social change to changes in economic conditions, changes in the forces of production. I will review Marx's discussion of the persistence of the Asiatic form of pre-capitalist landed property in order to illuminate the difference between attributing social change to changes in the *relation* to objective conditions which presumes a particular subject that knows itself in terms of its relation to objective conditions, and attributing social change to changes in the objective conditions alone.

Marx states:

> The Asiatic form necessarily hangs on most tenaciously and for the longest time. This is due to its presupposition that

the individual does not become independent vis-à-vis the commune; that there is a self-sustaining circle of production, unity of agriculture and manufactures, etc. (486).

The two conditions that he mentions are the presupposition about the relation of the individual to the commune and the unity of agriculture and manufacture. He begins with presuppositions which imply a subject that has presuppositions. Marx compares the Asiatic form with the struggle of the clan system to reproduce itself. Ordinarily the clan system results in warfare, because the only barrier to the community's reproducing itself in its relation to the earth (the objective condition of production) as to its own property is another community which also claims the land as its inorganic body. '*Warfare* is therefore one of the earliest occupations of each of these naturally arisen communities, both for the defense of their property and for obtaining new property' (491).

With warfare as a necessary condition for defending or obtaining new property, the development of slavery and serfdom becomes possible. They 'are only further developments of the form of property resting on the clan system' (493). Slavery and serfdom in turn 'corrupt and modify' the original form of the communities – the relation to objective conditions. However, this is least likely in the Asiatic form. Because the Asiatic form is based on a self-sustaining unity of manufacture and agriculture, 'conquest is not so necessary a condition as where *landed property, agriculture* are exclusively predominant' (493).

Conquest is not so necessary in the Asiatic unity of manufacture and agriculture, because new population can be absorbed, whereas where landed property and agriculture form the basis of community, increased population brings a need for additional land. Marx states that slavery which alters the relation to objective conditions does not do so in the Asiatic form. He attributes this to the unity of agriculture and manufacture, but also to the specific relation to objective conditions that is presupposed, the subjective conditions for its existence. The subjective condition is the consciousness of itself in terms of a higher unity that is divine. Membership in a community mediates the individual's relation to the land. This community, conceived as a divinity, and not the individual, is the sole proprietor. In antiquity, however, the individual is a proprietor and as such can lose his property. Private

149

property in this form implies both having and holding. In the oriental form, holding does not presuppose having. The individual cannot lose his property in the same way:

> In the oriental form this *loss* is hardly possible, except by means of altogether external influences, since the individual member of the commune never enters into the relation of freedom towards it in which he could lose his (objective, economic) bond with it. He is rooted to the spot, ingrown. This also has to do with the combination of manufacture and agriculture, of town (village) and countryside (494).

With the unity of town and country in the oriental system, the individual can never become free of the relation to the commune – he is possessed by the community. That which he holds he does not have (as his own). Hence there is little possibility of new development such as mercantile capital,

> In classical antiquity, manufacture appears already as a corruption (business for freedmen, clients, aliens) etc. This development of productive labour . . . which necessarily develops through intercourse with aliens and slaves, through the desire to exchange the surplus product, etc., dissolves the mode of production on which the community rests, and, with it, the *objective individual*, i.e. the individual defined as Roman, Greek, etc. Exchange acts in the same way; indebtedness, etc. (495).

The implication is that the Asiatic form, in which the individuals are not independent proprietors, but 'at bottom . . . the property, the slave of him in whom the unity of the community exists,' precludes the development that occurs on the basis of the individual proprietor form.

Marx's discussion of the tenacity of the Asian system does not indicate an identification of forms of life with economic conditions, nor social change with economic developments *per se*. Rather, it shows a treatment of a form of life as a relation to objective conditions, a totality of internal relations. Rather than concern with the empirical accuracy of the analysis, I want to show that Marx treats the change from one form to another in terms of internal relations of a specific subject (a community) and its specific objective conditions of existence.

The historic character of the separation of labor from its objective conditions

Marx formulates pre-capitalist forms in order to bring out the historic character of the property relation of capital. The exchange of labor for labor (objectified labor as exchange value for living labor capacity) is an historic relation not a 'natural' one. It presupposes the separation of labor from its objective conditions. 'The notion that production and hence society depended in all states of production on the exchange of mere labour for labour is a delusion.' In pre-capitalist forms, the reproduction of society as the reproduction of the worker 'is by no means posited through *mere* labour, for his property relation is not the result but the presupposition of his labour' (515).

While this might seem obvious for the case of landed property, Marx claims that it is also the situation of the gild system. Property there, too, rests on 'an objective connection between the worker and a community and conditions which are there before him, which he takes as his basis.' Of these objective conditions, Marx states:

> These too are products of labour – of the labour of world history; of the labour of the community – of its historic development, which does not proceed from the labour of individuals nor from the exchange of their labours. Therefore mere labour is also not the presupposition of realization (515).

Production and appropriation, the realization of the worker and the community, do not originate with the individual and his work, but the individual and his work presuppose objective relations and conditions. Even the objective conditions are products of labor. This may seem to contradict his earlier statement that 'the original conditions of production cannot themselves originally be products, results of production.' These seemingly contradictory statements are reconcilable.

Production can refer to individuals' labor, in which case the original conditions are presupposed to labor. They are not the products of the individual's work. On the other hand, production can refer to the community's activities, in which case the conditions of production are such only in so far as the community so treats them (produces them as such). For example, land for agriculture only becomes a condition of production when the community treats it as such, when the community knows agriculture.

We have seen that Marx treats the community as a natural condition which is not to be attributed to or reduced to the actions of individuals in some state of nature outside of community. Rather, a community is always the relations within which individuals stand. Therefore, in one case, he can state that the conditions of production cannot be the result of production. He means they cannot be the result of *individual* labor. In the other case, he can state that the conditions of production are products – products of the community, the historic development of the community. The realization of individuals in production presupposes property relations that are historic products of a community. The realization of individuals in production is not simply the result of the individual's labor.

With capital, however, labor appears independent of community or as itself producing community. This is because labor does not realize itself in property which presupposes community. Rather, labor is separated from property, therefore separated from community. The relations which form the community appear as external relations among individuals. This appearance, however, is the product of history, of the dissolution of all forms in which labor is one with its objective conditions:

> *Dissolution* of the relation to the earth . . . to which he relates as to his own inorganic being. . . . *Dissolution of the relations* in which he appears as proprietor of the instrument (497).

Just as the former relation of the producer to the earth as his own organic being presupposes a community, the latter relation as proprietor of the instrument presupposes the community of the gild-corporation system. According to Marx, these indicate, 'Labour still as his own; definite self-sufficient development of one-sided abilities, etc.' Labor is self-sufficient but its self-sufficiency is based on a one-sided development.

In addition, the relations of capital presuppose the dissolution of the relation in which the slave or serf is the basis of production, which in turn is a development of the landed property form:

Dissolution . . . of the relations in which the workers themselves, the living labour capacities themselves, still belong
directly among the objective conditions of production, and
are appropriated as such – i.e. are slaves or serfs (498).

Separation of subject from object personified in class relations

The unity of labor with its objective conditions is part of the
formulation of pre-capitalist forms. This internal relation is seen as
a pre-capitalist form in contrast with the separation of labor from
its objective conditions in capital. Instead of the objective conditions of labor realizing the purposes of labor, the objective
conditions, including the activity of labor, and the purpose are
divided. The division of labor as purpose from labor as activity
corresponds to the experience of activity that lacks intrinsic
meaning. This experience sometimes has moral value attached.
When it does, it is attributed to the character of a subjective
individual, an individual whose activity is seen to be original with
him as his own private motive: 'He's only in it for the money.' On
the other hand, it is sometimes attributed to objective conditions
that are likewise devoid of history: 'You can't live on love. You
need money.'

However, the separation of purpose and activity is an historical
relation. It is neither a subjective condition, nor an objective
condition alone. It is made possible by the historical separation of
labor from its objective conditions. That which mediates and
makes the separation possible is exchange value, an abstraction
that is external to the specific production, to the specific activity
and to the specific needs and purposes of labor. Exchange value in
the form of capital becomes the independent, for-itself, objective
condition of labor. The alien quality of this objective condition
confronts the worker in the person of the capitalist – as personification with its own will and interest (452).

Wage labor in not appropriating its objective conditions as its
own fails to realize itself as mastery. Labor only treats as its own
what Marx calls its subjective conditions, that which is needed to
reproduce the worker as labor power, the means of subsistence,
objects of consumption:

> Labour capacity has appropriated for itself only the sub-
> jective conditions of necessary labour – the means of
> subsistence for actively producing labour capacity; i.e. for
> its reproduction as mere labour capacity separated from the
> conditions of its realization (452).

The question arises as to why labor cannot be formulated as mastery in terms of its relation to the subjective conditions of labor, the objects of consumption with which the individual may produce himself as a particular type. Although Marx talks of the subjective conditions of necessary labor as means of subsistence with which the worker reproduces himself as labor power, why cannot the relation to the subjective conditions be formulated as a relation to the means of sustenance and means of self-realization, a relation of mastery in which the individual produces himself with the objects he consumes?

Marx suggests the answer when he states that objects of consumption are themselves produced. These objects, then, make possible the consumer as a particular type. Thus the consumer is made possible by production. The worker as consumer is not produced by his own purposes and activity. He is not master of his condition, because the object of consumption is produced by the labor of the worker and the purpose of capital. In consuming, the worker does not reproduce himself as subject, as master of his conditions of existence. Instead of reproducing himself as master, he only reproduces capital and himself as living labor power.

With capital, instead of mastery of the objective conditions as the condition for the realization of the worker, the worker becomes the condition for the realization of objective conditions, of products as values for themselves independent of the laborer. Because of the separation, analysis is made possible. Analysis remembers the unity from which the separation is wrested. This does not mean that analysis merely knows the early, 'natural' unity that is analytically prior to the separation. Rather, it knows the possibility of unity that is made possible with the analytic suspension of the separation, the possibility of a new unity based on the conditions produced with that separation.

The separation of labor from property, of subject from object, is at the same time the reversal of the relation of labor as mastery. Labor, instead of master and subject, becomes the slave and object of that which is objective. The objective conditions confront labor as subject, as master:

> Instead of their being realized [the objective conditions of
> labor] in the production process as the conditions of its
> realization [the realization of labor], what happens is quite
> the opposite: it [labor] comes out of the process as mere
> condition for *their* realization and preservation as values for
> themselves opposite living labour capacity (462).

This reversal of the subject-object relation is the consequence of the separation of the subject from its unity with its objective conditions. In earlier forms, this unity was realized as mastery, mastery as a 'natural unity of labour with its material [*sächlich*] presuppositions' (471). The separation of worker from the soil as his 'natural workshop' is a product of history; it is not natural. Marx sketches the relations of mastery that characterize the pre-capitalist forms and, in so doing, creates a picture that contrasts strongly with that of the relations of capital:

> The worker thus has an objective existence independent of
> labour. The individual relates to himself as proprietor as
> master of the conditions of his reality. He relates to the
> others in the same way . . . the individuals related not as
> workers but as proprietors – and members of a community,
> who at the same time work. . . . The positing of the
> individual as a worker, in this nakedness, is itself a product
> of history (471).

The metaphor of nakedness with which he portrays the worker is a metaphor for the separation of labor from its objective conditions. This nakedness is poverty; it is the exclusion of wealth in its objective form, the objective conditions of labor. Wealth in its subjective form, we have seen, is the individual:

> labour [is] separated from all means and objects of labour;
> from its entire objectivity. This living labour, existing as an
> *abstraction* from these moments of its actual reality; this
> complete denudation, purely subjective existence of labour,
> stripped of all objectivity. Labour as *absolute poverty*:
> poverty not as shortage, but as total exclusion of objective
> wealth (295).

The division of labor into capital and wage labor that comes with the separation of labor from its objective conditions not only produces relations of mastery and subjection but class relations of wealth and poverty.

Division of labor and relations of wealth and poverty

As the exclusion of objectified labor in the form of value, labor is *not value* or only use value. However, as use value, it is purely objective; it is not a subject-object unity. Rather, its subject or purpose is not its own; it is an alien, imposed purpose. Thus labor is use value, whose use is not its own:

> as the existing *not-value*, and hence purely objective use value, existing without mediation, this objectivity can only be an objectivity not separated from the person: only an objectivity coinciding with his immediate bodily existence. Since the objectivity is purely immediate, it is just as much direct not-objectivity. In other words, not an objectivity which falls outside the immediate presence [*Dasein*] of the individual himself (296).

Labor does not mediate between itself and its activity by positing purpose to be realized in the activity itself. In not positing purpose, it is purely objective, something that is used. This objectivity coincides with the individual's bodily existence. At the same time labor is an object, a use value for another, it is the subjective existence of the worker, the 'purely subjective existence of labour, stripped of all objectivity.' It is activity that is not itself value, value for itself, because it does not relate to the value it produces as its own. Instead of value, it is the 'living source of value.' I take it that is what Marx means in the rather tortuous passage above and the one that follows:

> Not-objectified labour, not-value, conceived *positively*, or as a negativity in relation to itself, is the not-*objectified*, hence non-objective, i.e. subjective existence of labour itself.
> Labour not as an object, but as activity; not as itself *value*, but as the *living source* of value (296).

Labor, as the potential for objectifying itself in products, is subjective wealth. Marx, in the following pasage, also calls it general wealth, wealth that has not taken a *specific* form in objects:

> [Namely, it is] general wealth (in contrast to capital in which it exists objectively, as reality) as the *general possibility* of the same, which proves itself as such in action (296).

We now have a contradiction; labor is absolute poverty, the exclusion of objective wealth and, at the same time, labor is general wealth, the general possibility of wealth which it proves in its activity as production. However, this contradiction is not the result of faulty reasoning. Rather, it is a real contradiction, that is a contradiction realized in the separation of labor from itself as value, the division of labor into capital and wage labor:

> Thus it is not at all contradictory, or rather, the in-every-way mutually contradictory statements that labour is *absolute poverty as object*, on one side, and is, on the other side, the *general possibility* of wealth as subject and as activity, are reciprocally determined and follow from the essence of labour, such as it is presupposed by capital as its contradiction and as its contradictory being, and such as it, in turn, presupposed capital (296).

The contradiction is the separation of subject from itself as object, the division of purpose and means for realizing that purpose. This contradiction is already posited in the exchange of labor for wages. In this exchange, labor 'surrenders its creative power,' its general wealth, to capital for a fixed sum, for exchange value:

> It is clear, therefore, that the worker cannot become *rich* in this exchange, since, in exchange for his labour capacity as a fixed, available magnitude, he surrenders its *creative power*, like Esau his birthright for a mess of pottage. Rather, he necessarily impoverishes himself, . . . because the creative power of his labour establishes itself as the power of capital, as an *alien power* confronting him (307).

The contradiction which appears as result of production, the contradiction that wealth in products is produced by labor while

157

labor itself is poor, is not an external result of production such as low wages or uneven distribution, as if distribution were externally related to production. Rather, it is presupposed to production in the act of exchange. That is, because the exchange is an exchange of labor and wealth, use value and exchange value, the exchange posits that separation in its own reality. Hence, the contradiction is not the result of production, but presupposed to production with the exchange relation:

> He divests himself [*entäussert sich*] of labour as the force productive of wealth; capital appropriates it, as such. The separation between labour and property in the product of labour, between labour and wealth, is thus posited in the act of exchange itself. What appears paradoxical as *result* is already contained in the presupposition (307).

Poverty is not an empirical category for Marx. It is an analytic formulation of the condition of wage labor. This means that poverty is not something to be discovered in the world; it is produced in analysis. Thus characterizing social class on the basis of income is irrelevant to Marxist analysis. Rather, income is a consequence of the analytic poverty of wage labor, its condition of being separated from its objective conditions.

Whereas the unity of subject and object in production is the realization of labor, the process by which labor as purpose realizes itself in its objective conditions, the separation of subject and object is the de-realization of labor. This curious formulation means that as labor realizes itself, it does not recognize itself in its products. In other words, the reality produced by labor is perceived as an alien reality:

> Living labour therefore now appears from its own standpoint as acting within the production process in such a way that, as it realizes itself in the objective conditions, it simultaneously repulses this realization from itself as an alien reality. . . . This realization process is at the same time the de-realization process of labour. It posits itself objectively, but it posits this objectivity, as its own not-being, or as the being of its not-being – of capital (454).

Instead of recognizing its products as its own, instead of treating objects as presupposing itself as subject, labor relates to its products as alien things, objects without history. The subject does not recognize itself in the object. This relation is not a failure of perception, but is produced by the division of labor in which the subject is divorced from itself as object. Hence, labor can only know itself as subject *or* object; it cannot recognize one in the other because it is not a unity.

Instead of treating objective conditions as the condition for the realization of labor, labor becomes the condition for the realization of objective conditions, for the realization of products as values for themselves independent of labor. This reversal makes possible the treatment of objects as independent things instead of as relations. An object presupposes a subject to which it is the object; otherwise it is not an object, but a thing. Therefore, objects are relations. The treatment of objects as things is a concrete form of life the opposite of which is an analytic form of life.

The separation of subject and object places analysis outside of the subject-object relation. If the relation were instead a unity, then analysis would not be known as such, for it would not be separate from the form of life itself. The form of life that is a subject-object unity is an analytic form of life, a self-conscious form of life. To reiterate, this unity is not the 'natural unity' of pre-capitalist landed property, but the unity that analysis knows as the solution to the disunity of capital.

The problematic of analysis: separation of subject and object

I have been reformulating Marx's description of capital as a form of life in terms of its internal relations. I have been calling such a description an analytic history. The internal relations of a form of life are the relations of production, the relation of labor to its objective conditions which presupposes the relations of a community. The relations of production are property relations. However, with capital, the property relation is the opposite or negation of a property relation. That is, labor does not relate to its objective conditions as its own, as its property.

We have seen how earlier forms were characterized by a 'natural unity,' whereby labor related to the conditions of production as its extended body. This original unity of subject and object is not problematic according to Marx. This is the natural condition of self-realization. Rather, it is the separation of subject and object which is problematic. One might formulate the Marxist method as the treatment of the separation of subject and object as problematic. The rules of grounding concepts and individuals in historically specific forms of life highlight the problematic character of a form of life in which concepts and individuals appear as things without history. As things without history they are conceived as either objectivities independent of the purposes that make them meaningful or as subjectivities, purposes without the relations and objective conditions which make those purposes possible.

Similarly, the rule to treat forms of life as internal relations highlights the problematic character of a form of life in which the relations appear to be those of externalities. A separation of subject and object is a concrete form of life, one which does not re-member grounds. As such it is the problematic of analysis:

> It is not the unity of living and active humanity with the natural, inorganic conditions of their metabolic exchange with nature, and hence their appropriation of nature, which requires explanation or is the result of a historic process, but rather the *separation* between these inorganic conditions of human existence and this active existence – a separation which is completely posited only in the relation of wage labour and capital (489).

It might seem that the separation between the active existence and the inorganic conditions of existence which Marx claims is completely posited only in capitalism is also posited in the slave relation or the serf relation. According to Marx this is not the case:

> In the relations of slavery and serfdom this separation does not take place; rather one part of society is treated by the other as itself merely an inorganic and natural condition of its own reproduction. The slave stands in no relation whatsoever to the objective conditions of his labour; rather labour, itself, both in the form of the slave and in that of the serf, is classified as an inorganic condition of production along with other natural beings, such as cattle, as an accessory of the earth (489).

Thus the serfs and slaves are not persons within the ancient form of life, for they do not have a position in relation to the objective conditions of their existence. They are themselves an objective condition of existence for the reproduction of persons. In the wage labor situation, the workers are not only a condition for the existence and reproduction of capital. They are persons that capital recognizes as such in exchange; they are not just another force of nature. The laborer is both exchanger and labor power. As exchanger, he relates to himself as owner of labor power. He has a subjective existence in relation to his body as object. Yet, while the worker has a subjective existence as an exchanger, he is at the same time just another objective condition of production for capital.

As exchanger, the individual is master of that which he exchanges, hence he is a master within the exchange relation. However, the exchange relation of capital is, as we have seen, not an exchange of equivalents. The worker engages in the exchange in order to realize the means of subsistence, exchange value. Capital engages in the exchange in order to realize the use value of labor as surplus value. In the exchange, labor relates to itself as exchange value.

As exchange value, the worker is not master, but an objective condition for the reproduction of capital which is indifferent to his existence as laborer. Capital only relates to the laborer as exchange value and as labor power, not as master. Hence, labor is a living contradiction. It is posited in exchange as master but realized in production as labor power, mere force of nature rather than master of nature.

Marx posits the resolution of this contradiction in a mode of existence in which the unity of subject and object is presupposed and posited, a self-conscious form of life characterized by unity instead of disunity and indifference. The production would not be limited by specific relations and conditions of production. Rather, production would presuppose the suspension, transformation and transcendence of all previously produced conditions. The suspension and transcendence of those conditions would be itself the condition and aim of production. The conditions of such production would include presupposing and positing its *general, social* character just as earlier production was presupposed as and limited to a *specific* form.

If the social nature of production is posited and presupposed,

161

then both the conditions of labor and the products of labor are immediately social – the inorganic body of the individuals as *social* individuals, producers who both presuppose and posit each other as condition for their existence. This means that each individual's labor is social or general immediately, part of the total production immediately, not through the mediation of exchange value:

> But with the suspension of the immediate character of living labour, as merely *individual*, or as general merely internally or merely externally, with the positing of the activity of individuals as immediately general or social activity, the objective moments of production are stripped of this form of alienation; they are thereby posited as property, as the organic social body within which the individuals reproduce themselves as individuals, but as social individuals (832).

I have been reformulating Marx's problematic as the separation of the subjective and objective aspects of social life. The dissolution of the separation produces the possibility of social life that is a unity, a unity inherent in the notion of the social individual, a self-conscious form of life.

The basis of merchant capital

In reformulating Marx's problematic in terms of the separation of labor, the separation of purpose from the means of realizing itself, I have taken the unity of labor as the point of departure. The separation of labor presupposes and produces the two essential social classes – capital and wage labor. A question that arises is whether the relation between capital and labor is not an external one. The whole analysis so far has been predicated on the formulation of labor as an internal relation, a relation of purpose to itself as objective conditions. Given this formulation, the separation of labor as the relation of capital and wage labor, is 'improper and forcibly imposed.'

However, it is possible to conceive of the two classes as the analytic origin of capital. In other words, rather than separation which presupposes an original unity, one might begin with a duality. In this case, the relation would not be an internal one at all, but an external one. Thus I will now turn to the process by which capital realizes itself. Instead of focusing on labor, I will see if *capital* can be conceived in terms of external relations rather than internal ones.

The first form of capital is merchant capital. I will review Marx's analysis of the history of merchant capital. Merchant capital is realized in the simple exchange relation which Marx calls simple circulation. In order to have exchange of unlike items (if they were the same there would be no reason for exchange), there must be some way to calculate exchange value. Value allows unlike items to be compared quantitatively and then exchanged as equivalents.

> Considered as values, all commodities are qualitatively equal and differ only quantitatively, hence can be measured against each other and substituted for one another (are mutually exchangeable, mutually convertible) in certain quantitative relations. Value is their social relation, their economic quality (141).

As a value, a commodity can be equated with all others. Value, then, is a general measure. As such, it allows for exchange. Thus value is also a medium of exchange. As value, the commodity is money:

> As a value, a commodity is an equivalent for all other commodities in a given relation. As a value, the commodity is an equivalent; as an equivalent, all its natural properties are extinguished; it no longer takes up a special, qualitative, relationship towards the other commodities; but is rather the general measure as well as the general representative, the general medium of exchange of all other commodities. As value, it [the commodity] is *money* (141).

Exchange value originates as a calculation, a comparison between commodities. In its natural existence, a commodity is not immediately exchangeable for any other. Its exchange value must first be determined. The transformation of a commodity into exchange value occurs through abstraction. The exchange value is expressed in terms of some common denomination or unit in which the other commodities can likewise be expressed. Marx specifies this common denominator as labor time. The exchange

163

value of a commodity is calculated on the basis of the amount of labor time it takes to produce it in relation to the amount of labor time it takes to produce another commodity. For the purpose of merely making a comparison, one can simply determine exchange value in the head. However, in actual exchange, the abstraction must be symbolized in an object:

> In order to cover the excess of one value over another in exchange, in order to liquidate the balance, the crudest barter, just as with international trade today, requires payment in money (143).

Even the simplest exchange relation, barter, requires money. It might seem that what distinguishes simple exchange, including barter, from complex exchange is precisely the absence of money. However, the direct exchange of one commodity for the desired other commodity depends on conditions of place and time, the availability of the desired commodity and an owner of that commodity who desires the commodity owned by the first exchanger. Treating a commodity as an exchange value, should make the two items exchangeable in a certain relation regardless of the desires of the particular owners.

In order for the commodity to realize its generality as exchange value, it cannot retain its particularity as a use value. In order to realize itself as exchange value, it must be exchanged with something that symbolizes the exchange value of the commodity and which can then be exchanged with any commodity. This thing which symbolizes exchange value is money. In other words, although the commodity as exchange value is itself money the owner has the problem of finding an exchanger with the desired commodity with whom to exchange it. To alleviate this problem, a symbol of exchange value is developed.

The use of money as symbol of exchange value is the result of the process of exchange. A particular commodity that is available in the community becomes used as a medium of exchange and 'becomes transformed into money, into a symbol only little by little.' In other words, money is not the origin of exchange. Money is not a natural thing, but an historic product, the result of exchange:

> The process, then, is simply this: The product becomes a

commodity, i.e. *a mere moment of exchange.* The commodity is transformed into exchange value. In order to equate it with itself as an exchange value, it is exchanged for a symbol which represents it as such. As such a symbolized exchange value, it can then in turn be exchanged in definite relations for every other commodity (145).

Once exchange value becomes symbolized in a commodity as money, it takes on the additional character of representative of general wealth. As such it becomes an end in itself as well as a medium of circulation. Instead of being a means for facilitating exchange, exchange can now take place in order to accumulate money:

> If I sell in order to buy, then I can also buy in order to sell. In the former case money only a means to obtain the commodity and the commodity the aim; in the second case the commodity only a means to obtain the money and money the aim (201).

In this latter case, money is no longer a mere medium of exchange. As such it would remain in circulation following its circular course 'always anew like a perpetuum mobile.' In other words, if all exchange were selling in order to buy, then whenever money was received in exchange it would again be used to acquire objects for consumption. But, as representative of wealth, as end in itself, the aim is to withdraw it from circulation in order to possess it as wealth. This forms the basis of merchant capital, the buying of commodities in order to then sell them. The distinction between selling commodities in order to realize money with which to buy other commodities to consume and buying commodities in order to sell them and realize money as end is represented by the formulae C-M-C and M-C-M, respectively:

> money which enters into circulation and at the same time returns from it to itself [buying in order to sell] . . . is at the same time the first concept of capital, and the first form in which it appears (253).

Capital is the movement of money in the process of buying in order to sell. This is merchant capital, which Marx also calls

165

commercial capital and circulating capital. In this form it has not yet become the foundation of production – industrial capital. 'Capital comes initially from circulation, and, moreover its point of departure is money.'

Merchant capital: external to production

If capital comes from circulation, then it is not a product of labor; hence, it is not an internal relation of production. It is externally related to production. This would mean that merchant capital is only externally related to the reproduction of the community, to labor. The movement of circulating capital is not internal to production:

> This motion can take place within peoples or between peoples for whose production exchange value has by no means yet become the presupposition. The movement only seizes upon the surplus of their directly useful production, and proceeds only on its margin. Like the Jews within old Polish society or within medieval society in general, entire trading peoples, as in antiquity (and later on, the Lombards), can take up this position between peoples whose mode of production is not yet determined by exchange value as the fundamental presupposition (253).

Trading peoples, then, 'live' on the 'margins' of society. Their work is not integral to the society as mode of production. This is not to say that they do not have importance in the society or that their influence is not great. Only that merchant capital is not a presupposition for labor. It might have tremendous influence, however, on the development of the society, on subsidizing political ventures, wars, etc. But the relation of capital to production remains an external one. It is not an objective condition for the existence of labor as such and, therefore, the relation of labor and capital is not a separation of an internal relation, but a relation of two discrete beings.

Merchant capital is not, however, an independent, self-sufficient form of life. It presupposes the circulating commodity which 'steps outside circulation and directly satisfies a need.' He calls this 'consumption-directed circulation' (254). While the aim might be to realize money and withdraw it from circulation, it can only be used by exchanging it for a commodity to be consumed.

The movement within pure circulation can never realize capital, for in the exchange for the commodity to be consumed, money is lost. On the other hand, if money is withdrawn from circulation, stockpiled, it is not 'realized' because it has no substance: 'it merely represents the non-substantial general form of wealth.' In realizing itself as substance by exchange, it disappears as money.

Merchant capital is not a form of life. Its internal relations, buying and selling, do not constitute a self-moving totality. Rather, the process of circulation in which capital is realized comes to an end with consumption. The realizing of merchant capital is also the loss of merchant capital. For its realization consists in its exchange with a commodity to be consumed, but with that exchange and consumption, capital disappears. Circulation does not reproduce itself, but comes to an end with consumption. In order for circulation to reoccur, some outside force must move it. In other words, its grounds are presupposed but not posited by circulation. Circulation does not provide for its self-renewal:

> The repetition of the process from either of the points, money or commodity, is not posited within the conditions of exchange itself. The act can be repeated only until it is completed; i.e. until the amount of exchange value is exchanged away. It cannot ignite itself anew through its own resources. *Circulation therefore does not carry within itself the principles of self-renewal. The moments of the latter are presupposed to it*, not posited by it (254–5).

'Commodities constantly have to be thrown into it anew from the outside' (255). Thus circulation presupposes the production of commodities:

> now, circulation itself returns back into the activity which posits or produces exchange values. It returns into it as into its ground. . . . This is their [commodities'] point of departure, and through its own motion it [circulation] goes back into exchange value-creating production as its result. We have therefore reached the point of departure again, *production* which posits, creates exchange values; but this

time, *production which presupposes circulation as a developed moment* and which appears as a constant process (255).

The development of trade as an ongoing process, even while it retains its character as an external force in relation to production, presupposes a regular surplus production. With the development of circulation, the organization of production becomes altered. Production now presupposes circulation and is carried out in order to exchange the product. As this type of production develops 'the sphere of needs is expanded; the aim is the satisfaction of the new needs, and hence greater regularity and an increase of production' (257). The relation between capital and production becomes qualitatively different when 'exchange value attacks the whole of production.' Capital ceases to be merchant capital, which disappears in circulation, and becomes industrial capital which maintains, reproduces and multiplies itself in circulation.

Industrial capital: internal to production

Capital becomes industrial capital, reproducing and multiplying itself in circulation, when production becomes the production of surplus value. In other words, the difference between merchant capital and industrial capital is the exchange with labor. Without the exchange with labor, the exchange of commodity for commodity, pure circulation, can never realize capital; it can never maintain or reproduce capital:

> The only aspect in which capital is here posited as distinct from direct exchange value and from money *is that of exchange value which preserves and perpetuates itself in and through circulation* (262).
>
> Its own animation consists exclusively in that; it *preserves* itself as a self-validating exchange value distinct from a use value only by *constantly multiplying itself* (270).

The process of realization, then, consists in the exchange between capital and labor. This exchange is made up of two parts which are qualitatively different. That is, one is an exchange; the other is not:

168

(1) the worker sells his commodity, labour, (2) the capitalist
obtains labour itself . . . i.e. the productive force which
maintains and multiplies capital . . . the reproductive force
of capital, a force belonging to capital itself (274).

Through the first exchange, the reproductive force of capital now
belongs to capital. The second process is not an exchange, but the
appropriation of labor by capital. This is 'directly opposite
exchange.' The relation is not one of exchange, but of compulsion.

Unlike the case of merchant capital, industrial capital is a form
of life. It is a totality of internal relations. I reformulated Marx's
analysis of capital as providing a history of the relation of labor to
its objective conditions of existence. However, the analysis of
capital so far suggests that capital does not come from labor but
from circulation.

However, with the production of surplus capital, a new cycle
begins with presuppositions that are internal to the production
process. With the production of surplus value, the moments of
capital – wages, machinery, raw material – are now produced by
labor, they do not come from outside:

> *surplus value or the surplus product* are nothing but a
> specific sum of objectified living labour – the sum of surplus
> labour. This new *value* which confronts living labour as
> independent, as engaged in exchange with it, as capital, is
> the *product of labour* (451).

Thus from the side of capital, analysis shows capital to be a
relation of labor to its objective conditions, an internal relation of
production and not an external relation of capital (with origins in
circulation outside of production) and labor.

Legitimizing and legalizing property relations

The treatment of a form of life as a totality of internal relations not
only has consequences for analysis but, as one might expect, for
the form of life that makes analysis as such possible – the form of
life that appears to be and which treats itself as a totality of external
relations. What seems legitimate and proper for a relation
between externalities, labor and capital, no longer seems legitimate

169

and proper if analysis shows it to be an internal relation – relation of living labor to itself as objectified labor. The production of surplus capital I presupposes the existence of values belonging to the capitalist and thrown by him into circulation, the exchange with living labor capacity. But the presupposition of surplus capital II is nothing more than the existence of surplus capital I:

> True, in order to create surplus capital II, he had to exchange a part of the value of surplus capital I in the form of means of subsistence for living labour capacity, but the values he gave in that exchange were not values which he originally put into circulation out of his own funds; they were, rather, objectified alien labour which he appropriated without giving any equivalent whatever, and which he now re-exchanges for alien living labour (457).

The exchange that produced surplus capital I was a simple exchange between objectified labor owned by the capitalist and living labor owned by the worker. The exchange is based on the laws of the exchange of equivalents which, according to Marx's analysis, is measured by the quantity of labor or labor time contained in them. As such, 'the legal expression of this exchange presupposed nothing other than everyone's right of property over his own products, and of free disposition over them.'

In highlighting the difference between the presuppositions of capital I and capital II, Marx's analysis contrasts with the treatment of capital by other political economists. A presupposition of capital I is the accumulation of exchange values 'perhaps by means of savings garnered from products and values created by his own labour, etc.' or merchant capital accumulated in trade. This accumulation is a condition and presupposition for the arising or becoming of capital. Marx considers it part of its *history of formation* which he contrasts with its *contemporary history*. Once capital has arisen, then such presuppositions become 'results of its presence.' The analytic origins of capital that already exist as such are not the origins of the formation of capital. To fail to analyze the origins of capital as an already existing phenomenon and to conceive of its origins concretely in terms of the preconditions of its coming to be, is to do a concrete explanation. For Marx, concrete explanations are bourgeois apologetics:

170

The bourgeois economists who regard capital as an eternal and *natural* (not historical) form of production then attempt at the same time to legitimize it again by formulating the conditions of its becoming as the conditions of its contemporary realization; i.e. presenting the moments in which the capitalist still appropriates as not-capitalist – because he is still becoming – as the very conditions in which he appropriates *as capitalist* (460).

Concrete explanations can be conceived as bourgeois apologetics, because they fail to reveal the analytic origins. They attempt to treat capital idealistically as an eternal and natural form of production, a general property relation realized in simple exchange. However, being able to conceive of the origins of its formation means that it is not a general property relation, a natural form of production:

These attempts at apologetics demonstrate a guilty conscience, as well as the inability to bring the mode of appropriation of capital into harmony with the *general laws of property* proclaimed by the capitalist society itself (460).

The 'general laws of property' refer to the right of property over one's own products, free disposition over them. As such, these general laws do not correspond to the situation of wage labor, where the product of wage labor is not its property. One might consider the general laws of property as the ideals of capital and the situation of wage labor as its reality.

Thus, a concrete explanation of origins in terms of the simple exchange of property leaves unaddressed the contradiction between its ideals and its reality. Because the ideals and the reality cannot be brought into harmony, explanation can be *either* idealistic *or* realistic. It cannot reconcile the two; it cannot see the origins of those ideals in the origins of the real conditions and relations. To do so would be to see the contradictions as historical and not natural. It is not that concrete theorizing does not recognize the contradictions. Rather, it does not see their history. It sees the contradictions as natural and not as historical.

To see contradictions as natural, is to assume that ideals as distinct from reality are natural, given with the human condition, part of the subjective reality of the human; and that reality is objective, an objective condition outside of the human that is also natural and not historical. In this way, capital can be explained 'ideally,' as a form of production that corresponds to general laws of property. Or it can be explained 'realistically,' as a form of production that assumes certain preconditions such as the accumulation of capital. The contradiction or relation between the real and the ideal is not accounted for historically.

Marx's analysis accounts for the relation between the ideal and the real, the legitimations of a form of life, historically. He does this by comparing the presuppositions, the property relations, of capital I with capital II. The interesting development is that the *right of property*, which is the legal expression for the exchange, becomes the *right to an alien product* on the part of capitalist and the *duty to relate to one's own labor or one's own product as to alien property:*

> We see that by a peculiar logic, the right of property undergoes a dialectical inversion [*dialektischer Umschlag*], so that on the side of capital it becomes the right to an alien product, or the right of property over alien labour, the right to appropriate alien labour without an equivalent, and, on the side of labour capacity, it becomes the duty of respecting the product of one's own labour, and one's own labour itself, as values belonging to others (458).

The paradoxical result is that the law which expressed the unity of labor with its product, the property relation of labor, now allows for the separation of property and labor:

> Furthermore, the right of property originally appeared to be based on one's own labour. Property now appears as the right to alien labour, and as the impossibility of labour appropriating its own product. The complete separation between property, and, even more so, wealth, and labour, now appears as a consequence of the law which began with their identity (458).

The separation of wealth and labor, property and labor, legitimized by law, brings us back to the class relations of capital. The problem of wealth and poverty as the problem of social classes is a problem of the internal separation of capital and labor. The legal relations confirm and legitimize this separation. Analysis shows the

172

legitimacy of capital to rest on property relations of simple exchange. By contrasting the analytic origins of the legal relation in simple exchange with the analytic origins of capital in the exchange with labor, analysis de-legitimizes capital and its legal relations.

We had initially reformulated Marx's analysis in terms of an internal relation of production from the standpoint of labor. We now see that even from the standpoint of capital as exchange value that realizes itself in circulation, once posited, capital is an internal relation of production, a relation to the conditions of production.

If capital is an internal relation of labor, how is it that it appears as an external relation? How is it that labor and capital are able to be conceived as external relations? Marx attributes this conception to bourgeois apologetics, to using relations of simple exchange to legitimize relations of capital. However, analysis requires an account of the possibility of that conception. It is not enough to attribute a conception to individual purposes. In other words, analysis does not account for theorizing as a mistake, intentional or otherwise or to poor reasoning. It is not that Marx is smarter than others or that Marx intentionally tries to de-legitimize, whereas others intentionally want to legitimize capital.

I will show how Marx's analysis of the relations and processes of capital reveal these to be external to each other, although internal to capital. Thus it is not that Marx simply accuses other theorists of a mistake that he corrects. Rather, Marx's analysis shows in what way such a conception is correct, how it is possible as such.

Inner unity versus external, independent processes

The internal relations of capital appear as external ones because in a certain way they are external to each other. This externality is the result of capital's not being value immediately, but is separated from itself as value. In order to realize itself as value, it must go through three exchanges:

> While capital is reproduced as value it is at the same time posited as not-value, something which has to be realized as value through exchange [with labour, with consumers, with raw material] (403).

Capital is separated from itself as self-multiplying value. The processes of realizing capital take place as external relations. Despite their inner unity in capital, they occur as processes independently of each other. Capital is the unity of these external processes.

It is not just the relations of capital that appear as external, so do the relations of money – the relations of simple exchange. With money, the act of exchange is split into two acts, buying and selling. Although exchange is a unity, it is a unity of external, indifferent acts, the acts of buying and selling. Buying may take place separately from and independently of selling.

While exchange implies an identity, the identity of the commodities being exchanged, this identity is mediated by money. There is a difference between money which mediates and the commodities which are being exchanged. Thus it is a mistake to conceive of buying and selling as immediately identical. With the mediation of money, selling in order to realize exchange value in money is different from buying in order to realize use value.

Similarly, it is a mistake to conceive of the exchanger as the immediate unity of seller and purchaser. The political economists whom Marx criticizes conceived of each exchanger as both purchaser and seller, 'each is posited in the double and antithetical aspect, and hence in the living unity of both aspects':

> When it is said that he who sells also buys in as much as he buys money, and that he who buys also sells in as much as he sells money, then it is precisely the *distinction* which is overlooked, the specific distinction between a commodity and money (197).

The failure to recognize the distinction between money and commodities, the failure of the political economists who formulate exchange as this identity, is a failure of analysis. It is the failure to remember grounds. Instead, it treats unity as given, as natural, as presupposing no separation.

Marx points out the inconsistency of this theorizing. On the one hand, it recognizes that money is necessary and that it is distinct from commodities. On the other hand, it asserts that there is no distinction between money and commodities. Money as the unity of exchange value and use value, is seen as identical with the commodity form, as just another commodity. However, the difference between money and commodity is crucial. The commodity that is money is different from other commodities. It is in this difference that the contradictions of money are revealed:

> It is entirely wrong, therefore, to do as the economists do, namely, as soon as the contradictions in the monetary system emerge into view, to focus only on the end results without the process which mediates them, only on the unity without the distinction, the affirmation without the negation (197).

In Marx's theorizing, analysis is the inquiry into the possibility of unity, the origins of unity. Thus Marx inquires into the analytic origins of capital, the relations and processes in which capital realizes itself as such. Just as the exchange relation of money is a unity divided into external, indifferent acts, capital also is a unity divided into external, indifferent processes:

> The three processes of which capital forms the unity, are external, separate. . . . As such the transition from one to the other, their unity as regards the individual capitalists, is accidental. Despite their *inner unity*, they exist *independently* (403).

The unity is a separated unity, its internal relations are indifferent to each other. The unity of money is the separation of buying and selling. The unity of capital is the separation of labor, consumption and raw material and machinery. Capital is the production and realization of exchange values. But the process of production and the process of realization are separated:

> The main point here – where we are concerned with the general concept of capital – is that it is this *unity of production and realization*, not *immediately* but only as a *process* which is linked to certain conditions, and as it appeared, *external* conditions (407).

The indifference of the various moments of the realization process of capital, the contradiction between the inner unity and the external independence of the moments, is the foundation of all contradictions in capital.

CHAPTER 6

Contradiction: mediation as uniting versus mediation as dividing

In chapter 5 we saw that capital was a form of life whose internal relations were separate and whose moments were, therefore, indifferent to each other. That means that the internal relations did not know themselves as such, but only as external relations. For instance, labor treated its objective conditions which were its own product as alien property. Capital treated labor which was a condition for its existence with indifference. The process of producing was separated from the process of realizing capital, the relation of buying separated from that of selling.

A form of life whose internal relations appear as external ones, whose concepts and acts appear as things having no history, whose subjects recognize no grounds, is a concrete form of life. I have indicated the source of contradictions in separation. In this chapter, I will show how Marx analyzes money and capital in terms of contradictions and their consequences for a concrete form of life. In other words, I will reformulate Marx's analysis in order to show how a concrete form of life is possible, how the contradictions do not allow grounds to be remembered.

How mediation produces contradictions and concrete theorizing

I have formulated a concrete form of life in terms of the repression of grounds. I prefer the word, 'repression,' to that of forgetting, for the latter implies an element of will: 'If they had only made an effort, they would not have forgotten.' Rather, the forgetting itself is grounded in the contradictory conditions of a form of life. The contradictions are grounded in separation. With separation, the internal unity is forgotten. In its place is the mediation. A mediation both unites and divides.

Orienting to the mediation means not orienting to the relation which it mediates. Thus the character of the relation is forgotten or repressed in the recognition of the mediation as a thing. The mediation becomes the unity of the separated elements and becomes more important than that which it mediates:

> Thus in the religious sphere, Christ, the mediator between God and humanity – a mere instrument of circulation between the two – becomes their unity, God-man, and, as such, becomes more important than God; the saints more important than Christ; the popes more important than the saints (332).

Similarly, exchange as mediation between producers becomes independent of the producers. As mediation between the extremes (the buyer oriented to use value and the seller oriented to exchange value), exchange becomes a power alien to the producers:

> As the producers become more dependent on exchange, the exchange relation establishes itself as a power external to and independent of the producers. What originally appeared as a means to promote production becomes a relation alien to the producers (332).

Instead of money being subservient to the producers and exchangers as their mediation, money seems to become autonomous and the producers and exchangers appear as merely its moments.

Furthermore, the relation of labor to its objective conditions, of producers to their products, is not seen as such because the unity of money, the appearance of money as a thing, is seen instead. By seeing the object in terms of its monetary price, one fails to see the object in terms of the labor that produced it. Hence, the relation between exchangers as a relation among producers is obscured. Instead, the exchange relation appears as a relation to money, to a thing. In other words, seeing the mediation is the same as not seeing the unity that was separated and which the thing mediates. The mediation seems to become autonomous, and the autonomous relata lose their autonomy and become moments of the mediation

> because the movement, or the relation, which *originally* appears as mediatory between the extremes necessarily

develops dialectically to where it appears as mediation with itself, as the subject [*Subjekt*] for whom the extremes are merely its moments, whose autonomous presupposition it suspends in order to posit itself, through their suspension, as that which alone is autonomous (332).

Instead of the producers, the mediation becomes the subject.

The mediation is the relation expressed to a higher power but expressed one-sidedly. That is, one side of the relation, one of the relata, takes precedence over the other. Thus, in the exchange of commodities, exchange value takes precedence over use value. The same happens with capital:

> Within capital itself, one form of it in turn takes up the position of use value against the other as exchange value. Thus e.g. does industrial capital appear as producer as against the merchant, who appears as circulation (332).

Within capital, mercantile capital takes precedence over, in the sense of appears autonomous in comparison with, industrial capital. Mercantile capital is the mediator between production (industrial capital) and circulation (the consuming public) or between exchange value and use value, 'where both sides are posited alternately, production as money and circulation as use value (consuming public) or the former as use value (product) and the latter as exchange value (money)' (332).

Marx similarly states this to be the case within commerce. The wholesaler appears as a higher power, as mediator between manufacturer and retailer, or between manufacturer and agriculturalist, or between different manufacturers. In turn, and in the same way, the commodity brokers take on more importance than the wholesalers. Also the banker appears autonomous to the industrialists and merchants:

> Money becomes an end rather than a means; and the higher form of mediation, as capital, everywhere posits the lower as itself, in turn, labour, as merely a source of surplus value. For example, the bill-broker, banker etc. as against the manufacturers and farmers, which are posited in relation to him in the role of labour (of use value); while he posits himself toward them as capital, extraction of surplus value; the wildest form of this, the financier (332).

Class struggle can be seen in terms of manufacture and banking. The terms of the struggle are metaphors for the separation of subject and object in use value and exchange value. This is not to say that class struggle between labor and capital is not real. It is to say, rather, that class struggle is the analytic consequence of the separation of use value and exchange value, that is, the separation inherent in the commodity form. Thus class struggle may take different forms. For instance, the struggle between manufacturer and banker does not mean that the struggle between capital and labor has ceased, only that it has taken the form of a struggle between manufacture as labor and banks as capital.

Just as the class struggle can be seen on the level of manufacture and banking, it can be seen on the level of the individual's internal struggle between himself as end or use value, and himself as means or exchange value: 'Should I take a job during my vacation? Should I take a better paying job that I know I'll hate?'

Of course, the individual's internal struggle cannot result in suspension of the conditions of the struggle. This is because the terms of the struggle are presupposed to the individual. The individual's internal struggle can only lead to a one-sided resolution in which the individual satisfies one side of himself, while depriving another side. However, class struggle can result in a suspension of the terms of the struggle either from the side of capital or exchange value or from the side of labor or use value. This is the progressive character of the struggle.

Thus, if labor realizes itself as unity in its struggle with capital, then capital is dissolved. If on a higher level, industrial capital (as use value to financial capital) realizes itself as unity in its struggle with financiers (as exchange value), a unity taking the form of a single industrial capitalist, then again capital is dissolved as such. It is not that the dissolution of capital is something that must necessarily occur with or without struggle. It is rather that the dissolution of capital can only come with struggle that results in unity. Struggle corresponds to the condition of a self-contradictory form of life, the struggle of two opposing tendencies that constitute a unity.

As the producers come to depend more and more on exchange, exchange comes to appear more and more as independent of the producers, 'and the gap between the product as product and the product as exchange value appears to widen' (146). Money symbolizes this exchange relation. According to Marx, it represents value as a relation of one commodity to another in terms of (socially necessary average) labor time which is the only element common to all commodities. Thus the relation among producers establishes the relation (exchangeability) among commodities and consequently the relation of a product to itself as exchange value. This originally social relation among producers becomes externalized in money. Although money appears as an autonomous thing, it must be understood analytically as a relation. Thus Marx talks about the contradictions that are 'immanent in the money relation, in the relation of the product to itself as money' (146).

With the development of money 'as an external thing alongside the commodity,' the exchange relation ceases to be a relation of immediate equality:

> As soon as money has become an external thing alongside the commodity, the exchangeability of the commodity for money becomes bound up with external conditions which may or may not be present. . . . The commodity is demanded in exchange because of its natural properties, because of the needs for which it is the desired object . . . . There thus arises the possibility that the commodity in its specific form as product, can no longer be exchanged for, equated with, its general form as money (148).

A second contradiction of the exchange relation derives from separating the act of exchange into two mutually independent acts: purchase and sale. In this way, their immediate identity ceases, as compared to exchange with barter for example, where to exchange one's product *is* to get another one. With the separation of purchase and sale through the mediation of money as exchange value, these two moments may not balance.

Originally, there was an immediate equality, one commodity is equated with the other immediately with the exchange. But when the commodity is exchanged for money, the equivalence of one commodity with another may now involve momentary non-equivalence. That is, the exchange value of commodity A may be 10, and the exchange value of commodity B may be 10. However, since commodity A is exchanged for 10, rather than exchanged immediately for commodity B, it is possible that commodity A may not realize the exchange value equivalent to that with which it would be necessary to purchase commodity B at a later date, i.e. 10 may not purchase commodity B tomorrow. Instead of immediate identity, they may enter into disproportion with one another just as the relation between the commodity and its exchange value may likewise enter into disproportion:

> They will of course always attempt to equalize one another; but in the place of the earlier immediate equality there now stands the constant movement of equalization, which evidently presupposes constant non-equivalence. It is now entirely possible that consonance may be reached only by passing through the most extreme dissonance (148).

A third contradictory feature of production based on exchange value is the separation of the movement of exchange from the exchangers, the producers of commodities. 'A mercantile estate steps between the producers; an estate which only buys in order to sell and only sells so as to buy again.' The separation of exchange (commerce) from the exchangers, the development of the mercantile estate, 'corresponds to the rise of exchange value as an independent entity, as money, torn away from products' (148).

The purpose of the commerce among merchants is the gaining of money, exchange values. The merchant expects to receive back the money he has laid out plus more, whereas this is not the case for the consumer who is the one who provides the final exchange value for the commodity:

> Exchange within the mercantile estate, and exchange between the mercantile estate and the consumers – as much as they must ultimately condition one another – are determined by quite different laws and motives and can enter into the most acute contradiction with one another. The possibility of commercial crises is already contained in this separation (148).

The mercantile estate may corner the market or stockpile in order to control the supply and raise the prices. Furthermore, when there is a shortage of a commodity such as grain, the grain merchants try to sell it at a high price in order to make a high profit which is possible due to the greater demand than supply.

In addition to the above contradictions, money contains a fourth contradiction by virtue of being a particular commodity once it is not a mere mental abstraction, but is objectified. Because it is a particular commodity, it is subject to the conditions of exchange. That is, its value can fluctuate based on demand and supply or changing costs of production. This conditioned exchangeability contradicts its essence as unconditional exchangeability. This is because it is treated as a commodity subject to the fluctuations of the market and the costs of production. However, as money, it represents general unconditional exchangeability. General unconditional exchangeability refers to the property of money where the particular qualities of money (gold and silver) do not determine whether or not they can be exchanged, but they can always be used in exchange.

A fifth contradiction contained in the separation of the commodity from its exchange value – the money relation – is realized in money as medium of exchange. In this capacity, the attribute which is essential is that of quantity, of amount in which it circulates. This contradicts its character as measure. As measure, it only served a mental function for calculating the relationship between two commodities by relating them to a third. As measure, the symbol of exchange value did not have to be around in any particular quantity:

> Money as measure . . . is required only as an imagined unit once the exchange value (labour time) of an ounce of gold compared to any one commodity has been determined; its actual presence is superfluous, along with, even more so, its available quantity: as an indicator (an indicator of value) the amount in which it exists in a country is irrelevant; required only as accounting unit (208).

Thus as medium of exchange it contradicts the requirements of money as measure of exchange value. As measure, there is no need for it to exist in any particular quantity. As medium of exchange, the amount of gold and silver available for circulation affects circulation and, therefore, production.

A sixth contradiction is between money as means for accomplishing exchange in order to realize human needs and money as an end in itself. By becoming an end, money can be withdrawn from circulation in order to serve the need for possessing wealth in general – the potential for buying any and all commodities. Money was set up as a means for accomplishing exchange but, as soon as it takes a material form, it represents wealth in general and is treated as an end in itself. Instead of being a means for facilitating exchange, exchange now occurs only in order to accumulate money:

> If I sell in order to buy, then I can also buy in order to sell. In the former case money only a means to obtain the commodity and the commodity the aim; in the second case the commodity only a means to obtain the money and money the aim (201).

In this latter case, money is no longer a mere medium of exchange. As medium of exchange, it would remain in circulation following its circular course 'always anew like a perpetuum mobile.' If everybody sells in order to buy, then when one person receives money for his commodities, he then uses it to buy something else from somebody who in turn uses the money realized from that sale to buy something else. In this situation, money functions only as long as it remains in circulation.

But in its third character as representative of wealth in general, money is no longer merely a medium of exchange, a mere means. As an end in itself, it can be withdrawn from circulation. In fact, the aim is to withdraw it from circulation in order to possess it as wealth:

> It represents a greater or lesser amount of general wealth according to whether its given unit is possessed in a greater or lesser quantity. If it is general wealth, then one is richer the more of it one possesses, and the only important process, for the individual as well as the nation, is to pile it up. In keeping with this role, it was seen as that which steps outside circulation (229).

Thus the sixth contradiction contained in the concept of money is its negating itself as medium of exchange where its function or essence is to remain in the circulation process. In its function as general form of wealth and material representative of wealth, it 'steps outside circulation.' Marx analyzes money in terms of the separation of the product from itself as value expressed in an external, material form. What is in essence a unity (the product and its value) must become in practice a separation. The

183

separation, which is necessary as soon as exchange becomes developed, is the basis for contradictions and crises.

Contradictions within the completed form of money

So far we have traced the contradictions among the various properties of money. The final feature of money, as the general form of wealth and the material representative of wealth not only contradicts the function of money as medium of exchange, but involves internal contradictions as well. Marx uncovers the contradictions of money in its 'completed character' as representative of wealth in general: 'As the general form of wealth the whole world of real riches stands opposite it. It is their pure abstraction' (233). In other words, money is merely the representation of wealth abstracted from its content and expressed in a different material form. The real content of wealth consists of all that has been produced. However, it is only the mere abstraction that is treated as wealth. 'Where wealth seems to appear in an entirely material tangible form, its existence is only in my head, it is pure fantasy' (233). The material that constitutes wealth, i.e. money, is only a representation of wealth. It functions as wealth only because people treat it that way as a result of the development of exchange. It has value only because of the use people make of it for conducting exchange. Therefore, its value is due to people's treating it that way, its value is symbolic, which means that its value exists only in the mind, yet people treat it as having intrinsic (rather than symbolic) value independently of them.

In order to realize the wealth that money represents, it must be exchanged for the particular products which constitute real wealth. In other words, it must disappear in circulation in order to realize itself as general wealth.

As medium of exchange it remains in circulation, 'but for the accumulating individual, it is lost and this disappearance is the only possible way to secure it as wealth' (234). If we all keep it and do not throw it into circulation, then exchange cannot take place. If exchange cannot take place, no wealth is realized. This means that there is no real wealth for the money to represent and, therefore, money loses its character as wealth. 'I can really posit its being for myself only by giving it up as mere being for others. If I want to cling to it, it evaporates in my hand to become a mere phantom of real wealth' (234). Accumulating money (restraining from spending) means that certain products cannot be sold (exchanged). If they cannot be sold, production declines. Then the wealth that money represents does not accumulate and the money, therefore, represents less wealth. The notion that

> to accumulate it is to increase it turns out to be false. If the riches do not accumulate, then it loses its value in the measure in which it is accumulated. What appears as its increase is in fact its decrease (234).

Although people may think that money is independent of circulation when they treat it as wealth in itself, its value as money depends on the circulation of products. 'Its independence is a mere semblance, its independence of circulation exists only in view of circulation, exists as dependence on it' (234).

Although it may appear as and be treated as the general commodity, a standard that is not variable, it is actually a particular commodity subject to the variations in the costs of producing it and subject to the fluctuations of the market: 'It pretends to be the general commodity, but because of its natural particularity, it is again a commodity, whose value depends both on demand and supply and on variations in its specific costs of production' (234).

Unlike general wealth, wealth in particular products is related to an individual's qualities and particular abilities. It cannot be separated from the person by any accident.

In contrast with wealth that is related to the development of an individual's qualities and abilities, money is, on the one hand, secure because it is independent of any individuality on the part of the owner. On the other hand, it is at the same time insecure because it can be separated from the individual by any accident:

> As absolutely secure wealth, entirely independent of my individuality, it is at the same time, because it is something completely external to me, the absolutely insecure, which can be separated from me by any accident (234).

We discussed above how its qualities as measure contradict its qualities as medium, and how its qualities as medium contradict its qualities as wealth: 'it has entirely contradictory qualities as measure, as medium of circulation and as money as such' (234). In addition to these three functions, but only because of them, the embodiment of wealth – gold and silver – can take on a different function as display of wealth in the form of jewelry or treasure:

> As a particular commodity it can be transformed out of its form of money into that of luxury articles, gold and silver, jewellery; . . . or as money, it can be *accumulated* to form a *treasure* (216).

Although it can be treated as luxury items independent of its role in circulation, its character as luxury items presupposes its use value for circulation. Although appearing to be independent of circulation in the form of jewelry or treasure, it is dependent on circulation:

> Cut off from all relation to it, it would not be money, but merely a simple natural object, gold or silver. . . . Its independence is not the end of all relatedness to circulation, but rather a negative relation to it (217).

As wealth, its transformation into an article of display or as treasure is a way of signifying that one is so rich that one does not need it as money. In this way it has a negative relation to circulation. It is not independent of circulation, in its form as jewelry; it is only because it could be used to purchase things that not using it gives it its character as treasure or luxury item.

In analyzing the category of money, Marx shows its contradictory character as a thing that appears to be independent of its history, its origins in exchange. He uncovers its origins in exchange and the various forms it takes or functions it acquires as it ceases to be merely an abstract or ideal means of measurement and becomes objectified in a material thing separate from the product, its natural qualities and the exchangers. As it develops, it expresses the contradiction between exchange value and use value to a higher power. In its developed form as measure, medium of exchange and material representative of general wealth, certain of its attributes contradict or negate others. Its surface identity as one thing – money – is a negative unity, a unity of negations.

According to Marx, 'the special difficulty in grasping money in its fully developed character as money is that a social relation, a definite relation between individuals, appears as a metal, a stone, as a purely physical, external thing' (239), which is indistinguishable from its natural existence. The social relation is exchange. Gold and silver, in and of themselves, are not money.

We saw earlier that this was the criticism that Marx leveled against other economists – that they treated gold and silver as absolute wealth rather than as symbols deriving from social relations and social needs. 'It is not at all apparent on its face that its character of being money is merely the result of social processes' (240). That is, its character of being money is a result of people's using it for exchange:

> The memory of use value, as distinct from exchange value, has become entirely extinguished in this incarnation of pure exchange value. Thus the fundamental contradiction in exchange value, and in the social mode of production corresponding to it, here emerges in all its purity (240).

The 'fundamental contradiction' arises from forgetting the origins or use value of money – its origins in social relations. Marx's analysis is a display of treating money not as the thing which it appears to be, but as a result of social processes which include social relations and social needs. Marx's work is a form of analysis that treats its objects not as things, not as givens, as first, but as presupposing social relations. Analysis treats its objects as products of social processes. The purpose for inquiring into grounds is to realize the object as social property, i.e. the product of social processes.

The dissolution of pre-capitalist societies

For Marx the failure to remember the grounds of money, distinct from capital, results in the dissolution of the community that is based on money. This is because the members cannot recognize that wealth in the form of money originates with exchange. By attributing wealth to money independent of exchange, they are in danger of disregarding the basis of their community:

> In antiquity, exchange value was not the 'nexus rerum' [the reigning connection]; it appears as such only among the mercantile peoples, who had, however, no more than a

carrying trade and did not, themselves, produce. At least this was the case with the Phoenicians, Carthaginians, etc. But this is a peripheral matter. They could live just as well in the interstices of the ancient world, as the Jews in Poland, or in the Middle Ages. Rather this work itself was the precondition for such trading peoples (223).

In other words, in the ancient world as well as in the Middle Ages, there were people for whom money through trade was the *'nexus rerum.'* However, these trading people existed only because of the exchange among the communities of the Middle Ages. Marx explains that the trading peoples, therefore, would fall apart when they came into serious conflict with these communities:

Only with the Romans, Greeks, etc. does money appear unhampered in both of its first two functions, as measure and as medium of circulation, and not very far developed in either. But as soon as either their trade, etc., develops, or, as in the case of the Romans, conquest brings them money in vast quantities – in short, suddenly, and at a certain stage of their economic development, money, necessarily appears in its third role, (general representative of wealth) and the further it develops in that role, the more the decay of their community advances (223).

Exchange value is a result of exchange (and, conversely, the development of exchange presupposes exchange value). Money requires the exchange of commodities. The more money develops in its aspect as wealth without developing its role in circulation, the 'more the decay of their community advances.' Vast increases in gold that are not the result of increased commerce (i.e. increase in goods exchanged) bring the appearance of wealth, but increased gold does not mean that the community becomes wealthier. In order for increase of wealth to reproduce itself as such, it must become the basis of community, the basis of production. This only happens in conjunction with wage labor. Thus discovering new gold, or acquiring it through conquest, can lead only to wasteful consumption:

In order to function productively, money in its third role, as we have seen, must be not only the precondition but equally the result of circulation, and, as its precondition, also a moment of it, something posited by it. Among the Romans, who amassed money by taking it from the world, this was not the case (223).

If it is a result of circulation, an increase in money signifies an increase in goods circulated, which means increased production. In order for money to be the basis of this increased production, wage labor is used. Money in conjunction with wage labor can act as a 'driving wheel' for the development of all forces of production. It can be used to get more people to work more productively:

> It is inherent in the simple character of money itself that it can exist as a developed moment of production only where and when *wage labour* exists; that in this case, far from subverting the social formation, it is rather a condition for its development and a driving wheel for the development of all forces of production, material and mental (223).

In the world of antiquity, the coming into money by chance, rather than through commerce, could dissolve those communities because of the failure to remember that production and exchange are the real sources of wealth, and that an increase in gold must be used to increase production and exchange if that increased gold is to represent an increase in wealth. 'Where money is not itself the community [*Gemeinwesen*] it must dissolve the community' (224).

Marx compares this situation to that of the individual in modern society, who comes into money by chance and is undermined by it because he fails to remember that it is only in conjunction with production that money brings wealth. If the individual ceases to be productive because he now possesses money, and if he uses that money unproductively to buy for consumption rather than using it directly or indirectly as a source of production, e.g. purchasing material and hiring wage labor, then the individual will be undermined by his increase in money just as the ancient communities were but with one difference. Unlike the ancient communities, the individual in modern society, who ceases to produce but uses his money for consumption, is at the same time contributing to the industrial process. He provides money that gets thrown back into production. The 'dissolution . . . affects only his person.' The dissolution does not affect society. On the contrary, it is the 'enrichment of the productive section of society' (224).

189

In modern society, money acts productively. It becomes the means of general industriousness and is 'ingenious in the creation of new objects for a social need . . . . General wealth is produced in order to seize hold of its representative. In this way the real sources of wealth are opened up.' For the ancient communities, on the other hand, money has a dissolving effect:

> It is clear, therefore, that when wage labour is the foundation, money does not have a dissolving effect but acts productively, whereas the ancient community as such is already in contradiction with wage labour as the general foundation (224).

Not just in the ancient communities was the increase in gold and silver dissolving, but a similar consequence occurred during the mercantilist period, the period just before the development of industrial society. This was a period in which there was general greed for money on the part of states as well as of individuals. In aiming to gain possession of the representatives of wealth, gold and silver, countries engaged in production for exchange. In doing so, 'the real development of the sources of wealth takes place as it were behind their backs.' However, wherever gold and silver do not arise out of circulation – as in Spain – but are discovered physically: 'the nation is impoverished, whereas the nations which have to work in order to get it from the Spaniards develop the sources of wealth and really become rich' (225).

The problem of mercantilism is the failure to recognize that the grounds of wealth are in production and exchange not in the physical material with which wealth is represented. This 'failure,' of course, is a necessary condition of mercantilism as the hunt and desire for gold. However, this failure to recognize what real wealth is, and the treatment of money as real wealth, when combined with a system of production based on wage labor as an attempt to get the money, to 'make money,' results in the real development of the forces of production. This is in spite of the failure to recognize the truth about money:

> But it is inherent in the attribute in which it here becomes developed that the illusion about its nature, i.e., the fixed insistence on one of its aspects, in the abstract, and the blindness towards the contradictions contained within it, gives it a really magical significance behind the backs of

individuals. In fact, it is because of this self-contradictory and hence illusory aspect, because of this abstraction, that it becomes such an enormous instrument in the real development of the forces of social production (225).

Thus abstracting out a certain aspect and objectifying it in some thing leads to the treatment of the abstraction as a thing that is real in itself. In orienting to this illusory aspect, people then develop the forces of production in order to gain that which appears as wealth. In doing so, they develop the real source of wealth, but in a limited way.

We have seen how contradictions arise from the money relation, the relation of the product to itself as exchange value. Contradictions arise when the essential unity of production is broken and exchange value is abstracted from it, becoming symbolized in a material form. Separation within an internal unity then characterizes exchange, industrial development and accumulation of treasure. Therefore, each of these activities involves inherent contradictions, just as each of the features of money – measure, medium and representative of general wealth – contradict each other and yet appear as a unity in the form of money. The contradictions are found through the analysis of the concept of money formulated as the relation of a product to itself as exchange value.

A contradictory form of life and repression of grounds

Like the trading peoples and the mercantilist, the economists Marx criticizes fail to treat money and capital as having grounds. Rather, they treat them as natural conditions of production or expressions of natural property relations. Marx refers to the economists, who, on the one hand, distinguish money from other commodities in explaining that conditions of modern production require money, and who, on the other hand, in explaining money, do it in terms of simple exchange, formulating money as only another commodity. 'They take refuge in this abstraction because in the real development of money there are contradictions which are unpleasant for the apologetics of bourgeois common sense, and must hence be covered up' (197). I read this not as an intentional covering up necessarily, but a necessary covering up.

In order for the bourgeois exchange relation to be maintained, its contradictory character, its grounds in separation cannot be remembered. Separation cannot be remembered. Only unity can be re-membered. To re-member is to consciously member again.

The exchange relation of buying and selling provides an illustration of the *necessity* of not recognizing contradictions. The relation of buying and selling originates in the separation of exchange value and use value. It is an external relation; one side can take place independently of and with indifference to the other. At the same time the relation of buying and selling is an internal one. This means that the buying of a commodity is the selling of another commodity; the money used to buy the commodity comes from the selling of a different commodity. With the mediation of money, buying can take place independently of selling.

Although the relation of buying and selling appears to be independent, and is independent in practice, the relation is internal to exchange. This means that the money for buying comes from selling. Hence, no more value can be bought than was already sold. Therefore, if more value can be realized for one commodity because of stockpiling, less can be spent on other commodities. The commodities for which there is less money become devalued. This is a situation of economic crisis:

> In so far as purchase and sale, the two essential moments of
> circulation, are indifferent to one another and separated in
> place and time, they by no means need to coincide. . . .
> But in so far as they are both essential moments of a single
> whole, there must come a moment when the independent
> form is violently broken and when the inner unity is
> established externally through a violent explosion. Thus
> already in the quality of money as a medium, in the
> splitting of exchange into two acts, there lies the germ of
> crises, or at least their possibility, which cannot be realized,
> except where the fundamental preconditions of classically
> developed, conceptually adequate circulation are present
> (119).

In other words, the inner unity of buying and selling is re-established in crisis, in the depreciation of all commodities. Such economic crises are only possible when circulation and the division of labor have developed to the point that, instead of production oriented towards immediate subsistence, the specific product and the specific labor must be exchanged for money. In other words, when the production of exchange values is the dominant form of production:

> The splitting of exchange into purchase and sale makes it possible for me to buy without selling (stockpiling of commodities) or to sell without buying (accumulation of money). . . . At moments when purchasing and selling assert themselves as essentially different acts, a general depreciation of all commodities takes place. At moments when it turns out that money is only a medium of exchange, a depreciation of money comes about. General fall or rise of prices (200).

Thus, when stockpiling occurs (buying without selling), there is a general depreciation of all commodities. When there is an accumulation of money (selling without buying), there is a depreciation of money.

The economists do not recognize the contradiction in the independence and indifference, the externality, of the relations of exchange which are internal relations, an inner unity. They focus only on the end results and not on the process which mediates them. However, this 'failure' on their part is necessary if they are to act as merchants or theorize in terms of the activity and problems of merchants. In other words, bourgeois economics is true for the world of merchants, but it is a one-sided truth. To the extent that it is one-sided, however, it is also false.

To be a merchant is precisely to act in terms of the externality of the moments of exchange, to buy and sell in order to realize money. Not doing this, is not being a merchant. Hence, it is not that seeing exchange as external relations is a mistake or an intentional cover up; it is a necessary condition for being a merchant. In other words, the condition of being a merchant is engaging in the relations of exchange, buying and selling, as external relations. To be a merchant, is to realize money in exchange. As such there is no unity, only buying and selling as activities that are externally related.

Deriving tendencies from the concept of capital

By treating capital as a totality of internal relations, by examining the process in which capital is produced, Marx is able to show the tendencies of capital. With these tendencies, the contradictions can be seen. These possibilities are derived from the formulation of capital as exchange value that reproduces and multiplies itself in circulation. Given this formulation, the development of the world market can be seen as made possible with capital. 'The tendency to create the *world market* is directly given in the concept of capital itself.' The surplus value that is created at one point, 'requires the creation of surplus value at another point for which it may be exchanged' (407). In this way a constantly expanding sphere of circulation develops. Such expansion is a precondition of production based on capital. The sphere itself may be directly expanded or more points may be created within it as points of production.

Given with the possibility of a world market, is the possibility of developing new consumption, an expansion of the consuming circle:

> the production of *relative surplus* value, i.e., production of surplus value based on the increase and development of the productive forces, requires the production of new consumption; requires that the consuming circle within circulation expands as did the productive circle previously (408).

Marx describes three ways in which the expansion of consumption may occur:

> Firstly quantitative expansion of existing consumption; secondly: creation of new needs by propagating existing ones in a wide circle; thirdly: production of *new* needs and discovery and creation of new use values (408).

Thus Marx is able to treat needs as socially produced possibilities not as natural, absolute givens. In addition to these changes that are concomitants of the production of capital and its quantitative increase in surplus value, there is also produced a corresponding increase in qualitative differences among the workers. This is because the additional capital that is made available is able to develop a different branch of production. This, in turn, brings forth new needs which it satisfies.

The development of a new branch of production entails exploring nature to discover new things of use and to discover new, useful qualities in things which in turn spurs the development of the natural sciences. In addition it leads to the discovery and/or creation of new needs in society and the cultivation of the human being rich in social needs, that is, able to appreciate many different kinds of things, therefore more cultured than before:

> the discovery, creation and satisfaction of new needs arising
> from society itself; the cultivation of all the qualities of the
> social human being, production of the same in a form as
> rich as possible in needs, because rich in qualities and
> relations – production of this being as the most total and
> universal possible social product, for, in order to take
> gratification in a many-sided way, he must be capable of
> many pleasures (*genussefähig*), hence cultured to a high
> degree – is likewise a condition of production founded on
> capital (409).

In addition to developing a more cultured human being as the product of capitalism, there is also the development of new kinds of labor, new kinds of human activities and skills, and new needs which correspond to them.

Marx treats social needs not as independent, but as derivative, as presupposing a particular process by which they are produced. This is important. It means conceiving of social needs in terms of the process by which they are created and in which they are grounded. This approach differs from, and distinguishes Marx from, the ordinary treatment of social needs as object-like things that can be observed, measured or assessed, where the objective aspect is separated from the subject – the processes and relations by which it is produced and made intelligible.

While on the one hand, capital develops and utilizes all kinds of physical and mental qualities, on the other hand these are developed only in order to serve the reproduction and multiplication of capital, i.e. the development of these qualities as a means for capital production rather than as an end. The development of the human being through the development of new needs, capacities and abilities is not the aim of production. Instead the only end is

195

the constant increase in capital: production founded on capital creates

> a system of . . . general utility, utilizing science itself just as much as all the physical and mental qualities, while there appears nothing higher in itself. . . . Thus capital creates the bourgeois society (409).

Thus the bourgeois society is equated with a system of utility, a system where everything is treated in terms of its use for making money, i.e. reproducing and increasing capital. Marx indicates that this includes not just the appropriation of nature, but of the social bond as well, i.e. treating social relations in terms of its use for increasing wealth.

We have seen that by treating the concept as presupposing a process for its realization, we have been able to derive many characteristics of industrial society from that process. Unlike the approach which might notice that these characteristics are associated with capital or industrialization and then posit a reason for the connection, Marx derives them from the analysis of the concept or phenomenon, capital, itself. These characteristics are seen as internal to the concept, not external relations to it.

Deriving contradictions from the concept of capital

In addition to the exchange with labor, and the appropriation of labor, there are several other processes involved in the realization of capital. After capital (in the form of wages) is exchanged with labor and labor is appropriated, a product is produced. Capital now exists in the form of a commodity. In order to realize itself as value, the capitalist must exchange the product for money. Because capital is not immediately exchange value, but must realize itself by going through certain exchanges, devaluation is an integral moment of the process.

Devaluation occurs in one or two ways. If the process breaks down – the product cannot be sold – 'then the capitalist's money has been transformed into a worthless product, and has not only not gained a new value, but also lost its original value.' Such a possibility is given with the separation of the realization of capital into several processes: 'the separation by itself implies the possibility of such a miscarriage in the individual case.' In addition to the possibility of not being able to realize value, devaluation is implied in the fact that the product as such is not value. It has to enter into circulation before it can be realized as value:

> in any case devaluation forms one moment of the realization
> process; which is already simply implied in the fact that the
> product of the process in its immediate form is not *value*,
> but first has to enter anew into circulation in order to be
> realized as such (403).

Since capital is value which is realized only through processes of exchange, it is at the same time not-value because it first has to be realized. It is possible that the value may not be realized because of external conditions, conditions external to the individual producers. Thus, that which appears as a unity, capital, turns out to be made up of separate, external or indifferent processes. This analysis of capital as a unity mediated by exchange accounts for the continual crises of capitalism.

Because capital is made up of processes, each of which is the absence of or negation of the other, we may conceive of capital as a negative unity. It is both value and not-value. It is not an immediate identity, but a mediated one. In order for not-value to also be value, the mediation of exchange is required. According to my reading, any external mediation between the subject and object makes for an unself-conscious form of life and is problematic for Marx.

On the one hand, the concept of capital presupposes the unity of production with exchange value. Capitalism or the production of capital, is the production of exchange value. On the other hand, capital can only realize itself as exchange value through the process of exchange, which is separated from and external to the process of production. Exchange mediates the unity of capital as the production and realization of exchange value. Hence, capital is a mediated unity (of negations) rather than an immediate unity:

> Therefore, while capital is reproduced as value and new
> value in the production process, it is at the same time
> posited as *not-value*, as something which first has to be
> *realized as value by means of exchange*. The three processes
> of which capital forms the unity are external; they are

separate in time and space. As such, the transition from one into the other; i.e., their unity as regards the individual capitalist, is accidental. Despite their *inner unity*, they exist *independently* alongside one another each as the presupposition of the other (403).

The three processes of which capital forms the unity are: exchange with labor (wages); exchange with consumers as commodity for money; exchange with other producers as money for raw materials and instruments of production. Each of these processes contains its own conditions, e.g. the need for it, the availability of equivalent exchange value with which to purchase it, etc., which may exist as barriers to the realization of capital.

The indifference of the various moments of the realization process of capital, the contradiction between the inner unity and the external independence of the moments, is treated by Marx as a foundation of contradictions:

> So far in the realization process, we have only the indifference of the individual moments towards one another; that they determine each other internally and search for each other externally; but that they may or may not find each other, balance each other, correspond to each other. The inner necessity of moments which belong together, and their indifferent, independent existence towards one another, are already a foundation of contradictions (414–15).

Marx makes reference to 'the contradiction between production and realization of which capital, by its concept, is the unity.' This reference to the concept of capital reminds us that he analyzes capital as an object of knowledge, a concept, and that is why he is able to talk about contradictions of capital. Contradictions can exist only within language. If he were treating capital as a thing in the world, he could only report on his observations which he might formulate in terms of class conflict, but the word, 'contradiction,' would make no sense. A report on observations might include incongruities such as great displays of wealth surrounded by extreme poverty. Such an observation could be made in agricultural societies or industrial ones but it could not be considered a contradiction. Only within a formulation can we have a contradiction.

Marx formulates capital as the preservation, reproduction and expansion of itself as general wealth by means of a continual development of the forces of production. However, there is a limit on that development, a limit *'not inherent to production generally, but to production founded on capital.* This limit is double, or rather the same regarded from two directions.' Before discussing the limits or different aspects of the same limit, I want to call attention to Marx's statement, 'These inherent limits have to coincide with the nature of capital, with the essential character of its very concept' (415). Again, we see Marx clearly referring to capital as a concept. This is not to say that capital is not real or only exists in the mind. Only that a phenomenological analysis treats its object as a possibility or concept as opposed to a thing in itself, in order to call attention to its presuppositions as that which enables us to know the object as such and, therefore, as that which makes the object as we know it possible.

According to Marx's formulation and analysis, capital is self-contradictory. On the one hand, capital tends to overcome all barriers to production but, on the other hand, it sets up its own particular barrier. That capital 'contains a particular restriction of production . . . contradicts its general tendency to drive beyond every barrier to production' (415). The contradiction between its developing the forces of production and its restricting that development derives from the concept of capital as both value and not-value, unity and disunity, the separation and indifference of the moments of production and realization of which capital is the unity. These moments (exchange with labor, with consumers and middle-men, with other producers for material and instruments of production, etc.) 'belong together' and 'determine each other internally,' yet they take place as separate, external, indifferent processes. This separation, the need to realize capital as a separate process from that of production, constitutes the inherent limit of production founded on capital.

This limit can be considered from two directions, the limit on the development of living labor capacity and the limit on the development of objectified labor in the forces of production. Marx enumerates these limits on production as follows:

1. Necessary labour as limit on the exchange value of living labour capacity or of the wages of the industrial population (415).

The wages paid to labor are limited to the equivalent of the cost of purchasing the necessities for subsistence. The worker gets paid as if he worked the amount of time to produce the equivalent of the necessities – necessary labor time. He is not paid more than it costs to reproduce him as labor power. This is a limitation on the development of the forces of production which include the laborer. His development is limited by the exchange value of necessary labor:

2. Surplus value as limit on surplus labour time, and in regard to relative surplus labour time, as barrier to the development of the forces of production (415).

The workers can only produce more than necessary labor time to the amount that can be realized as surplus value, as money. Thus the production of goods is limited to their ability to be exchanged for money, even if the labor capacity to produce more is there. In regard to relative surplus labor time, which is produced through machinery or any other means that can reduce necessary labor time, it is only when more surplus value can be realized, that labor-saving machinery will be introduced. If labor power can be hired more cheaply, then the material forces of production will not be developed:

3. What is the same, the transformation into money, exchange value as such, as limit of production. This is:
4. Again the same as restriction of the production of use values by exchange value; or that real wealth has to take on a specific form distinct from itself, a form not absolutely identical with it, in order to become an object of production at all (416).

Thus the essential limit on production is the need to transform it into money. Even if the objects themselves constitute real wealth, contribute to the reproduction and development of labor, they will not be produced if people do not purchase them with money, e.g. lack of good housing for the poor if they cannot afford to buy it.

However, these limits come up against the general tendency of capital to forget and abstract from these four internal limits. The tendency is to forget and simply strive to produce as much as possible. Such production is considered 'overproduction' when it cannot be transformed into money. With overproduction the moments of production are recalled and production ceases. Forgetting these constraints and producing 'too much' results in devaluation:

> Hence overproduction: i.e., the sudden *recall* of all these necessary moments of production founded on capital; hence general devaluation in consequence of forgetting them (416).

There is another contradiction that is grounded in forgetting the various moments that constitute the production and realization of capital. This contradiction is due to forgetting that, as Malthus says,

> 'the very existence of a profit upon any commodity pre-supposes a demand exterior to that of the labourer who has produced it,' and hence the demand of the labourer himself can never be an adequate demand (420).

The tendency is for each capitalist to abstract his relation to his workers from the totality of the capital-labor relation. Each capitalist restricts the wages and, therefore, the worker's ability to exchange and consume, while hoping that the workers of other capitalists will purchase his own commodities:

> Every capitalist knows this about his worker, that he does not relate to him as producer to consumer, and (he, therefore,) wishes to restrict his consumption, i.e., his ability to exchange, his wage, as much as possible. Of course he would like the workers of *other* capitalists to be the greatest consumers possible of *his own* commodity (420).

However, it seems to each capitalist that the demand of the working class is an adequate demand. Therefore, the capitalists set production in motion to produce as much as possible, which they expect to be purchased by the workers of the other capitalists. This production, therefore, goes beyond the proportion that would correspond to what the workers could purchase:

> Since one production sets the other into motion and hence creates consumers for itself in the *alien* capital's workers, it

> *seems* to each individual capital that the demand of the
> working class posited by production itself is an 'adequate
> demand.' On one side, this demand which production itself
> posits drives it forward, and must drive it forward beyond
> the *proportion* in which it would have to produce with regard
> to the workers; on the other side, if the demand *exterior to
> the demand of the labourer himself* disappears or shrinks up,
> then the collapse occurs (420).

And again, we see Marx attributing the contradiction to separation,
in this case each capital is indifferent to and independent, i.e.
separate from, the other capitals:

> It is the indifference to and independence (competition) of
> one another which brings it about that the individual capital
> relates to the workers of the entire remaining capital not as
> workers, hence is driven beyond the right proportion (420).

According to Marx's formulation, capital is the reproduction
and expansion of wealth accomplished through appropriating
surplus value produced by labor. While it appropriates the surplus
value, it only pays labor for necessary labor, that which is
necessary to reproduce the worker as labor power:

> To begin with: capital forces the workers beyond necessary
> labour to surplus labour. Only in this way does it realize
> itself and create surplus value (421).

However, since the aim is surplus value, necessary labor only
comes in when there can be surplus labor that can be exchanged
for surplus value – wealth in the form of money. Therefore, if
surplus value cannot be realized for any reason, then necessary
labor is no longer called into being, i.e. workers are no longer able
to find work and earn wages that will pay for their subsistence.

By restricting labor according to the possibility or lack of
possibility of realizing surplus value, the creation of wealth is
restricted. This barrier to the creation of wealth is internal to the
process of capital at the same time that it contradicts the essence of
(the concept of) capital which is to expand wealth:

> By its nature, therefore, it posits a barrier to labour and
> value-creation, in contradiction to its tendency to expand
> them boundlessly. And in as much as it both posits a

barrier specific to itself, and on the other side equally drives over and beyond every barrier, it is the living contradiction (421).

In addition to the inherent limits on the development of production which contradict the essence of its concept: keep increasing and expanding production, is the inherent devaluation of capital. Although the formulation of capital is a process in which wealth reproduces and increases itself in circulation, it is at the same time a process of devaluation, a process of realizing itself as decreasing value.

Devaluation as a contradictory tendency

In order to understand how devaluation is involved, we first have to review the processes and moments of which capital is the unity:

> If we examine the entire turnover of capital, then four moments appear, or each of the two great moments of the production process and the circulation process appears again in a duality. . . . The moments are (I) The real production process and its duration. (II) Transformation of the product into money. (III) Transformation of the money in the proper proportions into raw material, means of labour. . . . (IV) The exchange of a part of the capital for living labour capacity (520).

The important point is to start from the recognition of the totality. We saw earlier Marx's critique of others' analyses, who treated circulation alone and did not consider production. Marx said that circulation should be considered a moment of production. The point, rather, is the emphasis on considering the two processes as a unity expressed by the concept of capital – the unity of the realization of capital. It does not much matter which is called the totality – production or circulation, and which is considered a moment of the other:

> we can take either circulation or production as the point of departure here. This much has now been said, that circulation is itself a moment of production since capital becomes capital only through circulation; production is a

203

moment of circulation only in so far as the latter is itself regarded as the totality of the production process (520).

Marx, then, shows how the separation into distinct processes, which appear indifferent to and independent of each other contradicts the inner unity of capital. This contradiction takes the form of devaluation, which is a contradiction of the essence of capital which is to increase continually:

> Capital exists as capital only in so far as it passes through the phases of circulation . . . in order to be able to begin the production process anew, and these phases are themselves phases of its realization – but at the same time, as we saw, of its *devaluation* (546).

Devaluation occurs because during each phase capital is fixed in one form, which means that it cannot be realizing itself in another form, i.e. the process of realization, reproduction and multiplication, is held up:

> As long as capital remains frozen in the form of the finished product, it cannot be active as capital, it is *negated* capital. Its realization process is delayed in the same degree, and its value-in-process negated. This thus appears as a loss for capital, as a relative loss of its value, for its value consists precisely in its realization process. This loss of capital means in other words nothing else but that time passes it by unseized, time during which it could have been appropriating alien labour, *surplus labour time* through exchange with living labour, if the deadlock had not occurred (546).

The unity of capital consists in movement, in the process of realization which includes both the circulation process and the production process; anything which impedes the movement is an impediment, a barrier to capital. The separation of the unity of capital, as unity-in-process, into its various phases and their existence as dependent on seemingly external and independent conditions, e.g. finding a market for its goods, creates its own barriers. Capital, fixated in any of its phases, which is posited by the separation of the unity into indifferent moments – is a negation of itself as subject, as unity-in-process:

This unity itself is motion, process. Capital appears as this unity-in-process of production and circulation. . . . But while capital . . . is the process of going from one phase into the other, it is at the same time, within each phase, posited in specific aspect, restricted to a particular form, which is the negation of itself as the subject of the whole movement. Therefore, capital in each of its particular phases is the negation of itself as the subject of all the various metamorphoses (620).

We saw above how during the time in which capital is frozen in the form of the product, it is negated capital, devalued, because it is time during which it could have been engaged in producing more surplus value. Similarly, the time during which it is fixated in any of the other phases is also a devaluation process at the same time that it is a realization process:

As long as it remains in circulation, it is not capable of producing. . . . As long as it cannot be brought to market, it is fixated as product. As long as it cannot be exchanged for conditions of production, it is fixated as money. Finally, if the conditions of production remain in their form as conditions and do not enter into the production process, it is again fixated and devalued (621).

The key to understanding capital, then, is grasping that capital is a process; a unity in process which is divided into aspects called moments, which are separated in time and space and indifferent to each other. This means that for the individuals attempting to realize capital, the realization is dependent on external, uncontrollable circumstances.

The separation, fixation and consequent devaluation is inherent in capital; it is not a mistake or a failure of remembering unity. On the other hand, this separation contradicts the essence of capital as unity, which is to maximize itself. Capital, then, invests certain procedures for minimizing the time that it is fixated and devalued. One of the methods is the utilization of the middle-man – a merchant – who will buy the product immediately in order to resell it. This way the capitalist does not have to wait so long to realize the exchange value of his products. Another method is the use of credit in order to continue or expand the production process even before the products have realized their exchange value. These methods bring with it a third, which is the production at maximum capacity for an extended period followed by a reduction of production after it has been found that the products are not able to realize their exchange value, i.e. the alternation of overproduction and underproduction:

> since the decomposition into these two aspects, in which the realization process appears at the same time as the devaluation process, contradicts the tendency of capital towards maximum realization, it therefore invents contrivances to abbreviate the phase of fixity; and at the same time also, instead of the simultaneous coexistence of both states, *they alternate*. In one period the process appears as altogether fluid – the period of the maximum realization of capital; in another, a reaction to the first, the other moment asserts itself all the more forcibly – the period of the maximum devaluation of capital and congestion of the production process (623).

Thus a period of maximum devaluation and restriction of production follows the period of maximum realization. The alternation of the two periods, according to Marx, is due to the use of credit:

> As we saw earlier that money suspends the barriers of barter only by generalizing them – i.e., separating purchase and sale entirely – so shall we see later that *credit* likewise suspends these barriers to the realization of capital only by raising them to their most general form, positing one period of overproduction and one of underproduction as two periods (623).

> The necessary tendency of capital is therefore *circulation without circulation* time, and this tendency is the fundamental determinant of credit and of capital's credit contrivances (659).

In other words, in order not to lose valuable production time during circulation time, the capitalist uses credit to keep him producing. This has the effect of seeming to allow for increasing production independent of circulation. However, production is not independent of circulation. When the product starts having difficulty realizing its exchange value on the market (i.e. in circulation), then production must eventually cease. In this way, according to Marx, we have the periodic crises of capitalism – depression, unemployment following a period of prosperity.

Falling rate of profit as analytic possibility

A final contradiction that Marx derives is that of the tendency for a falling rate of profit. Capital tries to eliminate wages which must be paid to reproduce the worker, his necessary labor. The capital that is paid as wages to the worker seems to reduce capital. Therefore, capital tries to limit or eliminate necessary labor. However, the belief that one can eliminate necessary labor and still produce capital is a delusion, as capital is the production and realization of surplus value, which is the production that takes place during surplus labor time. The concept of surplus labor time is only possible given that of necessary labor time. Surplus labor time is labor time beyond that necessary for reproducing the worker, for producing his wages. Hence the process of producing and realizing capital is again seen as involving contradictory tendencies. The contradiction arises from forgetting the essential unity of necessary labor time and surplus labor time:

> Capital itself is the contradiction in that while it tries to suspend necessary labour time, necessary labour time is the necessary condition for surplus labour time (543).

The contradiction 'is at the same time the reduction of the worker to a minimum, i.e., his existence as mere living labour capacity.' It takes the form of keeping down wages.

This contradiction is similar to the contradiction that is the basis of Marx's famous 'Law of the tendency of the rate of surplus value to fall':

> Whereas the rate of surplus value is determined by the relation of surplus labour employed by the capital to necessary labour, the rate of profit is nothing but the relation of the surplus value to the total value of the capital presupposed to production (753).

This means that the rate of profit depends on the relation of capital exchanged for living labor to capital in the form of machinery, raw material (constant capital). If the labor component remained the same size and produced the same amount of surplus value while the constant capital increased, then the rate of profit would decline:

> Presupposing the same surplus value, the same surplus labour in proportion to necessary labour, then, the rate of profit depends on the relation between the part of capital exchanged for living labour and the part existing in the form of raw material and means of production. Hence, the smaller the portion exchanged for living labour becomes, the smaller becomes the rate of profit (747).

With increased productivity, more capital necessarily goes to constant capital. At the same time, the rate of profit declines although the amount of profit may increase.

The empirical accuracy of Marx's analysis is not at issue here. Therefore, I will leave to others (e.g. Appelbaum, 1978) the explication and discussion of the empirical relevance of the theory of the falling rate of profit and the ways in which this tendency is counteracted according to Marx.

Rather, my purpose in introducing this contradictory tendency as well as the others discussed above is to analyze how it is possible for Marx to be able to theorize in terms of contradictory tendencies. According to my reading, the contradictory tendencies are made possible by the separation and indifference inherent in the simple exchange relation, the separation of the inner unity of use value and exchange value. This separation is expressed in capital to a higher power as the separation and indifference among the different moments of production. The separation is seen as such against the possibility of unity that analysis knows as the unity of subject and object, purpose and objective conditions for realizing that purpose. I have reformulated this unity in terms of Marx's work as the form of life of socialism.

A form of life that is contradictory is an internally violent form, a form that presupposes and produces struggles of opposing tendencies. Its necessary actions contradict its basic premises; devaluation and restriction of the development of the forces of production contradict its posited character as constantly expanding wealth and constantly expanding forces of production. The contradictions of capital derive from the separation of an internal unity:

> Capital as the unity of circulation and production is at the same time the division between them, and a division whose aspects are separated in space and time, at that. In each moment, it has an indifferent form towards the other. For the individual capital, the transition from one into the other appears as chance, as dependent on external, uncontrollable circumstances (622).

Because of its contradictory character, the form of life of capital must be concrete. That is, it must be lived in its separate moments while its unity, the grounds that make those moments possible, must be forgotten. This means that capital can appear only one-sidedly, either as a thing or as a single moment, rather than as a unity of opposing moments, a self-contradictory totality. It appears in a one-sided way as value in objectified form, the unity of a thing, rather than as a unity in process. In order to exist as capital, it must forget grounds, and treat itself as first, as its own foundation:

> Through the absorption of living labour time and through the movement of its own circulation, it relates to itself as positing new value, as producer of value. It relates as the foundation to surplus value as that which it founded. Its movement consists of relating to itself, while it produces itself, at the same time as the foundation of what it has founded, as value presupposed to itself as surplus value, or to the surplus value as posited by it (745).

Capital is a divided form that cannot recognize itself as such and still be capital. Therefore, it treats itself as subject. It treats surplus value as something it has founded. It does not treat its relation to living labor as the source of surplus value because it cannot realize the surplus value so produced until it goes through another exchange, which can affect the amount of surplus value realized. Therefore, it treats, and must treat, its relation to living labor as a mere moment of its movement, and considers itself the producer of value as well as the value produced:

> Proceeding from itself as the active subject, the subject of

> the process . . . capital relates to itself as self-increasing value; i.e. it relates to surplus value as something posited and founded by it; it relates as well-spring of production, to itself as product, it relates as producing value to itself as produced value (746–7).

In other words, in forgetting grounds and treating itself as subject, capital is a concrete form of life. Its forgetting allows for contradictory tendencies, tendencies which are in opposition and conflict. These contradictory tendencies are presupposed in the concept of capital. An analysis of capital reveals its essential contradiction: the separation of an internal unity into indifferent moments.

Separation is the condition of capital and the ground of concrete theorizing. The separation and its contradictions not only provide for the possibility of a concrete form of life, but for the possibility of overcoming these contradictions by suspending the separation, suspending the relations of capital.

Marx's analytic theorizing begins with the conception of a subject-object unity as a mode of social (re)production, the form of life of analytic socialism. From this ground, it is able to formulate capital as a separation, to see the contradictory tendencies that derive from it, and to conceive of how the separation and contradictions could be overcome.

To summarize, Marx shows how mediations (e.g. money, capital) presuppose and reproduce a division of the subject (into buyers and sellers, workers and capitalists) and a division of the object (into use value and exchange value). The mediation externalizes and objectifies the relation of a divided subject and object. It symbolizes the relation in a material form – a thing. Because it is expressed in the form of a thing, the relation of a divided subject and a divided object ceases to appear as such; the relation appears as a concrete thing only. Dialectical phenomenology shows how this appearance of thing-like objectivity is a symptom of a repressed or contradictory unity. We have seen how it accomplishes this analysis by inquiring into the form of life or relation of subject and object that is presupposed by the objectivity and which makes the objectivity possible as such.

CHAPTER 7

Marx's critique of concrete solutions to economic crises

Marx criticizes two different theoretical attempts to solve economic problems. One solution represents monetarist theorizing and the other socialist theorizing. Both are instances of concrete theorizing. Marx's critique highlights the difference between a concrete mode of theorizing and his own. My first illustration of concrete theorizing will be that of the economist, Darimon. My second illustration will be the time chit solution put forth by socialists of the time.

Although an unimportant theorist today, Darimon's work represents aspects of classical monetarist theorizing that persist today. But more important than Darimon's theorizing is Marx's response. I will, therefore, concentrate on Marx's critique as it displays basic tenets of his own theorizing. However, I also want to show how the monetarist theorizing violates the four rules elaborated in the previous chapters. Thus, besides showing the concrete differences between the two theorists' solutions to economic problems, I will show the analytic differences. We will see how violations of the four rules make a difference in the theorizing and the solutions produced.

Violating rule 1 to treat concepts as grounded

Darimon explains the economic crisis of the time as due to the flow of gold out of the country and the bank's need to maintain its reserves by discouraging borrowing and this at a time when the public most needed to borrow. Darimon attributed the gold-drain to crop failures and the subsequent need to import grain from

211

foreign nations that required payment in gold. In addition, he refers to the numerous expensive but unproductive undertakings associated with the industrial exhibition in Paris. Marx further cites the failure of the silk harvest and the consequent purchase of silk in vast quantities from China. Darimon 'forgets' also the speculations and ventures launched abroad plus the unproductive expenditures of the Crimean War, including borrowings of 750 million franks.

Marx mentions that the loss of capital is not due solely to the failure of the domestic production, because 'the losses in domestic production, in any case, were not an equivalent for the employment of French capital abroad.' In other words, even if there had not been a crop failure, there would have been a crisis, because more capital had been lost than would have been produced had the crops been successfully harvested. The crisis was a result of the loss incurred through capitalist speculation abroad and the financing of the Crimean War, as well as the grain and silk failure.

Darimon analyzes the economic crisis as due to the Bank's need to maintain its reserves of gold in order to back the currency at a time when there is a great demand for that gold. Given this analysis, his solution is for France to go off the gold or metal standard. Marx takes the monetarist analysis and carries it out to its logical end, showing its impossibility to solve the problem. He does this by showing what would happen if the metal basis were eliminated:

> Now suppose that the Bank of France did not rest on a metallic base and that other countries were willing to accept the French currency or its capital in any form, not only in the specific form of the precious metals. Would the bank not have been equally forced to raise the terms of its discounting precisely at the moment when its 'public' clamoured most eagerly for its services? (121).

On what basis can Marx suggest that the Bank would raise the terms of its discounting, even if it did not have to maintain reserves due to the elimination of the metallic base? If the payments to other countries could be made in terms of paper money rather than gold, would the banks raise the cost of lending money? They would no longer have to keep a certain amount of gold on hand in order to back the currency. Instead of backing the money with the precious metals, the nation's stock of products and its labor force would back it. However, due to the situation cited above, that wealth had diminished. Therefore, the price of the products would increase anyway as the supply decreased:

> The notes with which it discounts the bills of exchange of this public are at present nothing more than drafts on gold and silver. In our hypothetical case, they would be drafts on the nation's stock of products and on its directly employable labour force; the former is limited, the latter can be increased only within very positive limits and in certain amounts of time (121).

At the same time as grain and silk failures, Marx explains that the railway and mining use up the exchangeable wealth (wealth which can be circulated and is acceptable abroad) in a form which creates no direct equivalent and, therefore, no replacement. Thus the directly exchangeable wealth of the nation is diminished. This brings about an increase in bank-drafts. 'Direct consequence: increase in the price of products, raw materials and labour.' In order to compensate, the Bank would either raise the price of a loan (credit) or directly devalue its currency to reflect the decreased value of its paper.

With the devaluation, production would decline, because the devalued money would result in a relative increase in the price of the necessary goods. However, it is not because of the Bank's devaluation, nor raising the price of loans that prices rise. It is because there is less exchangeable wealth. In a market economy this means that prices rise. This occurs when there is a decrease in supply relative to demand; price rises precisely when the public most needs the item. The Bank's behavior is in keeping with this situation: 'a very ordinary operation.' Furthermore, 'the bank has to act in this way whether the notes it issues are convertible or inconvertible' into gold.

The economic crisis derives from the impact of a smaller supply of exchangeable wealth to back the dollar; the dollar is worth less; the price of goods is greater because of the shortage:

> The directly exchangeable wealth of the nation 'absolutely diminished.' On the other side, an unlimited increase in bank drafts. Direct consequence therefore, increase in the

price of products, raw material and labour. On the other side, decrease in price of bank drafts. The bank would have undertaken a very ordinary operation to devalue its own paper. With this devaluation, a sudden paralysis of production! (121–2).

Marx's critique rests on showing that the theorist fails to treat gold and silver as symbolizing the exchangeable wealth of a country, capital. The monetarist thinking fails to analyze the grounds of gold and silver. It treats the precious metal as a thing, a medium of exchange, rather than capital. Instead of analyzing the origins of gold and silver as capital, it treats gold concretely as a given thing used in exchange.

Violating rule 2 to treat individuals as grounded

In Darimon's thinking, if reasons for charging high interest rates are eliminated, the Bank will lower the rates. However, Darimon's proposal fails to recognize that actions and reasons are determined by – in the sense of gaining their sense from being embedded in – an historically specific form of life. Instead, the proposal assumes that the actions are outcomes of reasons and the reasons are specific only to those actions, rather than specific to a form of life.

Marx argues that the banks were acting in accord with the general laws of accumulation: demand and supply, that express the grounds of all actions that can be analyzed as specific to capitalism. 'Did M. Darimon require his figures to prove that supply increases the cost of its services to the same degree as demand makes claims upon them (and exceeds them)?' (119).

Marx claims that Darimon draws an unwarranted distinction between the operations of banks and the operations of the investors that are Darimon's public. The same laws of supply and demand characterize the actions of the banks and the 'public', the merchants who borrow the Bank's gold in order to purchase grain from other countries and sell it at a high price to the public at precisely the time when grain is in great demand by a hungry public. The hungry public is not included in Darimon's concept of public:

And do not the gentlemen who represent the 'public' vis-à-vis the bank follow the same 'agreeable custom of life?' The philanthropic grain merchants present their bills to the bank in order to receive notes in order to exchange the notes for the bank's gold, in order to exchange the bank's gold for another country's grain, in order to exchange the grain of another country for the money of the French public (119).

Marx goes on to inquire whether these 'philanthropic' merchants do what Darimon asks of the banks. Do they let the people have the grain on easier terms because the people at that time had the greatest need of it?

> were they perhaps motivated by the idea, that since the public then had the greatest need of grain, it was therefore, their duty to let them have grain on easier terms, or did they not rather rush to the bank in order to exploit the increase of grain prices, the misery of the public and the disproportion between its supply and its demand? (120).

Marx ends with the ironic statement: 'And the bank should be made an exception to these general economic laws.' The laws, of course, being those of supply and demand. Marx shows the contradiction in Darimon's own analysis, in that Darimon treats the actions of the Bank differently from the actions of merchants. Further, Darimon treats the Bank's acts concretely as a policy that he fails to analyze.

He treats the policy as a thing with reason and causes, a decision that can be made and changed, rather than a practice that is grounded and, therefore, not explainable as an *immediate* response to a particular condition, i.e. a reason. Darimon fails to recognize the real (analytical) foundation of the Bank's actions – the relations that constitute the form of life of the 'public' that Darimon is concerned about.

Darimon attributes the Bank's actions to its motive to maintain a certain reserve because of the metal standard. He reproaches the Bank for the consequences of this policy and, therefore, recommends eliminating the metal standard. Marx suggests that this is inconsistent. Why not reproach the grain merchants or, by implication, all merchants, for they also raise prices when the public is most in need? These actions are all in accordance with the economic laws of supply and demand – that money just like grain is a commodity – and that Darimon fails to realize this. He exempts money from the form of life that determines the production and exchange of commodities.

Thus Marx is arguing that only as appearance does the Bank, or by extension, any individual independently determine its own acts. The Bank is not an independent entity separate from its acts. Its acts are, together, the Bank itself, and the Bank is internal to (determined by) the form of life of capital. The actions of the Bank are made intelligible by the rules of capital production. The situation may be compared to a game where the moves of the players are made in accordance with the rules of the game and it is only to that extent that these are players or actors in the game. For Marx, it would be absurd to treat the acts of the banks apart from the rules that make these acts and the Bank itself intelligible. A move in a game can only be understood in terms of the game: its aim and its rules.

Violating rule 3 to treat a form of life as internal relations

In addressing himself to the theories of the monetarists, who attributed the crisis to the drain or outflow of capital in the form of gold and silver, Marx argues that the gold-drain is not a separate process from production, but is part of production. The crisis is the crisis of the particular mode of production which is based on the laws of supply and demand. It is not enough, in fact it is misleading, to attribute the crisis to the drain of gold, as if refraining from importing would eliminate the crisis by keeping gold at home.

Marx begins by giving reasons for the outflow of gold (or silver):

1 Drain as a result of domestic harvest failures in a chief food crop.
2 Increased prices in main imported goods due to crop failure abroad.
3 Drain because of crop failure in decisive industrial raw materials (e.g. silk).
4 Drain because of excessive imports (caused by speculation and war).

Because of the need to replace the shortage through imports, a part of its invested capital or labor is not reproduced; there is a

216

real loss of production. A part of the capital which has been reproduced has to be shifted to fill this gap. The price of the deficient production or yield rises on the world market as a result of the decreased supply and increased demand. The grain failures and the excessive imports are the most important cases, he feels. The impact of war is self-evident. It is economically the same as if the nation were to drop a part of its capital into the ocean. Marx states that '[it] is necessary to analyze precisely how such crises would look if money were disregarded, and what determinants money introduces into the given relations' (128). In other words, Marx analyzes production as a totality before inquiring into the effects of money.

Marx goes on to work out how a crop failure results in the depreciation of capital:

> Suppose that the entire English wheat crop were 1 quarter, and that this 1 quarter fetched the same price as 30 million quarters previously. [If] we postulate that the working day necessary to produce 1 quarter = A, then the nation would exchange A × 30 million working days (cost of production) for 1 × A working days (product). The productive force of its capital would have diminished by millions since every working day would have depreciated by a factor of 30 million (128).

With the crop failure, each working day produces a fraction of its previous production. Yet the costs of production are based on the 'normal' productivity, the average labor time required in the previous production. This average labor time (one of the costs of production) now produces a fraction of what it had previously. Marx concludes that every unit of capital would then represent a fraction of its earlier value, of its equivalent in production costs. He traces the effects of the grain crisis to other branches of production as follows:

> With or without metallic money, or money of any other kind, the nation would find itself in a crisis not confined to grain, but extending to all other branches of production, not only because their productivity would have positively diminished, and the price of their production depreciated as compared to their value, which is determined by the normal

cost of production, but also because all contracts, obligations, etc. rest on the average prices of products (129).

The increase in the grain price by a given factor would be the expression of an equivalent depreciation of all other products. The surplus sum which the nation must expend in purchasing grain is a direct subtraction from its capital, its exchangeable wealth. Thus, Marx is able to say, the rise in the grain price is the same as a fall in the price of all other commodities.

The major point that Marx is making in this discussion is that one cannot simply attribute an economic crisis to the export of gold, as a factor that is externally related to production. It must be seen in relation to the totality, that which produces it as a possibility:

> A crisis caused by a failure in the grain crop is therefore not at all created by the drain of bullion. . . . The depreciation of most commodities (labour included) and the resultant crisis, in the case of an important crop mishap, cannot therefore be crudely ascribed to the export of gold, because depreciation and crisis would equally take place if no gold whatever were exported and no grain imported (129–30).

The totality that is production in this particular historical mode is characterized by the laws of supply and demand. These laws are the basis of the type of production and the basis of the crisis.

After analyzing the basis of the crisis independent of gold and silver, he then goes on to examine their role in the crisis:

> Gold and silver in themselves can be said to intervene in the crisis and to aggravate its symptoms in only two ways: (1) When the export of gold is made more difficult by the metal reserve requirements to which the banks are bound; when the measures which the banks therefore undertake against the export of gold react disadvantageously on domestic circulation; (2) When the export of gold becomes necessary because foreign nations will accept capital only in the form of gold and not otherwise (130).

The necessity of exporting gold and silver, then, does not cause the crisis but can aggravate it. The economic 'crisis' must, therefore, be understood as produced by a form of life characterized by relations of exchange, laws of supply and demand, i.e. commodity production.

Violating rule 4 to treat the concrete as contradictory

A form of life, in which crises appear to be due to a shortage of gold which could be remedied by retaining gold instead of exporting it, is concrete in its self-understanding. It denies the grounds of gold in production. Gold appears to be a thing rather than a relation – an internal aspect of a form of life. Its character as capital is not analyzed. Therefore, it is not recognized that the crisis of gold is a crisis of capital – a loss of productive wealth which in a market economy results in an increase in the price of that wealth. This is the economic crisis.

Monetarists concern themselves with the appreciation of gold and silver and the reserves of gold. The rise in the costs of bank-loans, the appreciation of gold and silver, or the devaluation of paper currency relative to gold and silver, reduces or prevents production and produces crisis. Marx claims that the appreciation of gold and silver, however, is only one side of a relation, the side that surfaces during financial crises. Bourgeois economists fail to see the other side, the depreciation of gold and silver during prosperity for capital. They fail to theorize about crises and 'prosperity' as an internal relation, internal to the process of production:

> Since this depreciation of metallic money (and of all kinds of money which rest on it) always precedes its appreciation, they ought to have formulated the problem the other way round: how to prevent the periodic depreciation of money (in their language, to abolish the privileges of commodities in relation to money) (134).

According to Marx, this would have reduced itself to: how to overcome the rise and fall of prices. The way to do this, he states, is by abolishing prices:

> And how? By doing away with exchange value. But this problem arises: exchange corresponds to the bourgeois

organization of society. Hence one last problem: to revolutionise bourgeois society economically. It would then have been self-evident from the outset that the evil of bourgeois society is not to be remedied by 'transforming' the banks or by founding a rational 'money system' (134).

Bourgeois economists theorize about the crisis concretely – the appreciation of gold and silver, the rise in the discount rate, or the loss of gold. To be analytical, would be to inquire into how these phenomena are produced as internal to a form of life. The aim of the form of life is the realization of exchange value. Such realization depends on prices which vary with changes in productivity and the relation to supply and demand. Thus Marx states that to overcome the rise and fall of prices, abolishing prices, requires either doing away with exchange value, or doing away with changes in productivity. Yet the very aim of bourgeois production is the realizing and increasing of exchange value through increased productivity. Hence, the aim that characterizes bourgeois production presupposes and reproduces the very problem that it needs to eliminate.

Marx shows that the bourgeois economists fail to see that appreciation is one side of a relation where depreciation is the other, that the 'problem' of appreciation is inextricably bound up with the 'desirable' depreciation of gold. This failure, however, is essential to bourgeois economics. To recognize that the problem of appreciation is only the other side of the depreciation of gold and silver, and that both are internal to the production of exchange value, is to recognize that the 'problem' is the bourgeois mode of production itself. It is to realize that eliminating the 'problem' requires abolishing the bourgeois mode of production. Such recognition would also suspend the bourgeois economist as one who tries to solve economic problems within capitalism.

The time chit solution

Marx examines another proposed solution to economic problems – the time chit solution put forward by socialists. The problem was the fluctuation of the prices of commodities due to market conditions affecting the value of money. This is the same problem as the appreciation/depreciation issue that the bourgeois econ-omists were concerned with. Only this time the 'public' that is of concern is the working class and the value of its wages – its purchasing power. The aim was to equate the price or money value of commodities with their 'real' value (exchange value). Since the value of money fluctuates due to market conditions and, therefore, affects the price of commodities, the solution was advanced that the price of commodities be expressed in terms of the labor time it took to produce it (its cost of production).

This view of the problem may be compared to the view that saw the problem as the appreciation of gold. They both see the problem concretely, but from different positions. Whereas the bourgeois economists saw the problem of the appreciation of gold in terms of the increase in the discount rate, the 'socialist' theorists who put forth the time chit solution saw the problem in terms of the cost of necessities. With a decrease in the value of money, it would require more to purchase the same item.

Their solution was the abolition of money and the substitution of 'labor money,' or time chits. The time chits would represent the amount of time it took to produce a commodity. In this way, the price of a commodity would be equivalent to its value. Its price would be impervious to fluctuations in the value of gold.

If the hour of labor became more productive, then the chit of paper which represents it would rise in buying power and vice versa. If productivity kept rising, which was anticipated, such labor money might even constantly appreciate, which would be to the advantage of workers; they would realize their increased productivity.

According to Marx, however, if money is presupposed (even in the form of time chits), then we must also presuppose the accumulation of this money, as well as contracts, obligations, fixed burdens, etc., which are entered into in the form of this money. The accumulated chits would constantly appreciate together with the newly issued ones and thus, on the one hand, the rising productivity of labor would go to the benefit of non-workers, those who accumulate time chits (e.g. profit). On the other hand, the previously contracted burdens would keep step with the rising yield of labor. Those who owed a certain amount of time chits would continue to owe that much, even if what they had received for the equivalent of the time chit (its value) would now be worth

221

fewer time chits, the depreciation of all commodities relative to the time chits. This would favor lenders over borrowers.

The reason for replacing metal money (and paper money) by labor money denominated in labor time is that doing so would equate the real value (exchange value) of commodities with their price, money value. But according to Marx, this would not be possible. If an item were priced according to its cost of production – labor time – it seems as if it would be priced at its true value and would not be subject to the fluctuations of the market:

> The first basic illusion of the time-chitters consists in this that by annulling the nominal difference between real value and market value, between exchange value and price – they also remove the real difference and contradiction between price and value (138).

In other words, there is a contradiction between price and value. Price is determined by the market – supply and demand – while value is determined by the average amount of labor time embodied in a product relative to the average amount of labor time embodied in other products:

> Thus, it may seem a very simple matter that labour time should be able to serve directly as money (i.e. be able to furnish the element in which exchange values are realized as such), because it regulates exchange values and indeed is not only the inherent measure of exchange values but their substance as well (for, as exchange values, commodities have no other substance, no natural attributes) (168–9).

Marx goes on to show that despite this appearance of identity between exchange value and labor time, the exchange value of commodities is more complicated and contradictory:

> However, this appearance of simplicity is deceptive. The truth is that the exchange-value relation – of commodities as mutually equal and equivalent objectifications of labour time – comprises contradictions which find their objective expression in a *money which is distinct from* labour time (169).

The value of a commodity for exchange purposes is not the actual amount of labor time embodied in it, but the average amount of labor time it takes to produce it relative to other products. Not only is the average amount not necessarily the actual amount that any individual expends, but that average amount expended per item and its relation to the other products keeps changing as new and more productive techniques or machinery or cheaper raw materials are introduced.

The value of commodities as determined by labor time is only their average value. This average is not merely an external single calculation, but is determined by the constant changes in productivity. This average 'is the driving force and the moving principle of the oscillations which commodity prices run through during a given epoch.' The market value is always different, either below or above this average value of a commodity. It is not merely of theoretical importance; it produces mercantile speculation.

Market value only equates itself with real value by these constant oscillations. 'Supply and demand constantly determine the prices of commodities; never balance or only coincidentally, but the cost of production, for its part determines the oscillations of supply and demand' (138).

If the price of an item were indicated as the amount of labor time it took to produce it (its cost of production), that price would differ for items produced today as compared with the same items produced yesterday. This would mean that the 'price' would have to reconcile the difference by being average. Thus an item that takes three hours to produce today may be priced at four hours, if it had previously taken five hours to produce. Another item which had also taken three hours to produce may be priced at two labor hours today if it now takes one hour to product it. Hence,

> the confusion would reach a new height altogether. . . .
> This contradiction is in practice expressed in money prices,
> but in a veiled form. . . . Because labour time as the
> measure of value exists only as an ideal, it cannot serve as
> the matter of price comparisons. (Here at the same time it
> becomes clear how and why the value relation obtains a
> separate material existence in the form of money) (140).

With respect to the necessary alienation of price and value due to the constant changes in value, constant changes in productivity, Marx states that even in the form of time chits, money would be alienated from value:

> [It] would achieve a separate existence of its own in the time chit, an existence corresponding to this non-equivalence. The general equivalent, medium of circulation and measure of commodities would again confront the commodities in an individual form, following its own laws, alienated, i.e. equipped with all the properties of money as it exists at present but unable to perform the same services (139).

Since the time-chitters do not understand the ground of exchange value, since theirs is concrete theorizing, they can conceive of time chits as a way of avoiding the oscillations of the market:

> Given the illusory assumptions it is self-evident that the mere introduction of the time-chit does away with all crises, all faults of bourgeois production. That is, if the money price of commodities = their real value; demand = supply; production = consumption; . . . the labor time, which is materialized in the commodity, would need only to be measured in order to create a corresponding mirror-image in the form of a value-symbol, money, time-chits (138).

In his critique, Marx shows that the problems associated with money would not be solved by abolishing the form of money (gold and silver) and substituting a new form (labor time). Rather, the problems associated with money do not originate with its concrete form, but with the social organization of production mediated by exchange value (regardless of the concrete form of exchange value – whether time chits or gold). In this mode of production, the market price, determined by supply and demand, must always differ from the real value (exchange value) of the commodity (the labor time embodied in it). This is because the 'real' value itself is always changing and always expresses an average. Thus it is not that gold is a commodity and subject to the fluctuations of the market which causes the problems, but the problem is the commodity form itself, exchange value as the aim of production. The critique may be summed up as accusing the time-chitters of treating value as an absolute thing (labor time), rather than as social relations.

Marx explains that the preconditions for equating the price of commodities with their exchange value are the balance of supply and demand, balance of production and consumption, in other words the elimination of the market as such.

For the time chit solution to work, the bank that would issue the time chit in exchange for the product would be the general buyer and seller. This would eliminate the market. As general buyer and seller:

1 the bank would need the power to calculate and establish the exchange value of all commodities, the labor time materialized in them in an authentic manner.

2 the bank would have to determine the labor time in which commodities could be produced with the average means of production available in a given industry, i.e. the time in which they would have to be produced.

3 the bank would not only have to determine the time in which certain quantities of products had to be produced, and place the producers in conditions which made their labor equally productive (i.e. it would have to balance and arrange the distribution of the means of labor), but it would also have to determine the amount of labor time to be employed in the different branches of production.

The bank, then, would be not only the general buyer and seller, but also the general producer:

> In fact either it would be a despotic ruler of production and trustee of distribution or it would indeed be nothing more than a board which keeps the books and accounts for a society producing in common. . . . The Saint-Simonians made their bank into the papacy of production (155–6).

Instead of realizing that a society producing in common and the elimination of capital is the necessary means for eliminating the problems of the market, they believe that the establishment of the bank would in itself eliminate those problems. They fail to inquire where the power of the bank would come from.

Marx feels that aiming for the regulation of all production by means of a bank is based on the failure to recognize that it requires the power to force producers to labor at a set rate of productivity, the power to make all labor equally productive, and the power to determine what and how much should be produced. This would require wresting power from capital. Capital could no longer determine production, for the accumulation of capital requires the constant expansion of the market and revolutionizing of the means of production, which is what produces speculation, overproduction, stockpiling, fluctuations in price and crises. This is precisely what the bank must prevent.

If the bank were simply a book-keeping organ for 'a society producing in common' (as opposed to a society producing as individuals who exchange), then time chits would no longer be an issue, for there would be no discrepancy between price and value. Thus, in order for the time chit solution to work, the problem which it solves would have already had to be eliminated.

Realizing socialism: eliminating external mediation

This chapter has dealt with the difference between Marx's method of formulating the grounds of economic problems and other theorists' method of theorizing. We have been claiming that the other theorists never leave the level of the concrete; they stay on the level of money, relating money problems to concrete practices of the money system, such as maintaining a gold reserve. Instead of inquiring into the grounds of money, they treat money as a thing.

In view of that failure, we will see that, for Marx, the only solution to the problems created by a form of life in which money is grounded is to change the form of life itself by negating its grounds. In his critique, Marx had been demonstrating that changes in the kind of money – metal to paper currency or chits – cannot solve the problems associated with money precisely because money is not distinct from commodities. It is a commodity, though one with some special properties. Thus, all kinds of money remain subject to the conditions of commodity production, in particular the exigencies of exchange. But, it follows then that politico-economic actions that constitute capitalism cannot be founded in particular intentions; nor, therefore, can the crises of capitalism be overcome by the development or exercise of socialist ideals.

Where wealth must be realized as exchange value, there is no possibility of the totality of production being controlled by the totality of producers:

There can be, therefore, nothing more erroneous and absurd to postulate the control by the united individuals of their total production, on the basis of *exchange value*, of *money*, as was done above in the case of the time-chit bank (158–9).

In other words, exchange value presupposes individuals producing and exchanging with each other. This precludes the treatment of production as a totality by a united people. Exchange value arises within an exchange relationship, where issues of fairness or equality can only be resolved objectively by some standard external to the individuality of the subjects. This is necessary in a situation where exchangers cannot trust each other, where exchangers do not 'know' each other and cannot get to 'know' each other, where they are externally related (through the exchange) rather than internally related, recognizing themselves as essential to each other, within production, recognizing that each is responsible to and for the other:

> it is clear to the economists that the existence of money presupposes the objectification [*Versachlichung*] of the social bond; in so far, that is, as money appears in the form of *collateral* which one individual must leave with another in order to obtain a commodity from him. Here the economists themselves say that people place in a thing (money) the faith which they do not place in each other (160).

If they do not have faith in each other, how can they have faith in a thing? 'Obviously only because that thing is an objectified relation between persons; because it is objectified exchange value, and exchange value is nothing more than a mutual relation between people's productive activities.' This relation among productive activities is alienated from the producers themselves. Instead,

> money serves him only as the 'dead pledge' of society, but it serves as such only because of its social (symbolic) property; and it can have a social property only because individuals have alienated their own social relationship from themselves so that it takes the form of a thing (160).

In other words, it is a relationship among past labor, a relation

227

among productive activities that have already been objectified in products.

Exchange value can be suspended when people relate to each other as 'knowable,' because they recognize each other as living within the same form of life, as produced by and co-producing the totality within which they live. The suspension means that they can relate to and depend on each other without the mediation of exchange value; their productive activities are internal to production as a totality, and, therefore, they can treat each other as 'knowable' and responsible. Marx identifies this form of life as 'the free exchange among individuals who are associated on the basis of common appropriation and control of the means of production' (159). This would be a form of life in which individuals' activities are recognized as grounded. Individual acts would be recognized as directly general, that is, as acts that do not originate with the individual, but as acts that originate within a totality.

This form of life is the negation of the one presupposed by exchange value which is what money represents:

> Labour on the basis of exchange value presupposes, precisely, that neither the labour of the individual nor his product are *directly* general; that the product attains this form only by passing through an *objective mediation*, by means of a form of *money* distinct from itself (172).

On the basis of exchange value, labor is posited as general only through exchange. For labor to be general directly (to have value without exchange and the vagaries of the market), which is what the time-chitters erroneously attribute to the use of time chits, a different social arrangement is necessary. In this arrangement, labor would not be individual, that is, something that has no value for anybody else, until it is sold (exchanged) for something else, but would be general (valuable) from the outset, having value as a link in general production.

On this presupposition, it would not be exchange which gave labor its general character; but rather it would have presupposed a communal, general character to begin with. The individual in general is the community. The general or communal production would make the product into a communal, general product from the outset. On this foundation, labor would be posited as general, as communal, not through exchange as at present, but before exchange. That is, the exchange of products would in no way be the medium for the participation of the individual in general production which is consumption.

In the form of life analyzed by Marx, production by individuals is mediated by exchange value (capital and wages); consumption as the appropriation of wealth is likewise mediated by exchange value (money). In the negation of this form of life, production is the immediate ground of wealth, and wealth is the immediate ground of production. Neither production, nor wealth, would be mediated by exchange value. The individual's relation to wealth would be as an individual participant in the production of wealth:

> Thus whatever the particular material form of the product he creates or helps to create, what he has bought with his labour is not a specific and particular product (which requires exchange for its value to be realized), but rather a specific share of the communal production. He therefore has no particular product to exchange. His product is not an exchange value. The product does not first have to be transposed into a particular form in order to attain a general character for the individual (172).

In this mode of production, workers would not sell their labor power for wages. Where types of labor are differentiated according to wages, the elimination of wages would dissolve the sharp boundaries between them:

> Instead of a division of labour where people are assigned to particular jobs on the basis of selling their labour power to somebody who can then assign them, the people would organize their work themselves not on the basis of receiving wages for particular types of work, but on the basis of providing products for the consumption of the community of which they are a part. Instead of a division of labour, such as is necessarily created with the exchange of exchange values, there would take place an organization of labour whose consequences would be the participation of the individual in communal consumption (172).

Production as purposive activity would not be separated into purpose that is indifferent to activity. In the case of wage labor, workers' purpose is wages, not that which is produced by their labor. In the case of capitalists, purpose is the expansion of capital, not that which is produced by capital. This is one way of understanding the division of labor. Instead of a division of labor, a purpose and activity that is divided by exchange value, labor would be united with itself as purpose. Where exchange value is the mediation, production is alienated; it is split between the production of products and the realization of exchange value.

In Marx's negation of this form of life, individual production would not be mediated by exchange, would not be posited as social only because of exchange. Individual production and consumption would be produced directly by and would directly reproduce itself, as an individual, internal part of a totality:

> Instead of the social characteristics of production appearing only when the individual's production is treated as exchange values and then exchanged, the social character of production is treated as the basis of individual production and consumption. In the first case the social character of production is posited only *post festum* with the elevation of products to exchange values and the exchange of these exchange values. In the second case, the social character of production is presupposed, and participation in the world of products, in consumption, is not mediated by the exchange of mutually independent labours or products of labour. It is mediated, rather, by the social conditions of production within which the individual is active (172).

Instead of an alienated form of production, wealth that is only realized through exchange, Marx describes a form of life where production is itself wealth, where consumption is mediated by the particular subjective and objective conditions of production within which the individual is active.

The advocacy of time chits is the advocacy of a situation where the labor of the individual would be made directly into money, where labor would be directly general labor, where labor would be directly realizable as participation in consumption without having that participation be dependent on fluctuations in the market or inequality between price and value. However, the time-chitters fail to realize that this desire or demand can be satisfied only 'under conditions where it can no longer be raised, where the social character of production is presupposed and therefore there is no need to first transpose labour into the form of money through exchange' (172).

Concrete solutions: failure to inquire into grounds

The problem with the solutions of the theorists that Marx criticizes is that they do not analyze. They are concerned with problems associated with, and corrections at the level of, money. They do not inquire into grounds. Marx's critique shows that these problems (and solutions) are only the outcomes or concrete appearance of the real problem: a mode of production or form of life wherein the social nature of production is realized only through the mediation of exchange and exchange value with its attendant fluctuations and crises. Marx shows the negation of this form of life or mode of production to be one where the social or communality is presupposed by the production process itself. In the latter case, the relations of the individual to the products (i.e. consumption) would be internal to the social conditions of production, rather than divided between production and the external relations of exchange – the market.

Marx appears to be considering solutions to economic crises, but his talk accomplishes the possibility of overcoming a form of life that fails to recognize grounds. His analysis of the solutions reveals the contradiction in human activity that treats itself as independent acts of individuals, rather than as produced by a totality in which they participate and which they reproduce.

According to Marx's analysis, money becomes the social bond, the grounds of community (and lack of community) and individual activity. He contrasts this with a form of life in which individual activity would be recognized as immediately social, in which the individual and the community would be an internal relation – individual activity would be grounded in the totality and the totality would be grounded in individual activity.

Marx's critique of others' analyses is not just that their method is inadequate because it fails to understand the grounds of what they discuss. Marx's concern is not others' analyses *per se*, but a form of life that produces those analyses. His critique is an attempt to show that form of life, so that it may be consciously reappropriated by its subject – the community.

Marx claims that the solutions of changing the moves of the money game, e.g. going off the gold standard, eliminating reserve requirements, refraining from exporting gold, or substituting time chits, would not solve the problems associated with money – economic crises. These moves are concrete because they are based on treating money as a given, concrete thing. The solutions only alter the uses of money. Changing the concrete moves does not necessarily change the game. Instead of dealing with money concretely, Marx inquires into its social grounds, the form of life within which it arises. Rather than beginning from the concrete moves which those whom Marx criticizes treat as grounds, Marx inquires into the presuppositions of the money relation (the relation of a product to itself as exchange value), and therefore of those moves.

CHAPTER 8

Dialectical phenomenology's critique of concrete readings

The present book fits into a tradition of anti-positivistic, phenomenological readings of Marx. This concluding chapter examines works that I consider to be within that tradition by such interpreters of Marx as Habermas, Althusser, O'Neill, Lukács and Merleau-Ponty. For each of these theorists, I choose certain representative aspects, showing what those readings share with and where they differ from my own.

Running through the phenomenological tradition of reading Marx, is a difficulty of putting into practice a distinction that these interpreters recognize and which I refer to as the difference between an analytic and a concrete mode of theorizing. Each of the theorists' readings of Marx exemplify a non-positivistic, 'analytic' mode. However, despite their criticism of positivistic, concrete theorizing, I see each of them at some key point adopting it.

This lapse from analytic to concrete creates intractable problems in their own theorizing or in their interpretations of Marx. My four rules make explicit the analytic approach which these other readers use implicitly but inconsistently. Explicitly formulating an anti-positivistic method for understanding Marx's theorizing, makes my reading differ from theirs and helps it to avoid concrete theorizing. The conception of dialectical phenomenology accomplishes two ends. It displays the possibility of an analytic mode of theorizing, and it avoids falling into a positivistic reading of Marx.

Such a lapse into concrete theorizing by theorists discussed in this chapter seems to take one of several forms. On the one hand, the method of reading itself may be concrete despite attributing to

Marx an analytic approach. For example, Habermas (1971, 1973) considers Marx's method to be analytic critique and not positivistic description. Yet he tends to read Marx's concepts concretely. For instance, he reads Marx's discussion of modes of production as concrete description (1975). Similarly, Merleau-Ponty (1973), who does a rigorously analytic reading of Marx including the latter's concepts of 'proletariat' and 'history,' tends to use those same concepts concretely when he addresses himself to particular political movements and practical issues.

On the other hand, Marx himself may appear to be concrete within an analytic reading. For example, Althusser does what he calls a symptomatic reading of Marx, in which Marx's formulations are symptoms of something else. This corresponds to a phenomenological approach for which a text can only be known in terms of what the reader provides. Yet he fails to see Marx's method as doing the same, as overcoming the positivistic distinction between the knower and the object known. Rather, he sees Marx as discovering a new way of theorizing captured by the concept, 'structure,' which can now be used to replace previous ways of theorizing. However, his account of Marx's revolution in theorizing, his version of 'structure,' turns out to be a positivistic one.

Habermas: critique of objectivism

I will now examine specific works by these theorists, beginning with Habermas, in order to highlight the similarities and differences between their theorizing and reading of Marx and the reading presented in these pages as dialectical phenomenology. For Habermas as for dialectical phenomenology, knowledge does not emanate from its object. Instead, according to Habermas, all types of knowledge presuppose types of human interest. He offers a critique of objectivism (1971, p. 168): 'Objectivism deludes the sciences with the image of a self-subsistent world of facts structured in a law-like manner – it thus conceals the a priori constitution of these facts.' Just as Habermas rejects objectivism, he also argues that knowledge cannot be reduced to the individual and his experiences. He builds on Dilthey's critique of psychologism which he considers to be

based on the insight that experience itself is organized by

symbolic structures. An experience is not a subjective process of becoming conscious of fundamental organic states . . . the objective structure of valid symbols in which we always find ourselves embedded can be understood only through experiential reconstruction such that we revert to the process in which meaning is generated (*ibid.*, p. 171).

For Marx, knowledge, meaning and ordinary language do not originate with objects, nor with individual subjects. Rather, ordinary language grounds itself in ordinary social practices. Habermas makes reference to this grounding when he states:

> The meaning of linguistic symbols can be made clear through participation in habitual interactions. Language and action interpret each other reciprocally: this is developed in Wittgenstein's concept of the language game (*ibid.*, p. 171).

The concern with meaning leads Habermas to consider hermeneutics, the interpretation of a text. However, his hermeneutics differs in important respects from the method of reading Marx that I have been presenting here:

> The interpretation of a text depends on a reciprocal relation between the interpretation of 'parts' through what is at first a diffusely preunderstood 'whole' and the correction of this preliminary concept by means of the parts it subsumes (*ibid.*, p. 171).

The hermeneutic method which Habermas describes does not account for the interpretation itself as a text. That is, the relation of parts to whole and whole to parts is a way of reconstructing the elements of a text: vocabulary and grammar. If this reconstruction is the whole, we are still left with the problem of interpreting that whole. How is it that the text which I have reconstructed makes sense? This is not a question regarding the correctness of the translation, but the meaning or sense of that which has been translated. In other words, the text or whole as it is understood presupposes a form of life that is other than the text itself and which provides for its sense. Hence, the very reconstruction of the text through the hermeneutic method presupposes that which is other to the text.

Habermas seems to acknowledge the otherness or form of life

that provides for the sense of the whole with the concepts of 'practice' and 'experience,' by which he means the unstated to which all ordinary language makes reflexive allusion (*ibid.*, pp. 168, 173). Yet, he explicates hermeneutics as a method of understanding parts in relation to a 'diffusely preunderstood "whole",' whose understanding is then clarified in relation to those parts. The ambiguity arises with his notion of the 'whole.' By 'whole' he might mean a form of life that is other to the parts but which the parts presuppose for their sense. This would correspond to the analytic approach that I have been stressing. Or he might mean by whole the sum of the parts which would correspond to a concrete approach.

However, Habermas does seem to recognize this distinction in another context where he discusses the 'insufficiency of dialectical logic.' Dialectical logic applies to distorted communication. It therefore presupposes its other, the possibility of its negation: the logic of undistorted communication. Thus, with respect to dialectical logic, Habermas recognizes its historical specificity to a form of life that produces distorted communication. He suggests that the task of dialectics, in the sense of the Hegelian 'Phenomenology'

> is to reconstruct that which has been repressed from the historical traces of repressed dialogues. But what is dialectical is then only the structure of compulsion that dialectical thought explodes by assimilating itself to it. . . . Then however, our problem is merely deferred. For the structure of distorted communication is not ultimate; it has its basis in the logic of undistorted language communication (1973, pp. 16–17).

This is similar to my analysis of dialectical phenomenology as a historically specific mode of theorizing. As the grounding of abstractions, dialectical phenomenology itself presupposes a form of life that produces and presupposes abstractions. The abolition of that form of life simultaneously suspends dialectical phenomenology as critique. In a self-conscious form of life, dialectical phenomenology would not exist as such. Habermas's conception of undistorted language communication with its elimination of the need for dialectic corresponds to the notion put forth here of a self-conscious form of life.

Habermas: critique of Marx's theorizing

Habermas offers a critique of Marx's treatment of history. His
critique of history as a totality is based on rejecting a conception of
world history as a story of class struggle with a beginning and an
end. Such a version of world history, as Habermas points out,
presupposes a unity of world. However, global unity has only
come into existence historically. Therefore, in an approach which
makes a totality of history from the very beginning its premise
becomes untenable:

> Extension of contemporary conflict back to beginnings of
> history retains a merely heuristic character. So too the
> anticipatory presupposition of history's end remains
> hypothetical (1973, pp. 251–2).

However, history is a story. This is not to say that it is a subjective
creation of a story independent of facts and events. But neither is
history a record of facts and events. Rather, facts and events
should be likened to a text. History is a reading of that text. It is
neither purely subjective nor purely objective. Rather, it is the
grounding of those objectivations of facts and events in a form of
life that provides for their sense. A reading is always within a form
of life and makes reference to that form of life in its possibility.

Marx formulates history from within a form of life characterized
by the possibility of self-conscious community (Fischer, 1978). He
reads history in terms of repressed community (capitalism) versus
natural community (pre-capitalism) and self-conscious community
(post-capitalism). The tension between unity and separation (community and alienation) constitutes the dialectic in which he reads
history. Habermas reads Marx as extending the 'contemporary
conflict' of social classes back to the beginnings of history. But one
does not have to read Marx this way. On the contrary, his work on
pre-capitalist formations lends itself to a different reading.

In that work, contrary to Habermas's interpretation, Marx does
not talk about the struggle of a dominated class against a
dominating one. Rather, he reads pre-capitalist society as a unity
of production, the unity of labor as subject with its objective
conditions of existence. Marx formulates this unity of production
as a property relation. Property in land is given with membership
in the community. However, because the community is not

237

created, but given with human existence, the community sees itself as natural or divine.

Thus property in land was a grant from Nature or the divinity. The individual was not free, but was possessed. The individual was possessed by the community just as the objective conditions of the individual's existence were the property of the community conceived as Nature or a divinity. With the dissolution of that natural community due to migrations, etc., comes community that is recognized as historical but community still conceived as external to members' activity, hence still limited and still divine in some sense. Both the natural and historical versions of community as external to members' activity and, hence, divine are pre-capitalist forms. In spite of all the differences that distinguish the different forms of pre-capitalist landed property, the key feature that makes for 'pre-capitalism,' is the unity of labor with its objective conditions – its property.

Only with capital is this unity mediated and thereby divided. (It may seem that slavery mediates landed property in some pre-capitalist forms. However, Marx argues that slaves were conceived as objective conditions, like the land and the instruments of production, and not as subjects.) The subject of production in pre-capitalist society may have been divided into property owners and slaves, but such class societies of pre-capitalism continued to presuppose a unity of landowning class with the objective conditions of its existence. In capitalism, although labor (like slaves) remains an objective condition of capital and the capitalist class, it is also conceived as the subject of exchange (unlike slaves). Labor is posited as subject as well as object. The class that owns capital does not own the objective conditions of its existence. It must first exchange its capital for wage labor and then exchange its products for money. With the development of capital, the unity of subject and object is completely divided and mediated.

Capitalism and exchange separate members' activity from themselves as communal subject, bringing repression of community and the end of unity conceived as external and divine. In this form of life, the communal subject is divided, creating a dual subject and dual object. Class struggle is the attempt by labor to overcome this disunity and duality of subject and object in the face of capital's attempt to maintain it. With class struggle, socialized labor, which capitalism produces as a class in itself, becomes a class for itself.

238

Socialized labor refers to production that is accomplished by the co-operation of large numbers of people. Class struggle makes possible a reuniting of members and their activity as a united subjectivity which, unlike pre-capitalist unity, would be a completely historical accomplishment. This means a form of life in which community is not conceived as a thing separate from members' activity, an external divinity as it is in pre-capitalism. It also means members' activity is not conceived as independent of community as it is in capitalism. Rather, community is conceived as members' ongoing activity, social (re)production. This is how I interpret Marx's concept of socialism – a self-consciously social mode of (re)production, (comm)unity as a historical accomplishment not conceived as external to the members and their activity. This unity of the laboring subject with its objective conditions is a self-conscious unity, a unity in which individuals know that they (re)produce themselves and their community in their laboring activity.

This knowledge becomes the point of departure and point of return, i.e. production for human needs unmediated by capital: self-conscious production. The individual in such a society would be a free (because consciously producing its own being – the realization of needs), social (member of a community that collectively determines production) individual (because of the diversity of possible activities and relations that would be open to and contribute to the development of the individual).

This does not mean that individual struggles would no longer exist. It means that class struggle as the attempt to achieve unity and freedom would have accomplished its end. This does not imply that such an end is inevitable. Rather, it means that given class struggle (as a concomitant of a divided subject), its end would be self-conscious production. This raises the question of how to understand Marx's conception of a third, post-capitalist stage of history.

Some read Marx's formulation of the third, post-capitalist stage as a projection based on observation of empirical tendencies within capitalism. This is true in a sense. Yet it implies that Marx does not ground these empirical tendencies in the disunity of capitalism. The tendencies, concrete theorists assume, are there for anyone to observe empirically.

Others, more commonly perhaps, read Marx's version of history as a subjective and quasi-religious belief in the inevitability of a rational society taking the place of a non-rational one. Habermas's critique implies such a reading. This interpretation of millenarianism has Marx attributing an end or telos to history. History becomes the movement toward a rational society. Although this too is true in a sense, Marx's work cannot be reduced to a subjective or idealistic view. Unlike idealism, Marx's approach shows how the future is already contained as a possibility in the movement of the present. In other words, he provides grounds for the future in his formulation and analysis of the present as a separation of subject and object. The future is not something that is simply posited idealistically on the basis of personal hopes or desires. Rather, the future is a formulation that presupposes for its possibility his conception of the present as a separation of subject and object.

Analytically, for Marx, the unity to be produced by struggle and the socialized character of labor under capitalism make possible a socialist society, a society in which socialized labor realizes itself directly by producing without the mediation of capital and the capitalist. Thus production would be a unity of purpose and activity – self-conscious production. This is the type of rational society that emerges as a possibility from the capitalist stage of history as Marx analyzes it.

Marx's version of the movement of history is, therefore, neither an idealistic (subjectivist) belief, nor a positivist (or objective) claim to the inevitability of a rational society. Rather, it is the possibility of a rational society, conceived as self-conscious production or socialism, that is provided by the very process of producing capital. Thus Marx does not do a concrete reading of history, nor an idealistic one. Every reading presupposes a form of life that provides for its sense. A reading is never a purely subjective or purely objective account. Marx's reading of history is no exception. It grounds itself in capitalism's form of life formulated as a separation of subject and object.

Marx's reading of history is not simply that class conflict has always existed. Rather, it is that history, read in terms of a relation of subject and object, can be understood in terms of class or property relations. With the mediation by capital and wage labor of the relation between a social subject and its objective conditions comes a specific property relation and a specific class struggle. If this class struggle ends, and it can only end by eliminating the conditions by which it (re)produces itself, this means that the mediation is eliminated and the end of unself-conscious production is simultaneously accomplished.

As Marx points out, one must analyze the conditions of the present in order to understand the past as a becoming of the present. One may make an analogy between this conception of reading the past as grounded in an analysis of the present and the notion of a self-conscious reading in which the reader recognizes that the reading is made possible by a form of life in which the reader stands. Marx's analysis of history (and my conception of reading and theorizing) raises the question of its status as a science. Habermas wants to see a science of social life developed as a critique of ideology. This would be in opposition to a natural science characterized by empirical-analytic knowledge. The latter takes the form of empirically testable propositions that have the power of prediction and the interest of technical control. Empirical-analytic knowledge is associated with instrumental action.

Habermas claims that a science of social life sketched by Marx was obscured by identification with natural science. He claims that Marx eliminates reflection as a motive force of history, even though he retains the framework of the philosophy of reflection. That is, although Marx worked within the framework of a philosophy of reflection, he did not acknowledge that he did so. He identified his work with natural science.

That Marx identified it in that way does not mean that Marx intended by science what Habermas means by science. One could read Marx as intending a contrast with utopian socialism. In fact, whenever Marx uses the term science in relation to his own work it is almost invariably in contrast with the utopian socialism whose critique rested solely on moral or subjective grounds. Marx saw his critique as resting on analytic grounds: subjective-objective conditions.

Although Marx's work can be read as a critique of utopian socialism, and just as it can be read as a critique of subjective idealism (associated with the young Hegelians), it can also be read as a negation of still another version of social science: bourgeois theorizing. Habermas's distinction between natural science and a self-reflective social science, between positivism and a critical

241

science, resembles Marx's distinction between bourgeois theorizing and what he calls scientific socialism.

Habermas recognizes the critical intention in Marx's work. Thus he acknowledges that Marx adopts a critical method of theorizing. However, he claims that Marx fails to explicate his method and identify it adequately as critique or self-reflection of science. Consequently, according to Habermas, Marx's scientistic account of his own work tends to reduce critical reflection to the process of production and instrumental action. This means that Marx eliminates reflection as a motive force in history. The reduction of reflection to production, interpreted by Habermas as instrumental action, occurs within Marx's analysis as a result of combining instrumental action with the 'power relations that regulate men's interactions,' under the misleading term of social practice. The term misleads, according to Habermas, by resulting in the reduction of the cultural tradition (the institutionalization of power relations) to instrumental action.

Habermas seems to suggest that this reduction can only be avoided by separating the institutions of a cultural tradition from instrumental action or the relations of production from the forces of production. Although in this he agrees that relations and forces of production are aspects of production as a whole, he argues that attributing primacy to production makes it impossible to consider relations of production in their own right:

> These relations are subject to norms that decide, with the force of institutions, how responsibilities and rewards, obligations and changes in the social budget are distributed among members. The medium in which these relations of subjects and of groups are normatively regulated is cultural tradition. It forms the linguistic communication structure on the basis of which subjects interpret both nature and themselves in their environment (1971, p. 53).

Habermas, then, distinguishes between emancipation from external forces of nature and emancipation from the compulsions of internal nature. The former occurs through labor processes, such as machinery. The latter occurs through the revolutionary activity of struggling classes (including the critical activity of reflective sciences). In other words, transforming forces of pro-

242

duction does not necessarily transform the social relations of production, the power relations of domination. Habermas's problematic is relations of domination. Reflection is a means for recognizing domination and is, therefore, necessary for struggling against it. Habermas reads Marx's central concern and overall problematic as domination also. He then criticizes Marx for not acknowledging the importance of reflection for revolutionary struggle against domination, and, in fact, claiming that changes in instrumental activity are sufficient for transforming relations of domination.

Instead of reading Marx's problematic as relations of domination in the abstract, and the relations of capital as a particular instance, I read Marx as displaying the following problematic: the possibility of self-conscious production and its corresponding free social individual. Here, production is not the making of things but the activities in which a subject produces itself in the appropriation of its objective conditions. In self-conscious production a subject produces itself and knows itself in its relation to its object.

In this reading, Marx, unlike Habermas, does not separate consciousness from production. Consciousness is either self-conscious production or production that is not self-conscious. In self-conscious production, ideas or concepts as well as actions are known as grounded in purposive activity. In unself-conscious production, knowledge and actions appear as independent things and relations between things that are independent of purposive activity or subjectivity. This distinction accounts for the Marxian notions of social(ist) science and capitalist ideology.

Reading Marx with this problematic means that his subject-object is not relations of power, but unself-conscious production. In other words, Marx must explain how it is possible that a subject could fail to be self-conscious. He does this by showing how the subject is not a single subject, but a dual one – a divided subject-object. It is divided by the mediation of exchange value. He grounds this division in production that is not a single process, but several processes separated in time and space that contradict each other: a self-contradictory mode of production.

Whereas Habermas sees reflection as a means for something else, Marx sees it as an inherent part of self-conscious production. The problem for Marx is explaining how reflection can appear to be separate from production, independent of the self-constitution of a subject. Marx must show how abstractions are produced as abstractions. In order to do this, he must show their difference from concepts which are grounded objects of knowledge. By grounding the abstractions in the form of life that they presuppose, he produces concepts where before there were abstractions.

In analyzing the process by which abstractions like labor, capital and value are produced, Marx ends up with different conceptions of capital, labor and value and different concepts such as the use value/ exchange value distinction, the labor power/labor distinction, the capital/money distinction, the commodity/product distinction.

For Marx, the presence of abstractions means the absence of self-conscious production. Instead of accounting for the absence of self-consciousness – as if self-consciousness were a thing in the world that could be used to overcome relations of domination – Marx accounts for the absence of self-conscious production. Self-conscious production is not consciousness of domination, but activity by a subject that knows that it produces itself in its practices.

Whereas Habermas concerns himself with the absence of reflection, Marx concerns himself with the absence of self-conscious production. A reading presupposes a problematic from which the reading and the text derive their impulse. The problematic from which Habermas begins accounts for his reading of Marx. Beginning with a version of consciousness as a separate thing in itself, he then reads Marx as failing to treat consciousness as a motive force of history. However, Marx begins with a different problematic, self-conscious production, which accounts for his analysis of capitalism. Likewise my problematic, reflexivity in theorizing and reading, accounts for my reading of the *Grundrisse*. Thus one's problematic produces one's reading.

Althusser: two conceptions of reading and knowing

Althusser explicitly addresses himself to the practice of reading. He presents two alternative reading principles to account for Marx's reading of classical political economy. The first reading suggests that a reader, Smith, for example, may discover certain things and miss others:

> What Smith did not see, through a weakness of vision, Marx

sees. What Smith did not see was perfectly visible, and it was because it was visible that Smith could fail to see it while Marx could see it. We are in a circle – we have relapsed into the mirror myth of knowledge as the vision of a given object or the reading of an established text . . . this reduces Marx to Smith minus the myopia (Althusser and Balibar, 1970, pp. 19–21).

The significance of this reading is that it

> reduces to nothing . . . the historical distance and theoretical dislocation in which Marx thinks the theoretical difference that nevertheless separates him from Smith forever. And finally, we too are condemned to the same fate of vision – condemned to see in Marx only what he saw (*ibid.*).

He contrasts with this a second reading:

> What classical political economy does not see, is not what it does not see, it is what it sees; it is not what it lacks, on the contrary, it is what it does not lack; it is not what it misses, on the contrary, it is what it does not miss . . . the over-sight no longer concerns the object, but the *sight* itself, the oversight is an oversight that concerns *vision*: non-vision is therefore inside vision, it is a form of vision and hence has a necessary relation with vision (*ibid.*).

What political economy does not see is not a pre-existing object which it could have seen but did not see, but an object which it produces itself in its operation of knowledge and which did not pre-exist it: precisely the product of knowledge which is identical with the object:

> This introduces us to a fact peculiar to the very existence of science: it can only pose problems on the terrain and within the horizon of a definite theoretical structure, its problem-atic, which constitutes its absolute and definite conditions of possibility, and hence the absolute determination of the forms in which all problems must be posed, at any given moment in the science (*ibid.*, p. 25).

By implication, the seeing is no longer the act of an individual.

245

Rather, seeing is the result of the problematic; the problematic makes the object visible:

> Any object or problem situated on the terrain and within the horizon, i.e. in the definite structured field of the theoretical problematic of a given theoretical discipline, is visible. . . . The sighting is no longer the act of an individual subject endowed with the faculty of 'vision' which he exercises either attentively or distractedly. Vision then loses the religious privileges of divine reading: it is no more than a reflection of the immanent necessity that ties an object or problem to its conditions of existence which lie in the conditions of its production (*ibid.*).

The problematic structures the field in which an object may be visible. Thus, the field presents itself in its objects. Another way of saying this is that every object is a display of that which makes it possible, its grounds:

> It is literally no longer the eye (the mind's eye) of a subject which *sees* what exists in the field defined by a theoretical problematic; it is this field itself which *sees itself* in the objects or problems it defines – sighting being merely the necessary reflection of the field on its objects (*ibid.*).

To read Marx in this second way is to treat the text as a product, a product of a reading. To know the text according to this second mode of reading, is to know how knowledge of it is produced.

These two versions of reading may be compared with two conceptions of knowledge that Althusser reviews: the empiricist and the one attributed to Spinoza and Marx:

> For the empiricist conception of knowledge, the whole of knowledge is thus invested *in the real*, and knowledge never arises except as a relation inside its real object between the really distinct parts of that real object (*ibid.*, p. 31).

In contrast, Spinoza distinguishes between the object of knowledge and the real object:

> Spinoza warned us that the object of knowledge or essence was in itself absolutely distinct and different from the real

object . . . the *idea* of the circle, which is the *object* of
knowledge, must not be confused with the circle, which is
the *real object* (*ibid.*, p. 40).

According to Althusser, then, Spinoza makes a distinction
between the idea of the circle as the object of knowledge and a real
circle which can never be known as such. The distinction is similar
to but not identical with the one I make between a universal and a
particular. I do not conceive of a real object that differs from the
object known. Rather, the object as it is known is the only reality.
The concept or universal expresses this knowing, this reality,
linguistically or mentally. The concrete object is an instance of this
reality, a particular. (As we have already discussed, the concept
may express the knowing, the reality, one-sidedly.)

Althusser similarly cautions against thinking of knowledge as
coming to us via an infinite series of mediations, from reality itself.
He rejects the concept of origin, claiming that the concepts of
origin, original ground, genesis and mediation should be regarded
as suspect *a priori*. As my analysis talks of grounds and origins and
even mediations, it may seem contradictory to agree with
Althusser on this point. However, I share Althusser's rejection of
this ultimately empiricist mode of thinking. Therefore, I want to
distinguish my use of these terms from that which Althusser rightly
suspects.

In my work, origin refers to the process of production with all its
conditions. Origin does not refer to a reality or to a real object,
knowledge of which comes to us through mediations. Rather, an
object is always grounded in its process of production, the process
that we presuppose in our recognition and sense of the object, the
process by which our knowledge of the object is produced. This
ground is its origin. In other words, our knowledge of an object is
the product of an ongoing process of production and reproduction.
This notion of origin as an ongoing process of (re)production is to
be distinguished from a genetic notion of origin which refers to the
circumstances in which an object of knowledge first makes its
appearance. What I call origins in a process of production,
Althusser calls structure:

The object of Marx's study is therefore contemporary
bourgeois society, which is thought of as a historical *result*:
but the understanding of this society, far from being

obtained from the theory of the genesis of this result, is, on the contrary, obtained exclusively from the theory of the '*body*,' i.e., of the *contemporary structure of society* without its genesis intervening in any way whatsoever (*ibid.*, p. 65).

This is the same distinction Marx makes between a genetic history and a contemporary history. To illustrate, Marx's discussion of the enclosure acts, the importance of the discovery of the Americas and the expansion of trade is a sketch of a genetic history of capitalism. His analysis of how capital is (re)produced, on the other hand, exemplifies a contemporary history. The second type of reading treats the known object as a product and not as a thing whose meaning is simply given. The latter treatment characterizes everyday life.

Althusser: Marx's theoretical revolution

Althusser reminds us of Marx's critique of the 'naïve borrowing' from everyday life of the category 'price of labour' by classical political economy. As opposed to the knowledge and use of a term in everyday life, analysis (which is not naïve) inquires into the grounds of that term. Althusser presents the following quotation from Marx that brings together a concern for the production of knowledge with a critique of political economy. This quotation suggests that Marx's critique of political economy implicates everyday life as well:

> Classical political economy naïvely borrowed from everyday life the category 'price of labour' without any prior verification, and then asked the question, how is this price determined? (*ibid.*, p. 20).

Classical political economy recognized that demand and supply only explained the oscillation of labor's price above or below a certain figure. It was this figure that needed to be explained. According to Marx, in accounting for this figure, its object ceased to be labor, becoming instead labor power:

> *It thus unwittingly changed terrain* by substituting for the value of labour, up to this point, *the apparent object of its investigations*, the value of labour power, a power which

only exists in the personality of the labourer, and is as different from its function, labour, as a machine is from its performance (*ibid.*, pp. 20–21).

Marx carefully distinguishes labor from labor power. By 'labor' Marx means the actual work which he distinguishes from 'labor power,' which is capacity to do work in general. Classical political economy treats the knowledge or concept, 'value of labor,' as a given, a reality, concerning itself only with problems regarding that value, for example, how the value of labor relates to the price of labor and to the value of other commodities. In so doing it ends up conceiving of labor as labor power without acknowledging that it does so because it concerns itself with the determination of the value of labor. In other words, it addresses concrete, quantitative problems. Marx, on the other hand, questions the possibility of the concept, value of labor.

Classical political economists distinguish price from value in the following way. Price is the result of the relative oscillations of demand and supply. However, there must be some notion of the price of labor that can be determined even when demand and supply are in equilibrium. They then arrive at the subsistence level as the 'value' of labor.

The failure of the classical political economists to recognize the distinction between labor and labor power led them to conclude that they had explained the value of labor. Instead, they had actually accounted for the value of labor power:

> Hence, the course of the analysis had led . . . to their resolution of the so-called value of labour into the value of labour power. The result the analysis led to, therefore, was *not a resolution of the problem as it emerged at the beginning, but a complete change in the terms of that problem* (*ibid.*, p. 21).

Marx shows that it is not the value of labor (the value of the accomplishment of labor) that is being determined, but the value of labor power – the maintenance of human beings who can work. Thus labor is treated abstractly rather than as the acts of work or the products of work, thereby reducing labor to the capacity to work instead of treating it as the actual work that is accomplished.

Classical political economy shifts unself-consciously from labor to labor power. It never questioned the grounds of the ordinary conception of the price of labor. Rather, accepting the notion as given, it asked only how the price was determined. It did not ask how it was possible to conceive in the first place of something called 'price of labor.' This conception was taken as a starting-point and not as a result. Instead of a concern with grounds, it concerned itself with concrete and quantitative problems: whether labor power was getting more or less than its value, the relation of this value to that of commodities, to the rate of profit, etc.

Althusser (*ibid.*, p. 79) cites Marx as claiming, in a letter to Engels, that one of the best points in his book was the twofold character of labor as use value and exchange value. Marx stresses use value, the identification of labor with its specific usefulness, whereas classical economy tended to identify labor exclusively as labor power.

Marx's contribution does not come from reasoning about abstract value or use value. The knowledge of the distinction between use value and exchange value, between labor and labor power, is a result of grounding the concept, value, in its form of life, analyzing its possibility or its existence by showing that which produces and is presupposed by its sense. This contrasts with treating value as a concrete thing that is simply given or as a concept that comes from the mind rather than from a form of life.

Althusser distinguishes between Marx's analytic method and political economy's concrete method of treating 'economic facts.' According to Althusser, the latter method treats economic facts as absolute givens without questioning their givenness:

> Political economy gives itself as an object the domain of
> 'economic facts' which it regards as having the obviousness
> of facts: absolute givens which it takes as they 'give' them-
> selves, without asking them for any explanations. . . .
> Marx's whole attack is directed at this object, at its pre-
> tensions to the modality of a given object: Political
> Economy's pretensions being no more than the mirror
> reflection of its object's pretensions to have been *given it*.
> By posing the question of the 'givenness' of the object,
> Marx poses the question of the object itself, of its nature
> and limits, and therefore of the domain of its existence
> (*ibid.*, p. 159).

In the above statement, Althusser makes an important claim regarding the 'failure' of political economy. He tells us more than that political economy treats its object as given, whereas Marx does not. It is not that political economy makes a mistake or fails to perceive its object correctly. Rather, the object appears as a given thing, a unity, and political economy simply treats it as it appears, as a taken for granted thing in the world, a fact or absolute given. Hence, political economy does no less than a naïve or everyday treatment of the object.

The problem does not originate with political economy, but with its object which appears as an ahistorical, natural thing, an appearance that Marx questions but political economy does not. In other words, concrete theorizing as exemplified in political economy and dialectical phenomenology as exemplified in Marx's analytic theorizing presuppose a specific object: the commodity or value form.

Whereas Marx analyzes the value form by showing that which it presupposes, other political economists simply concern themselves with explaining the magnitude of value without analyzing value itself as a form of life. For Althusser, that which the object presupposes and which other political economists disregard is the object's complexity or structure. According to Althusser, Marx's theoretical revolution consists in substituting a model of determination by structure for a notion of linear causality:

> If economic phenomena are determined by their *complexity* (i.e. their structure) the concept of linear causality can no longer be applied to them as it has been hitherto. A different concept is required in order to account for the new form of causality required by the new definition of the object of Political Economy, by its 'complexity,' i.e. by its peculiar determination: the determination by a structure (*ibid.*, p. 184).

This new conception of causality, determination by a structure, constitutes Marx's new terrain, his transformation of the problematic of classical political economy. This is Marx's theoretical revolution. Just as I read Marx as substituting for linear causality the conception of embeddedness in a form of life, an analysis of the internal relations by which a social phenomenon reproduces itself, Althusser reads Marx as substituting determination by a structure, an analysis of the complexity of the object. Althusser's formulation seems almost identical to my own. Furthermore, just as my conception of form of life refers to a set of practices or mode of reproduction rather than a thing-like external structure, Althusser also stresses that his notion of structure refers to practices. Althusser describes Marx's revolution in theorizing as the development of

> a historico-dialectical materialism of *praxis*: that is, by a theory of the different specific levels of human practice (economic practice, political practice, ideological practice, scientific practice) in their characteristic articulations, based on the specific articulations of the unity of human society . . . Marx (introduced) a concrete conception of the specific differences that enables us to situate each particular practice in the specific differences of the social structure (Althusser, 1969, p. 229).

Thus, for Althusser, the complex structure or whole which determines an object is the complex of an historically given society. Such societies

> present themselves as totalities whose unity is constituted by a certain specific type of complexity, which introduces instances, that, following Engels, we can very schematically reduce to three: the economy, politics and ideology (*ibid.*, p. 231).

Althusser's conception of structure in terms of which one analyzes an object turns out to be a concrete one. He conceives of society as composed of external relations (articulations) among its specific parts, the economy, politics and ideology. Hence, society is the sum of its parts. This contrasts with my conception of society as a specific mode of social (re)production, the relations of subject to object, a totality of internal relations.

Although Althusser claims to take Marx's transformation of political economy for a fact without analyzing the mechanism that unleashed it and completed it, he does state that the change of terrain or transformed problematic was produced in very specific, complex and often dramatic conditions. I take it that Althusser means the political, economic and ideological conditions of the time. If, however, we accept Althusser's own critique of empiricism, we should not treat the transformed problematic as a thing that developed out of specific conditions of the time, but should treat its conditions of existence as its own internal structure, that which it presupposes and which makes it possible as an intelligible mode of theorizing, a relation of theorist to the object of theorizing. Otherwise, we are left with the same problem with which he begins his critique: empiricism itself. That is, one would have to look elsewhere than the theorizing and its object (capital), in order to account for the theorizing. He suggests that the conjunction of conditions that characterized the time in which Marx lived determined his theoretical revolution. His reference to Lenin's analysis of the Russian revolution illustrates Althusser's approach:

> Lenin's invocation of the 'existing conditions' in Russia was not a lapse into empiricism; he was analyzing the very existence of the complex whole of the process of Imperialism in Russia in that 'current situation' (*ibid.*, p. 207).

Despite Althusser's disclaimer that the term, 'conditions,' is not an empirical concept, the same critique applies. One must distinguish between an analysis of the conditions of sense, of possibility, and an analysis of the conditions of its concrete emergence in time and space. This is the same difference that Althusser recognized between an analysis of society in terms of its contemporary structure and an analysis of its genesis. Yet with respect to analyzing other objects such as individuals or Marx's theoretical revolution, Althusser implies that one should study the structure of the society rather than the internal structure of, or form of life presupposed by, individuals' activities or Marx's theorizing. Althusser fails to recognize this crucial difference. Yet it con- stitutes the difference between being analytic and being concrete. In treating the object known as independent of the practices pre- supposed in knowing the object, Althusser's theorizing and his concept of social structure turn out to be concrete, an alienated mode of theorizing. Thus his understanding of Marx's theoretical revolution, determination by a structure, ends up being in no way the same as my conception of Marx's theoretical revolution, embeddedness in a form of life, a relation of subject and object. That is why Althusser's work leads to a positivistic method of theorizing and why Althusser can renounce Marx's discussion of alienation as unscientific without seeing its essential relation to Marx's mode of theorizing and his analysis of capitalism.

O'Neill: critique of alienation

Althusser condemns all interpretations of Marx that bring in the concept of alienation or humanist philosophy, stressing instead Marx's scientific revolution as the discovery of social structure. In opposition, John O'Neill claims;

> Marx is not the critic of social structure as such. . . . His criticisms are ethical evaluations of the degree to which social structure realizes an ideal of authentic being, i.e. nonestranged or unalienated existence (1972, p. 119).

He recognizes a paradox in Althusser's work: that beginning with a phenomenological version of reading, he ends with positivist conclusions. 'For what is curious in Althusser's enterprise is the way he manages to reach positivist conclusions from what is an apparently phenomenological starting point' (1974a, p. 386).

O'Neill disagrees with Althusser that 'the subject of *Capital* is a process without a subject, namely a structure and not a historical process of alienation' (*ibid.*, p. 392). For O'Neill the critical question in *Capital* and in every work of Marx is, 'how is it possible that the being who produces everything should produce his own non-being? How is it that the presence of man is the history of the absence of man' (*ibid.*, p. 393). Thus, Marx's critique of political economy is essentially 'a humanist critique of the absence of man and his world-alienated production through the subjectivization of the principle of property' (*ibid.*, p. 399).

Unlike Althusser, for O'Neill, Marx's reading of classical economics, like Hegel's reading of the history of philosophy, is a

> phenomenology of the tradition of rationality, of the history of reason and unreason. Therefore, the object of capital is not its topic, i.e. the analysis of the structures of surplus value formation, but its *objective*, namely the recovery of the subjective axioms of objectification in alienated and non-alienated modes of experience. . . . For the same reason, *Capital* is not what Marx is writing about, because

the sense of its analysis feeds off the next stage of human development (*ibid.*, p. 396).

O'Neill is sensitive to Marx's analysis as a critique of production that is not self-conscious. He argues that 'what Marx is concerned with is human production which is *as such* rational and moral,' in other words, self-conscious production. For this reason, he rejects Habermas's interpretation that the foundations of Marx's method are positivistic and that the method, therefore, fails to provide an adequate conception of critical theory:

> By insisting that Marx tied the reflexivity of social science knowledge to the system of instrumental action, Habermas is able to argue that historical materialism lacks any adequate conception of critical theory and rests ultimately on a positivist epistemology (1972, pp. 247–8).

He rejects Habermas's reduction as well as Althusser's claim of an epistemological break between early philosophical Marx and later scientific Marx. Instead he reads historical materialism 'as a critique of the "mathematical" auspices of classical political economy and its imputations of individual conduct and social order' (*ibid.*, p. 260).

O'Neill: grounding alienation in relations of domination

While he is sensitive to and appreciates Marx's analysis in this regard, O'Neill interprets Marx as reducing the examination of all forms of estrangement to the 'basic' phenomenon of economic exploitation and alienation (O'Neill, 1972, p. 127):

> Marx believed that the basic source of the estrangement of man's freely, creative energies lay in the nature of the sociological and technological organization of work or labour. In Marx's later writings, the theory of alienation is isomorphic with the theory of the class structure of society (*ibid.*, p. 128).

For O'Neill, the power which derives from ownership of the means of production is only one type of power and authority relations that are inherent in any social structure. 'Unfortunately,

Marx's perception of the phenomenon of alienation is restricted to the forms of estrangement which appear in capitalist industrial society (*ibid.*, p. 129). The reason that O'Neill considers 'unfortunate' an analysis that restricts itself to the forms of estrangement attributable to capitalist society is the 'embarrassing conclusion' that 'once private property and the social division of labor are abolished, the phenomenon of alienation will disappear' (*ibid.*, pp. 153–4).

Furthermore, 'any social reform movement predicated on the basis of the abolition of *all* forms of the division of labor is fantastic' (*ibid.*, p. 135). This reading presumes that a division of labor refers to technical specialization, etc. Instead, I have been recommending reading division of labor to mean the separation of labor from its objective conditions of existence. In this way, one provides for a critique of alienation as well as grounds for its abolition.

Such a possibility is no longer tied to the abolition of private ownership of production but to the self-determination of labor by labor for labor. This, of course, presumes that labor has united and in so doing comes to recognize itself as social producer. Given a self-conscious unity of labor, the mediation of capital is not required. This reading no longer limits the possibility of alienation to the production of capital but to any activity conceived as a process of production, because in any activity the actor (re)produces itself as such. Alienation occurs with activity in which a divided subject has no control over the objective conditions of its existence.

In such a situation, the objective conditions of production would appear as objects without any subjectivity, as things given with nature or speech. Marx's analysis of capital, then, would be a prototype for analyzing all productions, all human activity, all objects that appear to have value or meaning independently of their relation to social (re)production.

Lukács: totality as process

Lukács's work may be understood as stressing the importance of thinking in terms of totality and social process as opposed to empirical things. The two former concepts correspond to my concepts of form of life and social (re)production. He quotes Marx: 'A cotton-spinning jenny is a machine for spinning cotton. Only in certain circumstances does it become capital' (Lukács, 1971, p. 13). He explains that

> the intelligibility of objects develops in proportion as we grasp their function in the totality to which they belong. This is why only the dialectical conception of totality can enable us to understand reality as a social process (*ibid.*, p. 13).

The consequence of seeing totality as a social process is that social existence can then be seen as a product, a product of human activity. Seeing human existence as a product of ongoing human activity results in the possibility of intervention, of social self-determination, self-conscious social production:

> Only when the core of existence stands revealed as a social process can existence be seen as the product, albeit the hitherto unconscious product, of human activity (*ibid.*, p. 19).

Lukács responds to a misinterpretation of the critique of empiricism. He explains that eschewing empirical reality is not an abandonment of reality:

> But in fact, to leave empirical reality behind can only mean that the objects of the empirical world are to be understood as aspects of a total social situation caught up in the process of historical change (*ibid.*, p. 162).

He quotes from the *Philosophy of Religion* by Hegel with regard to the impossibility of immediate knowledge. Following Hegel, he regards all knowledge as mediated. 'There is no immediate knowledge. Immediate knowledge is where we have no *consciousness* of mediation; but it is mediated for all that.' Hence, the true unity of knowing subject and known object is constituted in the process by which the knowledge is produced: the negation of the otherness of the object through the activity of a purposive subject.

Lukács does not account for the appearance of objects as things rather than aspects of a totality that is a process. He is more concerned to re-establish the dialectic of history such that objective forms of objects are transformed into a process. Recognizing this dialectic with respect to capital, provides for the possibility of the proletariat's discovery that it is itself the subject of this process:

> But if the reification of capital is dissolved into an unbroken process of production and reproduction, it is possible for the proletariat to discover that it is itself the subject of this process even though it is in chains and is for the time being unconscious of the fact (*ibid.*, p. 181).

Thus Lukács reads Marx as providing grounds for the proletariat's recognition of itself as the subject-object of history. However, his failure to explicate how analysis determines totality leads him into problems regarding the proletariat and class consciousness. That is, he fails to ground the concept of proletariat in totality as a process by which it produces itself as such. The proletariat and proletariat consciousness, then, become independent troubles ungrounded in a specific process of production that brings them into existence as such. In other words, for Lukács the proletariat and proletariat consciousness become divorced from the specific struggles in which they find themselves. In this way they become troubles to be solved by a party.

Merleau-Ponty: history, the proletariat and revolution

In *Adventures of the Dialectic*, Merleau-Ponty appears to resolve this problem for Lukács. He concerns himself precisely with Marx's reading of history and the proletariat. To begin his analysis of Marx's treatment of history, he considers Marx's reading of pre-capitalism as reflection from the point of view of capitalism on what preceded it (1973, p. 36). He interprets this as Marx's way of finding a meaning in history:

> When one says that Marxism finds a meaning in history, it should not be understood by this that there is an irresistible orientation toward certain ends but rather that there is, immanent in history, a problem or a question in relation to which what happens at each moment can be classified, situated, understood as progress or regression, compared with what happens at other moments, can be expressed in the same language, understood as a contribution to the

same endeavor, and can in principle furnish a lesson (*ibid.*, p. 38).

For Merleau-Ponty, just as Marx reads history in terms of a problem that is found to be immanent in it, Marx reads the proletariat similarly. The proletariat is not to be understood in terms of particular problems of particular workers, nor of a particular goal held by members of the proletariat. Citing Marx, he suggests a distinction between the concrete proletariat composed of individuals and the proletariat that is a product of analysis:

> The question is not what goal is envisaged for the time being by this or that member of the proletariat, or even by the proletariat as a whole. The question is what is the proletariat and what course of action will it be forced historically to take in conformity with its own nature (*ibid.*, p. 46).

Merleau-Ponty acknowledges theorizing as the process by which an object of knowledge such as the proletariat is produced:

> But then, even if Marxism and its philosophy of history are nothing else than the 'secret of the proletariat's existence,' it is not a secret that the proletariat itself possesses but one that the theoretician deciphers (*ibid.*).

But a problem seems to be inherent in this formulation: is this not to admit that it is still the theoretician who gives his meaning to history in giving his meaning to the existence of the proletariat? This would lead to a position of idealism or subjectivism where objects exist only in the mind. However, following Lukács, he claims that the proletariat is neither subject nor object for the theoretician. Rather, Marx introduces a new mode of existence: praxis (*ibid.*, p. 47). The theorist gives meaning to history or to the concept of proletariat by analyzing the practices that constitute the proletariat, in other words by conceiving of proletariat as praxis (its form of life). The problem that animates Merleau-Ponty's work in the *Adventures of the Dialectic* is the problem of treating the proletariat as the objectification of the dialectic:

> If one concentrates all the negativity and all the meaning of history in an existing historical formation, the working

class, then one has to give a free hand to those who
represent it in power, since all that is other is an enemy.
Then there no longer is an opposition, no longer a manifest
dialectic. . . . There is no dialectic without opposition or
freedom (*ibid.*, p. 207).

The problem of the absence of dialectic, the end of history,
becomes identical with the problem of revolution:

> It is no accident that all known revolutions have degener-
> ated: it is because as established regimes they can never be
> what they were as movements; precisely because it suc-
> ceeded and ended up as an institution, the historical move-
> ment is no longer itself. Revolutions are true as movements
> and false as regimes (*ibid.*).

Therefore, Merleau-Ponty renounces revolution without de-
nouncing it. He believes that revolutionary movements are
'justified by their own existence, since they are proof that the
society in which they arise does not allow the workers to live.'
However, he recommends a new liberalism, a non-communist Left
in which revolutionary movements are accepted only as:

> a useful menace, as a continual call to order, that we do
> not believe in the solution of the social problem through
> the power of the proletarian class, or its representatives,
> that we expect progress only from a conscious action which
> will confront itself with the judgment of an opposition. . . .
> For us a noncommunist left is this double position, posing
> social problems in terms of struggle and refusing the
> dictatorship of the proletariat (*ibid.*, p. 226).

Furthermore, 'a noncommunist left is no more linked to free
enterprise than to the dictatorship of the proletariat.' The critique
of revolution, of establishing revolutionary régimes, and ultimately
of Marxism owes itself to Marx's identifying the proletariat as the
embodiment of critique, of negativity. Given this identification,
Marxism is left in the embarrassing position for Merleau-Ponty of
advocating a non-dialectical solution – the dictatorship of the
proletariat or its representatives. He rejects this solution in favor
of posing social problems in terms of struggle, a form of action that
confronts itself with the judgment of an opposition.

The strength of both Merleau-Ponty's and Lukács's reading of Marx resides in their analytic treatment of the concept of the proletariat. For them, the proletariat becomes a reading rule. This means that the 'proletariat' represents a way of treating all activity as dialectical experience from which to learn. In this way, these theorists anticipate Habermas's concern for the relation of theory, praxis and the proletariat. In their theorizing, the relation of theory, praxis and the proletariat becomes a pedagogical relation in which theory learns from the proletariat who in turn translates this learning (theory) into new praxis. The proletariat stands for a reflexive relationship of theory to praxis, a mode of self-learning. Hence, Habermas identifies this pedagogical mode with a dialogical relation: theory becomes a dialogue with experience – the proletariat. Similarly, Lukács conceives of 'mode of production' as a pedagogical mode of production. For him, the Party represents Theory which learns from in order to inform the proletariat.

However, both Lukács and Merleau-Ponty revert to a concrete reading of the proletariat. Rather than seeing the party or theory as a metaphor for self-learning or self-consciousness, they interpret these concepts concretely. Instead of the party or theory representing the self-consciousness of the proletariat, the party becomes a separate entity. This makes the proletariat into a concrete existent that relates (externally) to a party rather than the party being an internal relation of the proletariat to its form of life. Instead of doing a critique of the Communist Party for becoming a separate entity from the proletariat, they begin from an external relation of proletariat and party which enables Merleau-Ponty to conclude that the problems in this relationship derive from Marx's conception of the proletariat as embodiment of the dialectic.

A concrete reading makes the proletariat into whatever actions are engaged in or intentions held by particular workers or those representing the workers. Such concrete reading makes it possible to adopt the conviction that any action or violence taken by representatives of the proletariat must be justifiable by virtue of Marx's analysis of the proletariat as the embodiment of the dialectic.

Instead of seeing the proletariat as the embodiment of a dialectic between self-conscious and unself-conscious action, a concrete reading has the proletariat referring to those actions that are intended to accomplish a solely political or economic revolution, those actions intended to be progressive in the development of a non-capitalist economy or to any actions advocated by individuals representing the proletariat, particularly a party.

In contrast, an analytic reading interprets the proletariat's revolutionary mode of existence as referring to the struggle by labor to overcome its existence as a commodity subject to the vagaries of the market. As labor unites in order better to accomplish its struggle, it realizes itself as socialized labor. This means that socialized labor that exists in itself (which is made possible by capitalism) becomes socialized labor for itself. This, in turn, makes possible the realization of socialism as a direct, unmediated and, hence, self-conscious mode of production by socialized labor.

Unable to distinguish their analytic reading of the proletariat as the embodiment of the dialectic from a concrete reading of the proletariat as a narrowly understood political or economic group, they must either, as in the case of Lukács, accept all actions by a party which represents the proletariat or they must find fault with Marx's analysis itself as leading to violence and repression as in the case of Merleau-Ponty:

> There must be something in the (Marxist) critique itself that germinates the defects in the action. We found this ferment in the Marxist idea of a critique historically embodied, of a class which is the suppression of itself, which, in its representatives, results in the conviction of being the universal in action, in the right to assert oneself without restriction, and in unverifiable violence (*ibid.*).

According to Merleau-Ponty, if one accepts the proletariat as critique, then one must accept anything done in the name of the proletariat. This problem highlights the need for a reflexive reading of Marx and of the proletariat. Reading Marx's analysis concretely results in precisely the problem that Merleau-Ponty rightly condemns: the problem of justifying tyranny or any action as the will of the proletariat and any opposition as the enemy of the proletariat. A reflexive reading precisely avoids such consequences. Instead of reading the proletariat as workers, one reads the proletariat in terms of its praxis, a form of life in which actors are separated from the objective conditions of their actions.

Such separation implies the possibility of unity. In other words, the proletariat becomes a reading rule for (producing) alienation and the possibility of overcoming alienation. The proletariat is not a group of individuals; it is a form of life. Hence, to act in the name of the proletariat is to act on the possibility of socialized self-determination, the possibility of the free, social individual, the elimination of all external mediations (between subject and object) that alienate the social actor from its conditions of existence, whether the mediations are the party, the bureaucracy, the state or capital. This leaves socially conscious praxis as the only mediation between subject and object.

Summary: consciousness and history

To sum up, each theorist treats Marx concretely. Habermas interprets mode of production as instrumental action – the production of things. Althusser conceives of social structure concretely as various levels of activity in society and their articulations: the political, economical and ideological. O'Neill, while criticizing Habermas's notion of production and Althusser's positivist conclusion, ends up doing the same with respect to the concept of social division of labor. Lukács recognizes the need to ground all concepts in a totality. However, Lukács must look to a party in order to determine action. He does not see struggle as inherent in the totality independently of an external party. Finally, Merleau-Ponty ends up treating revolution concretely. Because he treats it concretely, he must confront the problem that emerges when a revolutionary group – a party or a government – representing itself as the proletariat denies all opposition as anti-revolutionary or regressive and inimical to the proletariat.

In contrast, I suggest that all of these concepts reflexively refer to their conditions of existence, the dialectic of alienated labor: production in which the subject is divorced from its objective conditions of existence. They all point to the possibility of production that is a self-conscious unity of subject and object.

The contradiction between self-conscious social production and unself-conscious social production constitutes the problematic that is the impulse for the readings that make up this tradition. My own reading also originates with this problematic. All of the five

263

theorists discussed here seek to eschew the concrete view of Marx's method of theorizing. They all read Marx as grounding knowledge and individual experience. However, they end up treating concretely as objective things in the outside world some of Marx's key concepts: mode of production, social structure, division of labor, proletariat and revolution. To what can we attribute this consistent return to concrete theorizing by critics who explicitly reject it? Answering this question requires a consideration of the concept of consciousness and its relation to history.

Consciousness and production
The trouble in all these readings of Marx seems to derive from the separation of consciousness and activity such that consciousness becomes a thing, a content in itself rather than internal to activity, a form of life. There are two versions of consciousness here. The first, and the one that is at the heart of the difficulty, is consciousness as what individuals think, as emanating from individuals. The other, and the one adhered to in the method of dialectical phenomenology, is consciousness as internal to activity such that we talk of conscious activity. The latter I call 'subjectivity.'

In linguistics, there is a tradition associated with the name of Wittgenstein that acknowledges the autonomy of language. Language does not originate with the individual, but is understood as an ongoing, social form of life. I use the term 'form of life' similarly in order to reconcile the social character of activity with the social character of consciousness, rather than treating the latter as originating with the individual.

The concern with history and social change brings most theorists to consider consciousness. The first rule I put forth for reproducing Marx's method of theorizing deals with consciousness. It states: treat concepts as grounded in a form of life. Consciousness is always within a form of life that makes it possible. This means that consciousness, even critical consciousness, does not stand outside of its form of life. The first rule can be restated: consciousness is grounded in its process of production.

The unity of ideas or consciousness and production has been understood by some readers as the relation of superstructure to base. However, production is usually conceived as a separate sphere of activity (division of labor, instrumental activity, the economy) and consciousness another sphere (culture or ideology). The problem is often seen as a question of which comes first, consciousness or production, or as a question of their relative autonomy. Max Weber, for instance, reads Marx as attributing priority to production, while relegating consciousness to an epiphenomenal realm – the superstructure. Weber himself, on the other hand, claims that the relationship of consciousness and production is a causal chain with each, in turn, acting upon and influencing the other (Weber, 1958, p. 27). Therefore, the direction of the relationship cannot be known in advance but must be studied empirically.

For those, like Weber, who treat the relationship between consciousness and production as problematic, the two are conceived as separate. This means that either consciousness precedes activity, or activity precedes consciousness. However, some interpreters of Marx argue that consciousness as a rule does not stand separately. Instead, they stress that consciousness is itself integral to activity or production in the broad, social sense of producing or reproducing any social phenomenon. That is what my first rule does by grounding consciousness in a form of life. According to these interpreters, Marx begins from a notion of purposive activity as a unity of consciousness and action – conscious activity. Only when consciousness is separated (or alienated) from activity – taking the form of rationalizations for already existing activity – does the term 'superstructure' make sense. As Avineri points out:

> the distinction between 'material base' and 'superstructure' is not a distinction between 'matter' and 'spirit' (as Engels in his later writings would have had it), but between conscious human activity, aimed at the creation and preservation of the conditions of human life, and human consciousness which furnishes reasons, rationalizations and modes of legitimation and moral justification for the specific forms that activity takes (Avineri, 1968, p. 76).

Nevertheless, the importance of consciousness as a separate factor continues to crop up with regard to revolution and social change. Some theorists claim that Marx's work lends itself to the interpretation of revolutionary consciousness as a mere 'epiphenomenon of "objective" conflicts between productive forces and conditions of production' (Wellmer, 1971, p. 97). They argue

265

that this reduces the human by making social change independent of human volition. They prefer instead a conception of individual consciousness as a separate and crucial factor in the development of revolution and the movement of history. In contrast with this view of revolutionary consciousness and mode of production as being different and separate with one preceding or causing the other, I hold that Marx treats consciousness as grounded in its mode of production.

The present work shows consciousness not as a thing, the content of mind: personal intentions, attitudes, beliefs or facts, but as a way of being alive in history. This formulation of consciousness as a form of life becomes a way out of the dilemma posed by the base/superstructure distinction. Revolutionary consciousness means revolutionary form of life. Instead of talking about base and superstructure, economy and society, this mode of theorizing talks about (re)production. Hence a revolutionary form of life is a revolutionary mode of (re)production. To know any social phenomenon as a form of life, we must analyze how it is (re)produced.

Changing the terms, base and superstructure, to form of life or mode of (re)production is not to deny the problem of ideology. Rather, it addresses the problem of ideology as a form of life that is false. A form of life is false in not treating itself as history, as dialectical (re)production, hence, it is one that is unself-conscious. Dialectical phenomenology grounds social phenomena that appear to be things in themselves in a form of life by showing how they are produced.

A form of life or dialectical reproduction refers to any activity as an active, purposive relation of a subject to its object by which a subject comes to realize itself and its object. In acting on its object, the actor comes to know itself as subject of that object. In other words, the object makes possible or produces the subject as such. Conversely, in relating to the object, the qualities that make up the object for the subject come to be known. In this sense, the subject makes possible or produces its object as such.

This work shows how to see dialectic, the (re)production of a subject/object as a feature of every aspect of thought and action. Doing so, shows the falsity of a form of life that denies dialectic. In going farther and showing the grounds for a false form of life in separation and contradiction, Marx shows how such a false form of

266

life is also a revolutionary one. However, this notion of a revolutionary form of life tends to be puzzling. How can Marx account for revolutionary change or the movement of history if he denies a causal role to individuals and consciousness? What is a revolutionary form of life? How can there be human intervention that we know as revolution or radical social change?

My whole reading of Marx addresses this question. It does so by reading Marx as an inquiry into the conditions that make for a false or unself-conscious form of life. In so doing, his analysis shows the possibility of human intervention by grounding that possibility in the form of life itself, its internal relations. For Marx, a form of life is a subjectivity, a totality of internal relations. Revolutionary social change is made possible by the contradictory character of its internal relations, contradictions that cannot be resolved without radically changing the form of life. For Marx, in other words, the contradictions that make for an unself-conscious form of life also produce oppositions that make possible its eventual dissolution, and with it, the development of its opposite, a self-conscious form of life.

Consciousness and revolution

That its internal relations are contradictory makes capitalism a revolutionary form of life. But what do they mean for everyday life? How do they get transformed into revolutionary struggles and social change? The contradictions result in struggles of labor in opposition to those of capital. These opposing tendencies expressed as struggles of opposition otherwise known as class conflict, make capitalism an ongoing revolutionary form of life. These oppositions or struggles cannot be finally resolved except by suspending the form of life itself – the (re)production of capital.

Labor's struggle may be understood as a struggle to overcome its status as a commodity. While knowing itself as use value, as abilities and qualities that have social value independently of a market, it can only realize itself as exchange value. This means that, like any other commodity, it is subject to fluctuations of the market. In this form of life, labor's struggle to realize itself becomes a struggle to overcome the consequences of a market economy. It may be thought of as a struggle to assert itself as use value over itself as exchange value. Overcoming the consequences of the market ultimately requires suspending the conditions for (re)producing itself as exchange value. These conditions include capital and wage labor. Suspending these (labor's ceasing to produce itself as exchange value) would constitute a revolution in how people (re)produce their social existence. The struggles to overcome the consequences of being a commodity, the contradiction between being use value and exchange value, the struggles to overcome the vicissitudes of the market, constitute revolutionary struggle whether it is recognized as such or not.

The concept of revolutionary consciousness as separate from and preceding revolutionary activity makes no sense in this notion of form of life. As a single phenomenon, revolutionary conscious activity against capitalism begins with independent struggles of various segments of labor and culminates with united class-wide struggle. The latter comes about as labor learns the importance of unity from the experiences of individual struggle. Class-wide struggle (socialized labor for itself) brings with it the possibility of socialism, production by socialized labor for itself, without the mediation of capital and the capitalist class. Struggles come from the contradictions involved in (re)producing exchange value in its developed form as capital. Revolutionary consciousness and revolutionary activity by labor are not separate things, one preceding the other, but are united in the activity of (re)producing capital with its opposing tendencies – its positing labor as exchange value while presupposing it as use value, its positing capital as exchange value while presupposing it as labor.

As Marx indicates, revolutionary struggle may rely on religious, philosophical or other ideas for justification or explanation. But this differentiation between ideas and activity derives from the separation of purpose and activity, a situation in which activity does not realize itself as intrinsically purposive, the situation of labor under capitalism. This means activity that has only extrinsic value or meaning – alienated labor whose value or meaning comes from outside itself. Ideas, conversely, appear to be ungrounded things in themselves, whose existence seems to come from mind as subjective notions (the ordinary understanding of ideology) or from external things as objective facts (a different version of ideology). Both of these versions of ideology – ideas that are treated independently of their production – have been referred to in this work as concrete theorizing.

The differentiation between ideas and activity ends when

activity achieves unity with consciousness. The former presupposes a divided subject and object, a subjectivity divided into opposing tendencies. In capitalism, the divided object, use value and exchange value, presupposes a divided subject, proletariat and capitalist. Its opposite presupposes a united subject/object, the development of the free, social individual, as the beginning and end (the telos), the point of departure and the point of return, to use Marx's words, of all social activity. Reasons external to (the purpose of the) activity would not be needed to justify activity. Rather, all activity would be open to question in terms of the purposes it was intended to realize, purposes that always relate directly to the development of a free, social individual without the mediation of having to realize exchange value.

The need for revolutionary consciousness is a problem for theorizing that sees activity and consciousness as externally related, theorizing that merely reflects the condition of alienated labor without overcoming it. Theorizing that is dialectical phenomenology struggles to overcome alienated consciousness as the other side of alienated labor. Instead of a concern for revolutionary consciousness as a thing in itself, separate from but necessary for revolutionary activity, dialectical phenomenology concerns itself with the self-contradictory character of our form of life in which consciousness and activity are separated.

In so doing, dialectical phenomenology displays the possibility of a non-alienated mode of production. Like Marx's conception of the proletariat, the conception of dialectical phenomenology shows how one side of a contradictory whole presupposes an opposing side. Just as labor opposes capital, dialectical phenomenology opposes consciousness that appears as an independent, ungrounded thing – ideology. The opposition consists in showing grounds, the presuppositions that make that consciousness possible but which the latter denies or represses. In so doing, dialectical phenomenology shows the self-contradictory character of consciousness which denies or represses grounds much like labor shows the self-contradictory character of capital which denies or represses use value.

Posing the problem of a need for revolutionary consciousness is a version of alienated theorizing that does not know grounds, theorizing that does not know the essential unity of consciousness and activity. Hence, it does not see its formulation of the problem as a product of the separation of labor and consciousness. It is itself an unself-conscious mode of theorizing. A self-conscious one would inquire into its own possibility. It would ask, how is it possible to see revolutionary consciousness as a problem. It would then see that such a possibility presupposes an external relation of consciousness and activity such that one precedes the other. Even further, it would see that this conception fails to account for the possibility of consciousness. Instead, alienated theorizing treats consciousness as a thing, a problem to be dealt with by studies of public opinion and research on communications.

For concrete theorizing, consciousness is not a property of social activity, but a property of individuals independently of social activity. Given this presumption, alienated theorizing goes on to ask how the individual acquires its consciousness? The answer becomes through personal experiences and perception – biography – hence studies on public opinion formation. Or through the indoctrination by others – education and socialization – hence research on communications. If this is the case, the problem of developing a revolutionary consciousness would call for providing appropriate experiences and modes of perception or proper indoctrination by others – education and socialization. However, the solution presupposes two types of people: the providers of experience or the indoctrinators who have the right consciousness and the recipients or those who need to be indoctrinated. This is the same problem that Marx addresses in his third thesis on Feuerbach, in which he criticizes the materialist doctrine for having to divide society into two parts, one of which is superior to society. It raises the question of who will educate the educators.

The question points to the impossibility of the solution and the impossibility of the original problem. In other words, the problem of a revolutionary consciousness turns out to be a false problem or an inadequate concept, a form of false consciousness – a concept that denies grounds. Marx calls such concepts, 'one-sided abstractions.' They refer to concrete things in themselves of which analysis shows the impossibility by inquiring into grounds.

The problem of consciousness and the individual raises an issue that has plagued sociology since its inception. How does one account for social phenomena without relying on a utilitarian version of individual psychology, which Marx in his ninth thesis on Feuerbach refers to as the observation of particular individuals and of civil society (Bottomore and Rubel, 1956, p. 69)? As a reaction against psychologism or explaining social facts by recourse to individual mental states, sociology sets up supra-individual categories such as society, social system, social institution, role, etc. These categories, in turn, have led to the charge of reification, of failing to recognize that social facts were social creations made possible by individuals. This criticism, in turn, brought a turning to the study of individuals in interaction which had its own counter-reaction that such studies could not account for larger issues of economic exploitation or revolution.

By denying the notion of consciousness as a property of individuals and treating individuals and consciousness as a property of social activity, dialectical phenomenology runs the risk of seeming to deny the importance of the individual in favor of some supra-individual entity like capitalism, as if one could explain all aspects of social life *a priori* by reference to capitalism or class conflict. It should be stressed that I do not substitute some larger thing-like entity. Instead the rule to ground individuals and consciousness in a form of life refers to form of life as process of (re)production. Dialectical phenomenology treats individuals and their acts as products of social activity that they themselves (re)produce either self-consciously, or as with capitalism unself-consciously. In other words, the individual must be understood not as a thing within some larger entity like society, but as actively engaged in social (re)production.

Consequently the concept of individual consciousness as a thing, either an epiphenomenal thing (dependent variable) or as an independent thing in itself (independent variable) becomes dissolved by treating it in terms of process, the practices by which human beings (re)produce that consciousness, their acts and themselves. These practices engaged in by individuals constitute a mode of (re)production as either a self-conscious one, or an unself-conscious one. The (re)production of capital illustrates the latter type of (re)production. All acts and concepts may be similarly analyzed. This does not mean explaining them *a priori* by reference to capitalism or class conflict, but by showing the form of life that they presuppose, the practices by which people (re)produce them and in the process (re)produce themselves.

Conclusion

The theorists discussed in this chapter, despite the problems pointed out, do make up a tradition of reading Marx into which my own reading fits. However, on its own, the analytic tradition within Marxism fails to be consistent in its commitment to a non-concrete reading of Marx. By drawing on an analytic tradition within phenomenological social science (particularly the works of Blum, 1974a and 1974b; Brown, 1977; Douglas, 1970; Fischer, 1978; Garfinkel, 1967; McHugh *et al.*, 1974; Piccone, 1971; Psathas, 1973; Roche, 1973; Smart, 1976) as well as within Marxism, I put forth a method of theorizing and reading, the method of dialectical phenomenology, that seeks to avoid the pitfalls stressed in this chapter. Just as phenomenology made possible my reading of Marx's text, Marx's text made possible my reformulation of the phenomenological approach: dialectical phenomenology.

Opposed to a concrete method based solely or largely on empirical observation, this method begins with the recognition that all meaning or consciousness must be grounded as a social accomplishment in its mode of production. Dialectical phenomenology, as a mode of theorizing, inquires into grounds of social phenomena. It conceives self-conscious production, reflexive theorizing and analytic socialism as different aspects of the same form of life. Furthermore, it shows how alienated labor, positivism and the production of capital are different aspects of a concrete form of life. I use Marx's analysis of capital to illustrate this method of theorizing, dialectical phenomenology.

My analysis of Marx grounds itself in the dialectic of unself-conscious theorizing and its negation. The concepts that this analysis leads me to use – 'form of life,' 'mode of theorizing,' 'internal relations,' 'grounds,' etc. – should be understood as rules for reading. These concepts, in other words, add up to a way of reading Marx in terms of the dialectic of concrete theorizing and its negation. Similarly, Marx's concepts should be treated as reading rules. They are ways of 'reading' political economy in terms of the dialectic of alienated production and its negation.

An analytic reading inquires into the presuppositions of the sense of phenomena which appear to be things in themselves. A phenomenon such as money or greed appears concrete in so far as it appears to be a thing in itself – given, taken for granted, natural.

Treating social, human-made phenomena as given, makes them reified and hence oppressive. By contrast, analytic theorizing is critical and liberating. For such theorizing shows social phenomena to be ongoing social accomplishments and, therefore, subject to human intervention.

Thus, as Freire puts it: 'scientific revolutionary humanism cannot, in the name of the revolution, treat the oppressed as objects to be analyzed and (based on that analysis) presented with prescriptions for behavior' (Freire, 1972, p. 129). Instead, analysis must enter into the life of the oppressed, must learn the life of the oppressed in order to grasp with the oppressed the conditions of that oppression. Analysis becomes a critique of that form of life by 'laying bare' the conditions that produce it. By grounding social phenomena in the form of life that produces them as objects that appear to be independent, natural things in themselves, analysis becomes a critique of that form of life.

Treating concepts and actions as social products, allows us to recognize not only the historically specific character of our concepts and actions, but also the possibility of change from within. Such inquiry becomes a form of critical and liberating self-education. Analytic theorizing, thus, becomes a critique of alienated education as a form of alienated production. This notion may correspond to that intended by O'Neill's statement that the education of the people is always the education of the educators themselves (1974b, p. 64). Critical thinking, for O'Neill, makes language the instrument of decolonization (*ibid.*).

As I have conceived of it, in sum, dialectical phenomenology consists of: 1 the dialectic as a struggle between the divided elements of a social unity; and 2 phenomenology as the study of the process by which a form of life produces our consciousness or knowledge. Dialectical phenomenology offers a way to see just how subjects and objects that appear as separate and indifferent to each other reciprocally produce and presuppose each other.

This work reformulates sociology's concern with forms of life as a science of social (re)production. This conception should not be equated with a science of the economy in the restricted sense of producing things to be bought and sold. Sociology concerns itself with any subjects and their objects, not just the subjects of the economy. It analyzes any subject *qua* subject which necessarily means any object *qua* object.

273

Thus sociological theorizing as self-conscious study of a form of life begins and ends with social (re)production in the broad sense of human subjects producing and reproducing themselves and their objects. This reformulation of sociological theorizing grounds the conception of dialectical phenomenology and my consequent reading of Marx.

BIBLIOGRAPHY

Althusser, L. (1969), *For Marx*, trans. Ben Brewster, New York, Pantheon Books.

Althusser, L. and Balibar, E. (1970), *Reading Capital*, trans. Ben Brewster, New York, Random House.

Appelbaum, R. (1978), 'Marx's theory of the falling rate of profit: towards a dialectical analysis of structural social change', *American Sociological Review*, vol. 43, no. 1.

Avineri, S. (1968), *The Social and Political Thought of Karl Marx*, Cambridge University Press.

Berger, P. and Luckmann, T. (1966), *The Social Construction of Reality*, New York, Doubleday.

Berger, P. and Pullberg, S. (1966), 'Reification and the sociological critique of consciousness', *New Left Review*, no. 35, reprinted from *History and Theory*, Spring 1965.

Blum, A. (1970a), 'On theorizing', Douglas, J. (ed.), *Understanding Everyday Life*, Chicago, Aldine.

Blum, A. (1970b), 'The corpus of knowledge as a normative order', in McKinney, J. and Tiryakian, E. (eds), *Theoretical Sociology*, New York, Appleton-Century-Crofts.

Blum, A. (1973), 'Reading Marx', *Sociological Inquiry*, vol. 1.

Blum, A. (1974a), 'Positive thinking', *Theory and Society*, vol. 1, no. 3, Fall.

Blum, A. (1974b), *Theorizing*, London, Heinemann.

Blum, A. and McHugh, P. (1971), 'The social ascription of motives', *American Sociological Review*, vol. 36, no. 1.

Bottomore, T. B. and Rubel, M. (1956), eds, *Karl Marx: Selected Writings in Sociology and Social Philosophy*, trans. T. B. Bottomore with foreword by Erich Fromm, New York: McGraw Hill.

Brown, M. (1977), '"Ethnomethodology" as dialectical materialism', paper presented, annual meeting American Sociological Association, Chicago.

Douglas, J. (ed.) (1970), *Understanding Everyday Life*, Chicago, Aldine.

Bibliography

Durkheim, E. (1961), *The Elementary Forms of the Religious Life*, New York, Crowell-Collier.
Fischer, G. (1978), 'Self rule or 1984', in *Ways to Self Rule: Beyond Marxism and Anarchism*, New York, Exposition Press.
Freire, P. (1972), *Pedagogy of the Oppressed*, New York, Seabury Press.
Freud, S. (1959), 'Obsessions and phobias; their psychical mechanisms and their aetiology', Vol. 1; 'A connection between a symbol and a symptom', Vol. 2; 'Repression', Vol. 4; 'Fetishism' and 'Splitting of the ego in the defensive process', Vol. 5, in Strachey, J. (ed.), *Collected Papers*, New York, Basic Books.
Garfinkel, H. (1967), *Studies in Ethnomethodology*, New Jersey, Prentice-Hall.
Gould, C. (1973–4), 'The woman question: philosophy of liberation and the liberation of philosophy', *The Philosophical Forum*, vol. 5, nos 1–2, Fall–Winter.
Gouldner, A. (1970), *The Coming Crisis of Western Sociology*, New York, Basic Books.
Habermas, J. (1971), *Knowledge and Human Interests*, Boston, Beacon Press.
Habermas, J. (1973), *Theory and Practice*, Boston, Beacon Press.
Habermas, J. (1975), 'Towards a reconstruction of historical materialism', *Theory and Society*, vol. 2, no. 3.
Hegel, G. (1967), *The Phenomenology of Mind*, trans. J. B. Baillie, New York, Harper & Row.
Heidegger, M. (1971), 'A Dialogue on Language' in *On the Way to Language*, trans. P. D. Hertz, New York, Harper & Row.
Lukács, G. (1971), *History and Class Consciousness*, Cambridge, M.I.T. Press.
McHugh, P. (1968), *Defining the Situation*, New York, Bobbs-Merrill.
McHugh, P. (1970a), 'A common sense conception of deviance', in Dreitzel, H. P. (ed.), *Recent Sociology No. 2: Patterns of Communicative Behavior*, New York, Macmillan.
McHugh, P. (1970b), 'On the failure of positivism', in Douglas, J. (ed.), *Understanding Everyday Life*, Chicago, Aldine.
McHugh, P., Raffel, S., Foss, D. and Blum, A. (1974), *On the Beginning of Social Inquiry*, London, Routledge & Kegan Paul.
Marx, K. (1963), *Karl Marx: Early Writings*, trans. T. B. Bottomore (ed.), with 'Foreword' by Erich Fromm, New York, McGraw-Hill.
Marx, K. (1967), *Capital*, vol. 1, New York, International Publications.
Marx, K. (1971), *The Grundrisse: Karl Marx*, trans. David McLellan (ed.), New York, Harper & Row.
Marx, K. (1973). *Grundrisse*, trans. Martin Nicolaus, New York, Random House.
Merleau-Ponty, M. (1973), *Adventures of the Dialectic*, Evanston, Northwestern University Press.
Nicolaus, M. (1968), 'The unknown Marx', *New Left Review*, vol. 48,

276

March–April; reprinted in Blackburn, R. (ed.) (1973), *Ideology in Social Science*, New York, Random House.

O'Neill, J. (1972), *Sociology as a Skin Trade*, New York, Harper & Row.

O'Neill, J. (1974a), 'For Marx against Althusser', *The Human Context*, vol. VI, no. 2, Summer.

O'Neill, J. (1974b), 'Le langage et la decolonisation: Fanon et Freire', trans. Francine Lacon-Okuda, *Sociologie et Sociétés*, vol. VI, no. 2.

Ollman, B. (1971), *Alienation: Marx's Conception of Man in Capitalist Society*, Cambridge University Press.

Piccone, P. (1971), 'Phenomenological Marxism', *Telos*, no. 9.

Piccone, P. (1975), 'Reading the *Grundrisse*: beyond "Orthodox" Marxism', *Theory and Society*, vol. 2, no. 2, Summer.

Postone, M. and Reinicke, H. (1975), 'On Nicolaus' "Introduction to the *Grundrisse*"', Telos, no. 22, Winter.

Psathas, G. (ed.) (1973), *Phenomenological Sociology: Issues and Applications*, New York, John Wiley.

Roche, M. (1973), *Phenomenology, Language and the Social Sciences*, London, Routledge & Kegan Paul.

Rossides, D. (1978), *The History and Nature of Sociological Theory*, Boston, Houghton, Mifflin.

Rovatti, P. A. (1972), 'Fetishism and economic categories', *Telos*, no. 14, Winter.

Rovatti, P. A. (1973a), 'Critical theory and phenomenology', *Telos*, no. 15, Spring.

Rovatti, P. A. (1973b), 'The critique of fetishism in Marx's *Grundrisse*', *Telos*, no. 17, Fall.

Schmidt, A. (1971), *The Concept of Nature in Marx*, New York, Humanities Press.

Smart, B. (1976), *Sociology, Phenomenology and Marxian Analysis*, London, Routledge & Kegan Paul.

Weber, M. (1950), *General Economic History*, trans. Frank H. Knight, Glencoe, Free Press.

Weber, M. (1958), *The Protestant Ethic and the Spirit of Capitalism*, trans. Talcott Parsons, New York, Charles Scribner's.

Wellmer, A. (1971), *Critical Theory of Society*, New York, Herder.

Wittgenstein, L. (1967), *Philosophical Investigations*, Oxford, Basil Blackwell.

INDEX

abstractions: concepts versus,
20–2, 34; exchange values as,
163–4; grounding of, 236, 244;
individuals ruled by, 130
agriculture, 149, 152
alienation, 24–5, 123; Althusser's
rejection of, 253–4; consciousness and, 269; dialectic of community and, 237; of labor from
its products, 158–9; non-
alienated labor and, 134–8;
O'Neill on, 254–6; of proletariat, 263; as property right,
172; as relation of individual to
production of exchange value,
132–4
Althusser, Louis, 18, 23, 234,
244–55, 263
analytical theorizing, 16–17;
concrete versus, 233; proletariat
in, 262; reading Marx using,
272–3; as self-conscious theorizing, 62; subject and object in,
159–62
animated reading, 18–19
antiquity as pre-capitalist form,
110–12, 120, 150; exchange
value in, 187–8; money in,
189–90
anxiety, 79–80
aqueducts, 109
asceticism, 78, 79
Asiatic pre-capitalist forms,
107–9, 148–50

Athens, 97–8
Avineri, Shlomo, 265

Balibar, E., 23
Bank of France, 212–16
barter, 164
Bastiat, Claude Frédéric, 50
Blum, Alan, 16, 17
bourgeois society, 196; revolutionizing of, 219–20
bourgeois theorizing, 18;
ahistoricism of, 41–3; capital
legitimated in, 171; Marx as
negation of, 241–2; see also
concrete theorizing

Calvinism, 79
capital (capitalism): class struggle
in, 179; community self-
knowledge in, 148; contradictions of, 209–10; depreciation
of, 217–18; deriving contradictions from, 196–203; devaluation of, 203–7; development
of individual under, 122–3;
exchange in, 173–5; exchange
value – use value contradiction
in, 64–6, 68; fall in rate of
profit for, 207–8; formation of,
44–5, 82; gold as symbolizing,
214, 219; industrial, 168–9; as
instrument of production, 83–4;
labor in general in, 147;
legitimizing property relations

279

Index

capital (capitalism) – *continued*
of, 169–73; as history in Marx's
analysis, 139–41; mediation in,
178; merchant, 162–8; as
objectified labor, 41; overpopulation and, 98–100; positivist
theorizing in, 10–11; pre-
capitalist forms and, 104, 125;
produced by labor, 120; realization of labor under, 152; subjective conditions of labor
under, 153–5; subjects and
objects in, 6–8; surplus values
produced by, 93–4; tendencies
of, 194–6, 239; Weber on legal
system necessary for, 88
capitalists, 153, 201
Carey, Henry Charles, 50
causality, 52–3
circulation: consumption-directed,
166–7; of industrial capital,
168, 169; as moment of production, 203–6; of money,
184–6, 188–90; simple and
complex, 88–92, 163, 164; of
surplus capital, 194
classes, 162
class relations, subject and object
separated in, 153–6
class struggle, 8, 9, 179, 237–41,
257–68
collateral, money as, 227
commerce, mediation in, 178
commodities, 23; exchange of,
163–5, 180–1; exchange and
use values of, 64–6, 68–9;
money as, 71, 226; money distinguished from, 174–5; price
fluctuations for, 220–1; prices
of, 224–5; in simple and complex circulation, 88; value of,
222–3
Communist Party, 261
community (commune): in Asiatic
pre-capitalist forms, 108–9;
under capital, self-knowledge
of, 148; in Germanic pre-
capitalist forms, 112–15; in-

dividual as possession of, in
Asiatic pre-capitalist form, 150;
as mediator of production, 141;
natural, 105–8; in pre-capitalist
forms of antiquity, 110–12; in
pre-capitalist production,
143–8; property as membership
in, 117–18; as relations, 152;
self conscious versus repressed
and natural, 237
complex circulation, 88–92, 164
compulsion, 89–91
concepts: abstractions distinguished from, 20–2, 34;
grounded versus subjective or
objective, 70–101; grounding
of, 211–14
concrete theorizing, 16–17; in
analysis, 34–5; contradictions
in, 61–9, 210; dialectical phenomenological critique of,
233–74; Marx's critique of,
211–32; mediation producing,
176–84
conquests, 58
consciousness: production and,
264–7; revolution and, 267–71
consumption: created by production, 55–7, 59, 119; individuals reproduced in, 124;
money used for, 189; in world
market, 194
consumption-directed circulation,
166–7
contradictions: mediation in, 176–
210; in concrete theorizing,
61–9, 219–20; natural versus
historical, 171–2; in value of
labor, 157–8, 161
corruption, 74–5
credit, 205, 206
Crimean War, 212
critique: of concrete theorizing,
dialectical phenomenological,
233–74; of concrete theorizing,
Marx's, 211–32; dialectic in,
16–18
cultural tradition, 242

280